FDR in American Memory

FDR in American Memory

Roosevelt and the Making of an Icon

SARA POLAK

Johns Hopkins University Press

Baltimore

Johns Hopkins University Press
2715 North Charles Street
Baltimore, Maryland 21218-4363
www.press.jhu.edu

Library of Congress Cataloging-in-Publication Data

Names: Polak, Sara, 1981– author.
Title: FDR in American memory : Roosevelt and the making of an icon /
Sara Polak.
Identifiers: LCCN 2021005544 | ISBN 9781421442839 (hardcover) |
ISBN 9781421442846 (ebook)
Subjects: LCSH: Roosevelt, Franklin D. (Franklin Delano),
1882–1945—Influence. | United States—Politics and
government—1933–1945—Historiography. | Roosevelt, Franklin D.
(Franklin Delano), 1882–1945—Public opinion. | Roosevelt, Franklin D.
(Franklin Delano), 1882–1945—Commemoration. | Press and
politics—United States—History—20th century. | Presidents in motion
pictures. | Presidents—United States—Biography. | People with
disabilities—United States—Biography. | Public opinion—United States. |
Collective memory—United States.
Classification: LCC E806 .P625 2022 | DDC 973.917092 [B]—dc23
LC record available at https://lccn.loc.gov/2021005544

A catalog record for this book is available from the British Library.

*Special discounts are available for bulk purchases of this book. For more information,
please contact Special Sales at specialsales@jh.edu.*

For Vincent, Abel, and Ilias

CONTENTS

ACKNOWLEDGMENTS

When I wrote my PhD dissertation, it had a classically lengthy acknowledgments section. I have never belonged to the population of academics who labor unseen and isolated, and I still owe thanks to everyone I thanked then: students, colleagues, mentors, friends, and family. But here I thank only a handful of people who have helped me with very specific elements of this book.

I am grateful to everyone at Johns Hopkins University Press, but especially to Laura Davulis, who has, since our first conversation at Yale in the fall of 2014, explained so much to me about how university presses and editors think. And who has, by way of Audra Wolfe, referred me to Ellen Tilton-Cantrell. As my academic editor, Ellen has helped me to profoundly revise my manuscript. Hiring her was possible thanks to a Johanna Nijland grant made available by Nadine Akkerman and Susanna de Beer, who I thank for their solidarity.

Jaap Kooijman, Dario Fazzi, Jeff Brune, and anonymous reviewers have given incredibly detailed and helpful peer feedback. Josje Calff and Menno Polak have sifted out a wagonload of large and small mistakes, especially in the notes, and have helped me organize and obtain the images and the rights to publish them in this book. Marieke Gerritsen has taken the screenshot from *Annie*.

I am grateful to the Franklin D. Roosevelt Presidential Library and Museum in Hyde Park, New York, especially its former director, Cynthia Koch, and the Roosevelt Institute for American Studies in Middelburg, the Netherlands. Finally, I thank everyone at my own institute, Leiden University Centre for the Arts in Society, which has employed me and been a home throughout.

FDR in American Memory

Roosevelt and the Making of an Icon

A statesman is a dead politician. Since his death, Franklin Delano Roosevelt has consistently ranked as one of the top three US presidents, usually together with George Washington and Abraham Lincoln—regardless of whether the jury consisted of historians, experts of another kind, or lay people. Roosevelt, who served from 1933 to 1945 as the thirty-second president of the United States, hovers on the edge of lived memory. There are people still alive who remember living during his presidency, but for most, he is now a historical figure—recent, yes, but no longer directly relevant to politics. Roosevelt remains, however, a towering cultural figure: he embodies the time in which the United States truly came into its own as world leader, after his own key mentors, Theodore Roosevelt and Woodrow Wilson, had paved the way. This is precisely why FDR forms a particularly intriguing case study for the genesis of a cultural icon. He is simultaneously a political leader who played a constitutive role in the ongoing world order and the US political arena, and a figure of the past, who represents History with a capital *H*.

This book analyzes FDR as an icon in American culture, joining studies that have been made of other iconic American presidents.[1] I explore how Franklin Delano Roosevelt became an icon in American memory and, in particular, what role Roosevelt himself played in that process. I examine how the FDR icon has developed over time, who has had agency over it, and how it has functioned culturally and ideologically at different times up until the end of 2016. In this book, I study how Franklin Roosevelt is remembered through cultural artifacts—novels, popular biographies, films, documentaries, museums, and memorials—and how he himself contributed to that remembrance. The book analyzes the rhetorical means through which various agents (FDR himself, his family, friends, aides, party members, supporters, detractors, news media, film makers, memorial designers, museum curators, and others) have over time negotiated the creation of Franklin Roosevelt as a cultural icon, a figure that many Americans still see as embodying the United States. As the word *embodying* suggests, one particular focus is to show how

FDR shaped himself in a bodily sense, negotiating his disability to match public expectations.

Thus, the question who FDR "really" was—a question that guides an overwhelming number of biographies, documentaries, and other cultural and scholarly texts—is not at stake. Instead, I ask why and how a particular image or narrative of Roosevelt functions rhetorically in shaping the icon at any particular moment. This says something about the time, place, and culture in which an image or narrative operates, and about how the cultural artifact functions rhetorically. In other words, this book is driven by a wish to understand how memory is produced and icons function in culture, not by a desire to know which memories are historically correct.

How do memories, texts, and artifacts that negotiate the past work? And what interest do they serve in the present? These questions are at the heart of this book. Although FDR is a historical figure, this book is not a traditional historical work. It uses methods and concepts from literary and cultural studies—close reading, in particular. Many of the texts that I analyze are not literary texts, not even necessarily texts in the conventional sense. The Roosevelt icon is the central "text," but this text has a wide range of expressions. It starts with Franklin Roosevelt himself, as a historical person who, increasingly assertively, set out to shape his public image as a politician in order to be elected to various offices and, in 1932, to the presidency. During his presidency, Roosevelt publicly spoke, wrote, and signed a plethora of texts. He gave radio speeches and held press conferences and appeared in photographs and film footage. He wrote letters and otherwise created texts, images, and other artifacts that somehow represented him, initially for what was then the present, but increasingly to position himself with an eye to future remembrance. During his life, and especially after his death, he was also often represented by others. For instance, there are many films, documentaries, and novels that incorporate a Roosevelt character or that otherwise represent him.

I want to understand two things: first, what in the nature of these cultural texts and artifacts makes them so attractive? (How does their beauty work, in aesthetic and rhetorical terms?) Second, which—and whose—desires, needs, and ideologies in the present are served or fulfilled by a particular representation of the past?

Of the many artifacts representing Roosevelt during and since his life, which constitute and negotiate an accumulative FDR icon, I have picked the most important exemplars. All of the selected objects of study are indeed exemplary, in the sense that each one might have been substituted by others similar to it in the points that I highlight. I chose all, however, for their individual importance, both qualitative (in the sense that they prompt new perspectives on how the FDR icon and its memory can work) and quantitative (because they have been widely disseminated, and therefore, presumably, contributed to his remembrance relatively prominently). While the six categories I employ—novels, popular biographies, films, documentaries, memorials, and museums—are not entirely rigid nor mutually exclusive, I chose them because they all provide narrative representations of FDR. This is in contrast to, say, the many streets, avenues, drives, and parks named after him.

To be clear: this is not a work of political history, despite being about a politician. Much has been written about FDR's personality and its massive influence on American and global politics in the twentieth century (e.g., in works by Frank Costigliola, Warren Kimball, Geoffrey C. Ward, Kenneth S. Davis, James MacGregor Burns, and Doris Kearns Goodwin).[2] In contrast to such works, this book is not primarily interested in scrutinizing FDR's personality, and—perhaps more importantly—it focuses not on FDR's political impact but rather on the process by which he created himself as a cultural icon. It attends in detail to FDR's legacies and to the politics of iconification, but not primarily in the concrete context of political history. Thus, this book is both like and unlike important works such as David Woolner, Warren Kimball, and David Reynolds's edited collection, *FDR's World*, and William Leuchtenburg's landmark, *In the Shadow of FDR*.[3] For instance, although I pay some attention to the New Deal as a branding opportunity for later presidents, I do not, as Leuchtenburg does, explore in detail how later presidents in disparate social and economic circumstances have related to the politics of the New Deal.

What Is Cultural Memory?

This book is a study of Franklin Roosevelt in cultural memory. That is, I try to understand how Roosevelt is remembered, not primarily by those who knew him personally, but by the broader culture and society that produced him. I avoid the term *collective memory*, because this term apparently takes for granted that there is a single, agreed-upon recollection that everyone in a community, or even nation, shares. Particularly in a case where memory is highly contested and dependent on political, geographical, generational, and other factors, it makes more sense to think about *memory communities*, groups within society that share the same cultural memories, which are inflected by the groups' social location and position in the present.[4]

Cultural memory and remembrance are terms that have been used in many contexts. I use *remembrance* to refer to acts of remembering—and artifacts that inspire particular practices of remembering—past events or people. Remembrance involves agency and one or more people or institutions that consciously assume power over who and what is remembered. Remembrance is always ideologically charged, even if it denies this claim (as many remembrance practices indeed do). Cultural memory is the context and complement of remembrance: it is the sense of the past that lives in society, shaped on the one hand by society's needs and ideologies in the present, and on the other by the shared memories and previous experiences of remembrance within various memory communities. Cultural memory is thus much more elusive and diverse than remembrance. It is less concretely situated and more omnipresent.

This use of cultural memory as the broad collection of possible culturally acceptable narratives about the past that "live" in a culture stands in contrast to one of the most famous definitions, by Jan Assmann.[5] Cultural memory, as Assmann understands it, concerns events that are no longer part of *lived memory* in society, but that are culturally inherited, becoming fixed legends or myths and functioning as cultural touchstones. At the other end of the spectrum, he posits the concept of *communicative memory*, which comes into existence in everyday interactions between people. Communicative memory is evanescent and allows for diversity and contradiction; it is made up of the informal, loosely shaped memories people share and does not involve high political stakes. For Assmann, while the life of communicative memory is about eight decades (as long as there are people alive to recount what they lived through), cultural memory concerns objects in a remote past. Although Assmann's notion that cultural memory is not lived memory for many members of the memory community remains important, the interest of Franklin Roosevelt as a case study lies in the fact that, temporally, he falls in the gap between being part of lived memory and being remembered as a congealed icon of a no longer relevant past. So rather than thinking of cultural and communicative memory as separate, I would argue they flow into each other—a negotiation that is more easily observed in space than in time.

My use of cultural memory shares with Assmann's the idea that cultural memory is something that can be drawn from, but, in contrast to Assmann, I think of the repository of traces, including documents and lived memories (communicative memory), as part of cultural memory. Aleida Assmann has, in between the original poles set out by Jan Assmann, developed an elaborate hierarchy.[6] I rather see the negotiation as a process happening at a range of material and more abstract sites of memory, at which various remembrance practices can vie for dominance. This can be observed particularly around memorial sites, where different memory communities have clashed heavily about memorial design, accompanying signs and labels, and the remembrance practices offered. To stress the active agency involved, I follow Jay Winter's suggestion to use remembrance to denote ideologically charged acts of reconfiguring elements of memory.[7] Remembrance is thus the configuration of narrative elements that agents draw from cultural memory in order to have others invest in a particular version of a story. It is important to realize that there is a negotiation about what and how to remember, because denying this negotiation artificially increases the authority of the remembrance practices that emerge as dominant.

One important book that analyzes the seemingly serendipitous dynamic of cultural memory is Emily Rosenberg's *A Date Which Will Live, Pearl Harbor in American Memory.*[8] Its case study—the attack on Pearl Harbor of December 7, 1941—is, of course, not an active agent in determining its own remembrance and is dissimilar to Roosevelt in that sense. Nevertheless, Rosenberg does investigate how Pearl Harbor, as a concept, has been historically developed in cultural memory from 1941 into the twenty-first century. The first part of Rosenberg's book describes Pearl Harbor's immediate reception, close reading Roosevelt's official reaction to the event. Rosenberg then analyzes the impact of Roosevelt's words in the public debates and discourse surrounding Pearl Harbor in the first fifty years after the event. The second part of the book provides a detailed look at the development of Pearl Harbor between 1991, the fiftieth anniversary of the event—when it was invested with new academic and public interest—and September 11, 2001. The section examines the omnipresent comparisons of the attacks on the Twin Towers with Pearl Harbor.

Rosenberg implicitly acknowledges the difference between cultural memory and remembrance. She also pays particular attention to the historical development of fabricated elements in cultural remembrance that do not necessarily appear to have been fabricated. For instance, she draws attention to the fact that Pearl Harbor was immediately received in the tradition of great tragic American losses, such as the Battle of the Alamo and Custer's Last Stand. Both newspaper headlines and governmental war propaganda appropriated the old phrase "Remember the Alamo" to Pearl Harbor by "reiterat[ing] the 'remember' theme."[9] This theme was first introduced by Roosevelt in his Pearl Harbor speech: "Always will our whole Nation remember the character of the onslaught against us." Rosenberg shows how that theme survived in iconic textual and visual cultural artifacts through the Cold War, and then changed into a call for vigilance—"Remember Pearl Harbor, Keep America Alert"—that has lasted into the twenty-first century.[10] This is a good example of an instance in which FDR adopted an older topos, although Rosenberg does not explicitly make this point. By tapping into the "Remember" appeal, FDR helped to propel Pearl Harbor into cultural memory.

The academic field of memory studies often focuses on cases of redress and repair: doing narrative justice to people who have been wrongfully marginalized and who seem to have been forgotten, often because they left few traces in the form of archival records and other documents. Memory studies rehabilitates them by giving them a voice in one way or another, often through oral history or fiction.[11] Of course, FDR was and is hardly in need of being rehabilitated in memory. As such, questions about his place in memory sometimes do not seem to fit well within memory studies. Memory studies, moreover, tends to focus on how and why present rememberers do, can, or should engage in remembering a particular event or person, and less on how the object of remembrance positioned himself for future memory.

There is, however, a great deal of literature on this latter topic as well. In particular, there are works on the image-making of kings and politicians, such as Peter Burke's book, *The Fabrication of Louis XIV*.[12] Within celebrity studies, there are also works on the production of seemingly authentic brands, personas, or public images.[13] In a sense, my reading of FDR's production of himself as a cultural icon fits into that debate better than into memory studies, but it is relevant to both.

FDR created many sites of memory, some of which—most obviously the Franklin Delano Roosevelt Presidential Library—were interpreted from the start as attempts at memorializing himself. Such sites continue to memorialize FDR to some extent.[14] In researching such sites, I have increasingly come to think of Roosevelt as a brilliant example of how to rhetorically position oneself so as to be remembered as an icon. Of course, FDR was able to do so in large part simply because he was very powerful and led the United States through the most difficult and decisive years of the twentieth century, but his enormous talent and cunning in what I call *autofabrication* was certainly also a key factor.

Links between image-making in the present and later remembrance are little theorized. The image management of leaders is treated independently from memory studies. However, if the Franklin D. Roosevelt Library shows one thing, it is that image-making and memory-making are not separate. FDR created the library as an act of autofabrication, primarily to represent himself to the future rather than to his own present, as his dedication makes explicit. In the years since his death, the library has changed dramatically, sometimes in ways FDR envisaged and sometimes differently. But in any case, he—as the remembered object—is a key player in negotiating the remembrance itself. His autofabrication concerns more than his image in the eyes of his contemporaries; it projects itself forward into the realm of remembrance. Roosevelt steered his future remembrance by appointing friends and relatives as representers. By giving his documents to the National Archives and Records Administration (NARA), he added them to the repository of cultural memory. However, by housing them in a separate building on his own estate and having the National Park Service (NPS) manage his home on the same estate, he contributed to a particular remembrance of himself and his presidency.[15]

Autofabrication for the sake of one's future image can involve attempts to shape, manage, or contribute to future remembrance practices, as FDR did when he created the museum on the first floor of his presidential library and chose agents to manage its permanent and temporary exhibitions. It can also shape and inform future cultural memory, as FDR did through his literal and figurative contribution to the national archive on the museum's second floor. As noted, it is more difficult to identify agents (e.g., people, organizations) exerting power over cultural memory, because changes in cultural memory are harder to trace than those of explicit remembrance practices. Cultural memory, nonetheless, does reflect the needs and interests of society or dominant groups or institutions within society.

What Is Disability Studies?

Although FDR would probably hardly recognize himself as a logical object for the field of disability studies—or memory studies—he squarely fits in both. My reading of FDR's production of himself as a cultural icon leans on insights from disability studies as well as from memory studies. Thus, disability studies provides another important lens that makes this book different from more traditional treatments of FDR's personality and presidency. The concrete reason for adopting this approach is, of course, that FDR was disabled; his disability played a significant role in his creation of his own public image and has also been a key influence on how he is remembered. But disability plays a different role in this book than well-known FDR themes and topoi such as his complex relationship with Eleanor Roosevelt or his role in the Second World War (which the book also discusses at length), because disability itself provides a tool for analysis. In ways similar to categories like race, class, and gender, disability can offer a unique perspective on the assumptions and politics that usually guide the making of power structures and, more specifically, presidential icons.

As Kim Nielsen points out, "Disability history has much to gain from biography; and biography has much to gain from considering disability as an analytical framework."[16] Disability biography can write otherwise marginalized people and key aspects of their identities into history. Conversely, taking into account the role of disability in someone's life can offer a more profound understanding of that life and historical context. In this book, I intend to both show how important the experience of disability was to FDR's autofabrication and remembrance, and how this realization can help us to better understand FDR's historical context and the contexts in which he is remembered. I consider the ways that FDR used his unique experience of disability in his autofabrication and theorize this process in the context of cultural studies. I, thus, steer clear of the endlessly repeated "general narrative of Roosevelt's life" as "that of a determined and successful man who tragically suffered polio, but who overcame its effects and a potentially meaningless life with heroism, manliness, and sheer will."[17] But in addition to showing how FDR's disability informed his autofabrication, I will also show how his disability—specifically, some of the prosthetic metaphors that some disability historians seem to reject too summarily—were key to his becoming a national icon.[18]

I should note that there is some debate over whether FDR actually had polio. Recently, various medical historians have argued—based on records of the symptoms that FDR showed during his illness in 1921—that he may have suffered from Guillain-Barré syndrome. The question of whether this theory is right or wrong is not a relevant one for this book. What is important is that FDR believed himself to be a polio survivor and was seen as such both by contemporaries and by later representations. Because he thought of himself in those terms, he became a major champion for polio treatment and for research to create a vaccine. When Jonas Salk created a successful polio vaccine in 1955, the publication of this spectacular news was timed to be announced on April 12, the decennial of Roosevelt's death. In this and other ways, even if FDR may not in fact have had polio, he is historically and in cultural memory so tightly connected to American polio history that, for this book, the issue is irrelevant.

One of the most basic tenets of disability studies is the idea that disability is socially constructed, and that people are disabled by the constraints of a society that has inflexible norms regarding how one should be and look, and what one should be able to do. Very briefly put, if everyone in a society commonly used a wheelchair, doors there would be designed differently. Visitors who did not use a wheelchair might have trouble negotiating those doors because, standing up, they would be taller than average users in this scenario; thus, they would have similar kinds of issues that many wheelchair users encounter in most societies organized around nondisabled people. This idea—often referred to as the *social model* of disability—is pitted against an older *medical model*, which sees disability as a product of faulty biology and "conceptualizes disability as a long-term or permanent illness or injury, and proposes to 'fix' it, or at least to ameliorate its effects."[19]

Disability studies as an interdisciplinary field of study came into its own in the United States in the second half of the twentieth century, largely in response to disability rights activism. Thus, it is somewhat similar to memory studies, in the sense that it is an academic pursuit that grew out of a drive to repair past injustices, and emancipate groups that had not previously been given a voice. This is a key point in which the interdisciplinary field of disability studies and disability history specifically differ from medical history or the social history of medicine.[20] Originally engaging primarily the perspectives and practitioners of medicine, the latter fields would perhaps sooner be inclined to embrace a medical perspective on disability, whereas disability history regards the past from the perspective of disabled subjects.

In the tradition of disability studies, I consider disability as socially constructed and aim to center that perspective, which also immediately brings two complications. First, FDR did not say much about how he experienced his disability, and this book intentionally does not center on his psychological shaping or internal self-perception. It is practically impossible to know how FDR felt about being disabled, and—contrary to various other scholars—this is not something I wish to speculate about. However, while disability studies tends to consider disability as an identity category similar to race or gender, FDR resisted being identified as such, and showed few signs of accepting it as an identity for himself. During FDR's life, neither disability studies nor the idea that disability is primarily a social construction were prevalent yet, and the medical model of disability reigned unchallenged. So, the few references to FDR's disability that exist, both by himself and by others around him, generally employ terms that framed it as an "unfortunate shortcoming" to be obscured or "overcome": if not in actuality, then at least for the public eye. The second complication is that there is every reason to assume that part of FDR's astuteness in projecting a particular desirable public image came from his experience in projecting himself as nondisabled. His experience of disability does seem to have given him a unique perspective on how norms, power structures, and public performance are made. Thus, FDR may well have been intuitively aware of some of the basic ideas underlying the social model of disability, even if he did not use its language.

One clue that disability is not just one of many themes in the study of FDR, but potentially also a critical lens through which to observe power structures in autofabrication and remembrance, is the fact that many of his biographers themselves were polio survivors. In the 1950s and 1960s, FDR was routinely held up to polio survivors as a model of endurance and perfection, specifically in "overcoming" the effects of polio, meaning that these were invisible to the public and, insofar as they were visible, were never the focus of attention.[21] Hugh Gregory Gallagher—as well as other historians, such as Geoffrey Ward, who had survived the disease and were disabled as a result—clearly admired FDR as an example and role model. In different ways, Gallagher and Ward also both realized that disability was not only something that FDR had "overcome" as per the medical model, but also something that gave him an exceptional perspective on the social construction of embodied power relations that informed his presidency.

The dominant model in which scholars have tended to understand disability in recent years is *intersectionality*. Although I do applaud the trend to understand the dynamics of inclusion and exclusion based on a wide range of identity categories as interacting and intersecting with one another, FDR himself is relatively un-intersectional, in the sense that he belongs to the dominant majority in practically every way (race, gender, class, sexuality) except physical ability. I will offer an intersectional reading of that combination of factors and show, especially in chapter 5, that his overwhelming advantages in all categories *but* physical ability gave him enough privilege to function well *despite* his disability. Later, this combination of privileges was a prerequisite for his coming to be remembered as someone who was able to function especially well *because* of his disability. Although I will discuss at several points the relevant interaction of FDR's disability with his masculinity, whiteness, and wealth, centralizing intersectionality as a driving concept in this book would seem artificial, given the fact that, in FDR's case, one specific issue stands out so clearly against an overwhelming set of social privileges.

A Note on Language

There are many different terms to refer to aspects of disability. What has been considered acceptable or accurate terminology has changed a great deal since FDR first contracted symptoms of paralysis in 1921 and continues to be in flux. Throughout this book, I generally adhere to the *Disability Language Style Guide* (2018) of the National Center on Disability and Journalism. However, Franklin Roosevelt and his contemporaries, if they referred to disability at all, commonly used terms that frame disability as a deficiency or medical condition to be cured (e.g., "overcoming" polio, "rehabilitation," "invalidity," "lame"). Many of those terms make normative assumptions about how disability is or should be experienced, and, in doing so, implicitly erases the perspective of disabled people themselves. Therefore, from the position that disability is socially constructed, such terms are themselves disabling. Thus, I avoid them in this book, except, of course, in direct quotation.

Another debate among disability activists and communities is whether "people-first" or "identity-first" language is preferable, that is, whether it is better to use "person with a disability" or "disabled person." The first option projects disability as one aspect or attribute in a person's life, whereas the second considers it a crucial part of a disabled person's identity. Both approaches have their proponents among disability scholars and activists. Many scholars by now use the two interchangeably, because, as Paul Longmore writes, using just people-first language is "monotonous, [and] sometimes leads to ludicrous linguistic barbarisms such as 'people with blindness,' and ultimately fails in its laudable but ineffectual effort to combat stigma."[22] While it is often productive to think of disability as an identity category like race or gender, it seems beyond reasonable doubt that Franklin Roosevelt did not wish to consider his disability as formative for his identity. In fact, he did not wish for his disability to be referred to at all, so that it feels somewhat indiscreet to do so here. Discussing his disability is, however, indispensable to my analysis of his autofabrication and remembrance as an American icon in a much broader sense. Therefore, I aim for language that both stresses the social and cultural constructedness of disability (which is more relevant than the medical context for my purposes) and that is as neutral and accurate as possible (e.g., "using

a wheelchair" instead of "wheelchair-bound"; "living with the effects of" polio rather than "suffering the effects of" polio or "having overcome" it).

Regarding the use of people-first or identity-first language: I have observed
in the history of speaking and writing about FDR's disability an initial tendency, also among nondisabled people, toward identity-first thinking (that
would term FDR "lame" or "an invalid"). Later, after his death, a people-first
perspective (that would, as did FDR himself, acknowledge silently that he had
a disability but deny that this defined him) became prevalent. Since the 1980s,
there has been a notable reversion to an identity-first perspective, in which
disabled people embrace disability as a part of their identity, doing so as an
emancipating and assertive choice. Over the course of the book, I will both use
"people with disabilities" and "disabled people," attuning this to the historical
context of who, and what period, I am writing about. Specifically, there are
many disability scholars (including Paul Longmore, Geoffrey Ward, Hugh
Gallagher, Tobin Siebers, Irv Zola) and activists (Ed Roberts, Judy Heumann)
who have survived polio, many of whom refer to themselves as "polios." Again,
this is not a term I use in reference to FDR.

FDR as a Cultural Icon

In this book—first examining FDR's autofabrication and then focusing on his
place in cultural memory—I trace FDR's development as a *cultural icon*. This
is defined as a person (or artifact) that is identified by members of a culture
as representative of that culture. In the process of identification, icons are
judged by the extent to which they can be seen as an authentic proxy of that
culture. The icon can relate to the cultural identity represented in variable and
changing ways. Indeed, the extent to which a cultural icon can be imbued with
new meanings and operate in new contexts is a measure of its success. As Mariana Casale O'Ryan asserts, to the culture in which it exists, the cultural icon
is a "vessel" for identity questions.[23]

In addition to this core definition, other nuances of "icon" are also helpful
in framing this project. The word *icon* derives from the Greek *eikon*, which
means image. As Charles Sanders Peirce theorizes, an icon is something that
is perceived as being similar to something else.[24] This particular meaning of
icon (and especially of the adjective, *iconic*) is more specific than my broader
usage of the word elsewhere. Thus, when I use *iconic* in the Peircean sense,
meaning "representing something through resemblance," I will explicitly state
that I am doing so; when no qualification is included, I mean *iconic* in the

broad sense of being "representative of a culture." According to art historian Martin Kemp, icons are images that have taken on meaning beyond their original context and that consistently "accrue legends," often around the belief that the icon "involve[s] some kind of secret."[25] Indeed, iconic figures often tend to accrue legends, because they function as allegorical or metaphorical depictions of other narratives. Through such mechanisms, icons easily become incorporated in new contexts and take on both new and implied meanings (hence, secrets).

Presidential icons like Lincoln or Washington often function successfully as allegorical figures that carry a range of complex and chaotic pasts into narratives that remember their pasts in the present. Indeed, a key characteristic of an icon is its potential to transgress beyond the "parameters of its initial making, function, and context."[26] FDR is unusually adaptable, allowing for a considerable (though not limitless) range of allegorizations and synecdochic representations. He has become a versatile figure on screen—poignantly so, because it is a medium the historical FDR tried to avoid—whose narratives are often profoundly tied to his beleaguered body, inviting comparison with other bodies. Kemp's notion that icons tend to involve "some kind of secret" is important here; many texts and objects representing and remembering FDR seem irresistibly drawn to uncovering his secrets.

A telling example is Anthony Badger's essay, "The New Deal Without FDR: What Biographies of Roosevelt Cannot Tell Us." The essay puts forward a fierce argument blaming what Badger calls the "seemingly insatiable appetite for more and more biographical detail about Roosevelt" for obscuring and leading historians away from far more important analyses of the New Deal in structural, social, and economic terms. However, at the same time, Badger's essay itself does not engage at all in scrutinizing "the New Deal without FDR." Instead, most of the essay actually engages in the discussion about Roosevelt's personality, physical disability, and daily life that Badger feels is unhelpful to understanding what really matters:

> We now know what Roosevelt had for breakfast, what drinks he mixed for himself at cocktail hour, that he despaired of the food served at the White House. We know that from 1919 Eleanor and he slept in separate bedrooms. But does the biographical detail about Roosevelt that we now have in such abundance help us to understand the New Deal's legacy? . . . A rehabilitation counsellor, a paraplegic polio victim and Geoffrey Ward have documented just how crippled Roosevelt was and "the splendid deception" involved in the collaboration of the media which ensured

that neither photographic nor film evidence allowed the American people to see the true extent of his disability. Few Americans knew that the President was so wheelchair bound or had to be lifted like a baby to so many locations.[27]

Most of the essay is apophatic in this fashion—it denies that "biographical detail" can "help us to understand the New Deal's legacy," yet constantly engages in it, in a manner that is rather prurient. While supposedly assuming the moral high ground, Badger feasts on voyeuristic detail about the Roosevelts: the separate bedrooms, the despair about the food, Roosevelt's need to be "lifted like a baby." Each of the authors Badger mentions who have investigated "the effect of polio on Roosevelt" are in some measure speculative about the mental and psychic effects the disease had on him, but unlike Badger, none of them would be so crude about this as to describe FDR's disability by likening him to a baby.

But while Badger does objectify FDR by gorging on these biographical details, he inadvertently also shows the need for a disability perspective on FDR. His intent focus on FDR's disability is like the scholarly equivalent of *staring* at disability, a phenomenon Rosemary Garland-Thomson has framed as "an intense visual exchange that makes meaning."[28] The stare, she argues, is unlike the gaze "which has been extensively defined as an oppressive act of disciplinary looking that subordinates its victim," and it requires analysis both from the perspective of the starer, and the staree.[29] This is what this book sets out to do in its paired analysis of FDR's autofabrication and remembrance.

When Badger refers to the authors who have begun to analyze FDR from the perspective of disability, he calls them a "rehabilitation counsellor, a paraplegic polio victim, and Geoffrey Ward." He implies that a "rehabilitation counsellor" (presumably, Richard Goldberg, author of the 1981 biography, *The Making of FDR: Triumph over Disability*) or "a paraplegic polio victim" (presumably, Hugh Gallagher), are identified entirely and unambiguously by that label and so don't need to be referred to by name. Ward, the only historian who is named, is a polio survivor too, but unlike Gallagher, he generally passes as nondisabled—apparently successfully enough to be taken seriously by his colleague.

Badger probably incorporates so many biographical details in an attempt to parody, or at least exaggerate, the biographical historiography he is criticizing. At the same time, he cannot resist recounting page after page of trivial but also highly memorable Roosevelt anecdotes. Despite the title, the article is really more a part of biographical debates about FDR than of debates about the New Deal without Roosevelt. This is especially true because Badger keeps arguing with the views previous Roosevelt biographers have taken. He argues, for instance, that it was not the experience of polio that—as traditional FDR wisdom has it—"toughened [FDR's] inner core," but rather FDR's marital crisis in 1919, after Eleanor Roosevelt discovered that he had an affair with her social secretary, Lucy Mercer.[30] So Badger seems, in spite of his principles, irresistibly drawn toward joining the biographical debate and speculation about FDR.

I want to point out from the outset that this book is somewhat unorthodox in its tendency to treat scholarly works on FDR as primary sources themselves. Here, I treat Badger's essay as a remembrance practice itself: a text that is shaped by and that itself influences how FDR is seen and remembered in American culture more broadly. I admit that this tendency may sometimes be a little unfair. For example, I argue in chapter 5 that Hugh Gallagher has profoundly shaped the remembrance of FDR's disability through his speculative projections of what FDR must have felt in his book *FDR's Splendid Deception*. At the same time, I employ Gallagher's work as a rich source of information about that disability. Every historian, of course, has their own positionality that feeds into their selection of what to research and how to interpret their findings. But here, the contrast between Badger, who—seemingly without realizing—erases the disability perspective, and Ward and Gallagher, who—each in different ways—center it, is a very clear example of how historians (however "dispassionate") also contribute to cultural memory and remembrance.

This book, of course, risks falling into the same trap of being enticed by Roosevelt narratives rather than analyzing how their temptation works. I do not in the least wish to deny my own positionality and the context I grew up in, in which FDR was indeed an admired icon. I identify as nondisabled; my family is traditionally left-wing Democratic, "social democrats" in European terms. All but one of my grandparents were Jewish, and thus survivors of World War II against the odds, saved by an allied coalition led by Roosevelt. So I come from a context in which Franklin Roosevelt was a celebrated, if not often-mentioned, figure. However, it remains essential that this book retain a critical distance from its object to analyze how the FDR icon attracts and fulfills desires in different places and contexts. Indeed, this alluring quality is, I hope to show, precisely the decisive reason for FDR's success as a cultural icon after his death. FDR was also virulently hated and continues to be so in parts of US society that seem to have become more visible recently. But he tried—largely successfully—to be a seductive figure, a potential vehicle for a wide range of narratives, and a stakeholder in his own future remembrance. FDR was and remains a key player in historical and other representations of the 1930s and 1940s, and he was committed to staying relevant into the far future.

Chapter Structure

I will clarify briefly the central point of each chapter, and then I highlight some key topics the book takes up by exploring in some depth a site that is critical to FDR's autofabrication: the Franklin D. Roosevelt Presidential Library in Hyde Park, New York, which I consider the most important site remembering FDR.

The first three (of six) chapters focus primarily on how Franklin Roosevelt and the people around him negotiated the creation and spread of the "FDR icon," both in the then-present and for the future. The last three chapters approach the same topic from the other end: they focus on how FDR has been remembered since his death in 1945, and how the FDR icon has taken on different meanings, depending on the context in which it functioned. Thematically, those chapters revolve around the cultural memory of the New Deal, World War II, and FDR's physical disability.

The first chapter explores how FDR was shaped by his environment and how this relates to his own public image-making; I coin the term *autofabrication* to discuss this complex relationship. I focus on the ways that FDR actively projected a well-considered public image by drawing attention to himself and his political ideals, but also by obscuring many of his actual acts as a politician.

Chapter 2 shows how a wide range of family, close friends, staff, cabinet members, and aides assisted FDR in managing his image and steering his autofabrication. In part because of the need to negotiate his disability, FDR—together with his team—created himself as an iconic figure and well-known radio voice. Although this voice and FDR's public persona were widely perceived as "intimate," they were the product of a professional collective effort that used state-of-the-art techniques to steer and stay in touch with public opinion.

Chapter 3 zooms in on how FDR and his autofabrication apparatus projected a particular cultural memory of him into the future, in part through publishing *The Public Papers and Addresses* and creating the FDR Presidential Library and Museum. Eleanor Roosevelt, who survived her husband by seventeen years, also became an important narrator and disseminator of the FDR icon, both during his life and after his death.

Chapters 4, 5, and 6 concern the politics of representing FDR in popular culture and public history since 1945. These chapters show how artifacts and acts of remembrance have negotiated cultural memory since FDR's death, and how his impact on his own remembrance remains palpable even if it has found new cultural frames and appropriations. Cultural artifacts representing FDR form case studies grouped around three key themes in FDR memory: the New Deal, FDR's disability, and World War II. Each of these themes elucidates a central development within the politics of American culture between 1945 and 2014, so that, together, these themes draw up FDR as a relevant embodiment of key aspects of postwar America.

Chapter 4 focuses primarily on how the New Deal is "depoliticized" in cultural memory, showing that FDR himself initiated this process by engaging in (highly political) "depoliticization" strategies. Chapter 5 shows how FDR's disability and wheelchair use took on a crucial function in narrating FDR's role in "pulling the US through crisis." Chapter 6, through a reading of two novels and three films focused on World War II, analyzes the ways that Franklin Roosevelt can be understood as a cultural icon.

The FDR Library as a Case in Point

Traveling through the Hudson Valley to Hyde Park, it is impossible to miss that this is an affluent and beautiful part of New York State and has been for centuries. The Home of Franklin D. Roosevelt (a national historic site) and the Franklin D. Roosevelt Presidential Library and Museum share a grand estate with impressive views and colonial revival-style buildings. From the visitor center and the parking area, you can already catch glimpses of the fairly removed Springwood Home, the Rose Garden, the horse stables, and other traditional outbuildings, as well as the understated Dutch colonial architecture of the FDR Library and Museum. The visitor center is commanding but unpretentious. There, you would typically buy a ticket for a guided tour of the home, followed by a self-guided museum visit. In front of the center is a wind vane in the shape of a sail—one of FDR's most passionate hobbies—mounted on the base of a wheelchair. In its courtyard is a sculpture of Franklin and Eleanor Roosevelt on garden benches, whom you can join for a photo. Inside, an NPS ranger awaits, standing on a massive but detailed floor mosaic of the grounds. You can join the ranger for the start of the tour or elect to first watch the twenty-minute introductory documentary, *A Rendezvous with History*, in the visitor center's large cinema. Although the site is, of course, wheelchair

Kinetic sculpture by Henry Philippe Loustau, *The Four Freedoms* (2006). Courtesy of Harvey Barrison

accessible and also offers an audio description guide for blind visitors or visitors with low vision, it does not explicitly upfront a holistic approach to accessibility.

The Franklin Delano Roosevelt Presidential Library and Museum, in the middle of this majestic setting, is an excellent example of a site that is crucial to Roosevelt's autofabrication. It also provides a helpful entry point to many other matters this book takes up. The FDR Library at Hyde Park is situated on the Roosevelt family estate, yards away from Springwood, the home in which FDR grew up, and where his overbearing mother lived until her death in 1941. Franklin and Eleanor Roosevelt are buried in the Rose Garden between the two buildings. The FDR Library is the first presidential library in the United States, and the very idea of a presidential library—an archive and a museum dedicated specifically to one president—was Franklin Roosevelt's. Previously, US presidents had not been obliged to publicize their presidential records, and in many cases, they did not. If they did, the archives would usually go to the Library of Congress. The FDR Library, designed and built by Roosevelt on his home estate and deeded to the federal government, houses his records and a museum, which initially displayed his personal collections and "oddities" sent to him by admirers. The FDR Library was revolutionary; it established a practice followed by all presidents since, laid down in federal law in 1955.[31]

The FDR Library was dedicated in 1941. Eleanor Roosevelt bequeathed Springwood, the home, to the NPS upon FDR's death in 1945, as he had wished; a year after his death, it was opened to the public.[32] Thus, the estate came to house two major tourist attractions in the Hudson Valley, steps away from each other. One might read Springwood as the home of FDR's self-fashioning, the privileged social and cultural environment where he was formed and educated, and the library as a key site of this autofabrication. The library is the place in which he most explicitly offered his own representation of himself— immediately also read as self-memorializing.[33] He did so not through a statue or other visual tribute, but by publicizing his documents and collections, though the library's adjacency to his lifelong home created a clear connection to his private life. The very fact that FDR built the library beside the home, and that he deeded both to the federal government, shows that that this entanglement itself was part of his autofabrication, a strategy to give the impression of continuity and transparency between his political and private life. That continuity was emphasized by the fact that the museum initially showcased many of Roosevelt's private collections of stamps, ship models, and stuffed birds.[34]

The FDR Library Museum showcases stories of FDR's autofabrication as a collective effort. For instance, the museum has recreated 1930s and 1940s living rooms and kitchens in which visitors can listen to parts of FDR's famous radio "Fireside Chats," as if they were doing so at the time they were held and in the situation in which they were heard by his contemporaries. At the same time, the FDR Library makes concrete the division between various materials. The full body of documents, letters, and other papers that FDR signed, wrote, and spoke is stored in the archive on the second floor of the building, which the overwhelming majority of visitors do not see. On the other hand, the recordings, letters, pictures, and film footage that carefully and selectively construct the public image and voice for the benefit of the museum visitors are located on the ground floor.

The museum exhibition simultaneously treats FDR as an individual who became president and as a symbolic embodiment of the nation. The elision between these two kinds of representations contributes to shaping FDR as an icon. For instance, visitors can see the actual shoes and leg braces that shaped and are shaped by FDR's legs, and they are invited to put themselves into FDR's shoes figuratively. The exhibition thus intertwines public and private aspects

Museum exhibit titled "Our Plain Duty: Franklin D. Roosevelt and America's Social Security," August 2010. Courtesy of the Franklin D. Roosevelt Library and Museum, Hyde Park, New York

of FDR, using the private aspects to create a sense of authenticity—a strategy that FDR himself used during his presidency. At the same time, this is a strategy that allows for a kind of intimacy with FDR via his prosthetic devices that he himself would rarely have chosen (FDR would sooner upfront his dog, smile, or cigarette pipe as a prop to suggest embodied intimacy) and that addresses itself primarily to a nondisabled audience, suggesting what Tobin Siebers has called "disability drag."[35]

The museum and the library as a whole have undergone dramatic changes in the process of remembering FDR beyond his death. In the FDR Library, the museum that visitors see reflects the modern sensibility of its twenty-first-century curators, who are employed by NARA. The private nonprofit Roosevelt Institution has built the wing housing special exhibitions. NARA and the Roosevelt Institution, along with the NPS that administers the home, are institutions with a direct or indirect link to FDR. NARA is a federal body established during FDR's presidency, while the home was deeded to the NPS as one of its early historic sites. The idea that the NPS should manage national historic sites alongside US natural heritage also dates from the 1930s; FDR was a warm supporter.[36]

The Roosevelt Institution is a partisan body, a private nonprofit organization dedicated to furthering the legacy of the Roosevelts.[37] Roosevelt intended the library mainly to open his archives to the public, but under the influence of presidential foundations, presidential libraries have increasingly become shrines to the presidents they remember.[38] The FDR Library is actually, among presidential libraries, the least celebratory and the most even-handed in addressing also the problematic and painful sides of Roosevelt's presidency. Like the involvement of the nonpartisan federal bodies in Hyde Park, this even-handedness is in line with Roosevelt's own wish to be remembered not just as a hero, but as an example for future generations to learn from and improve on.[39]

In other aspects, too, the library both propels him as a heroic American icon—presumably, in ways he would have applauded—and portrays him in ways he might have liked less, or in any case, that he could not have foreseen. For instance, his wheelchair, an element FDR carefully kept out of the public view, is now emphasized in the home as well as the library museum. It is framed consistently as a mark of Roosevelt's resilience in the face of adversity, but as such, it is more a product of cultural memory—that is, of what agents in the present consider a relevant aspect of the past—than of a culture of remembrance that Roosevelt himself tried to instigate through autofabrication.

The FDR Library Museum, as it operates in the present, is a product of FDR's autofabrication for the future but also revives his voice in a modern context. On the one hand, the museum depoliticizes him through the personal and nonpartisan treatment of his person and presidency. On the other hand, it shows how the many positive outcomes of his presidency—particularly the victory over the Great Depression, the United States' global success in winning World War II, and the Four Freedoms and the UN—were clearly results of FDR's foresight and courage. The museum suggests that these outcomes were always intended to be positive for the United States and the world as a whole. This framing depoliticizes FDR's, at the time, often controversial acts, suggesting they were a result of global consensus, unequivocally benefiting the entire world.

FDR's disability is a central vehicle at Hyde Park. The FDR Library Museum displays many of the prosthetic devices he employed, exhibiting one of his wheelchairs at the home. The tour most visitors take is led by an NPS guide and leads from the Wallace Visitor Center to Springwood, past the

Roosevelts' graves, and then to the self-guided space of the museum. On the way from one building to the next, guides point out the long path on which FDR tried to learn to walk again. Different guides no doubt treat this in different ways, but, in the four or five tours I have taken between 2010 and 2015, it struck me that they generally stressed the bravery and hopelessness of this insistence to walk again. Alison Kafer, in *Feminist, Queer, Crip*, analyzes the underlying assumption in such treatment that disability has "no future," in ways that FDR's career clearly belies.[40]

Between the visitor center, the library, and the home, there is a wind vane with a wheelchair as its basis, reminding visitors of its centrality to FDR's life. The parts of the site regular visitors enter are all on the ground floor, easily accessible to anyone, and the ramps at most doors are explicitly original, made for FDR. Thus, every part of the site directly or indirectly shows that FDR used a wheelchair, and FDR's disability functions to connect the home, the library, and the visitor center. As such, FDR's disability is now assertively present as a conduit between all the other, more static sites, thus acquiring a function in FDR memory that is itself prosthetic. However, the site does not make visitors explicitly aware of this fact: it treats accessibility primarily as a matter of ontology, and not, as Tanya Titchkosky has advocated, as a "space of interpretive encounter."[41]

In postwar years, the museum has mostly been somewhat ahead of other similar institutions in terms of accessibility but never radically so. It has developed from a narrow focus on the wheelchair accessibility FDR himself required to a broader interpretation of access, including the previously mentioned interpretation tools for blind or low-vision visitors. Although on the whole, the FDR Library offers fair accommodations to disabled visitors, it also engages in a disability drag, which is problematic, because "playing disabled" is very different from its lived experience and tends to cast it as deprivation and a reason for pity. Thus, the library does not explicitly center on a disabled perspective.

The FDR Library Museum regularly revives FDR's First Hundred Days, most recently in a special exhibition in 2008, just before Barack Obama entered office. The more general exhibition tends to depoliticize the New Deal through personalization: the focus is on the many letters to Roosevelt on display, written in response to the first Fireside Chats. In their individuality and their treatment of FDR as an older brother or family friend, such letters personalize both the American experience of the Great Depression and the New Deal. In a short documentary film about Roosevelt's legacy, written and narrated by Bill Clinton as his contribution to the FDR Library Museum, Clinton says over photographic and film footage of the Great Depression and the New Deal: "Even though Franklin Roosevelt was the architect of grand designs, he touched tens of thousands of Americans in a very personal way. To ordinary Americans, Roosevelt was always more than a great President, he was part of the family. My own grandfather felt the same way. He believed that this president was a friend, a man who cared about his family's future. My grandfather was right about that."

Of course, the fact that this is Clinton's voice and text politicizes Roosevelt's legacy. On the other hand, letting individual people—"ordinary Americans," such as, presumably, Clinton's grandfather—represent the beneficiaries of the New Deal may persuade viewers that Clinton's grandfather was right and that "this president . . . cared about his family's future." Pulling the representation and remembrance of the New Deal into the personal and the familial draws it away from political debates about government spending.

Clinton's documentary also highlights FDR's role in World War II, which shaped FDR's status as one of the most iconic US presidents. Be it as the *primus inter pares* of the "Greatest Generation," or as the eager interventionist who was proven right by the attack on Pearl Harbor, FDR is remembered as embodying the United States at war. In the documentary about FDR's legacy that is played at the FDR Library, Clinton lists what Americans studying the 1930s and 1940s will perceive through understanding FDR: "The victory of democracy over fascism, of free enterprise over command economics, of tolerance over bigotry. And they will see that the embodiment of that triumph, the driving force behind it, was President Franklin Delano Roosevelt. Though he was surrounded by turmoil, he envisioned a world of lasting peace. The triumph of freedom in the face of depression and totalitarianism was not foretold or inevitable."

Clinton posits Roosevelt as the embodiment of—and driving force behind—the victory of American ideology over fascism, communism, and anti-Semitism. He casts FDR as the personification of that triumph, so as to make it graspable to a twenty-first-century audience. "Freedom" in "the triumph of freedom" might be read as "Roosevelt" and stressing that his triumph was "not foretold or inevitable" pushes home the sense that, while history may seem to follow a clear storyline, it does not, in fact, do so.

Clinton's contribution to the FDR Museum clearly shows one of the ways in which FDR is kept relevant in modern remembrance practices. Clinton emphatically connects his own presidency to Roosevelt's. The fact that he was presumably asked to make the contribution shows that it works both ways. Hyde Park, as the site of the Roosevelt Historic Home and the FDR Presidential Library, exemplifies many of the key autofabrication, remembrance, and negotiation strategies that this book highlights—strategies that FDR, his contemporaries, and later agents employed in representing him. Together, these strategies model how FDR moved from politician to statesman to icon.

"I am a juggler"

FDR's Public Image–Making

On February 23, 1942, FDR delivered his twentieth Fireside Chat, a glowing war speech, in which he framed himself and early-1942 America in sweeping historical and geographic contexts. He began the speech by mentioning that it was George Washington's birthday and ended it as follows:

> And General Washington ordered that these great words written by Tom Paine be read to the men of every regiment in the Continental Army, and this was the assurance given to the first American armed forces:
>
> "The summer soldier and the sunshine patriot will, in this crisis, shrink from the service of their country; but he that stands it now, deserves the love and thanks of man and woman. Tyranny, like hell, is not easily conquered; yet we have this consolation with us, that the harder the sacrifice, the more glorious the triumph."
>
> So spoke Americans in the year 1776,
>
> So speak Americans today![1]

Thus, Roosevelt framed the American war effort in 1942 as a contemporary version of the American Revolutionary War, typical and constitutive of true Americanness. In the process, he associated himself with General George Washington; significantly, with the military leader rather than the president, albeit in a moment when Washington quoted the high rhetoric of Thomas Paine to inspire his army. In the rest of the Fireside Chat, FDR exhorted his "fellow Americans" to look at a map of the world to understand the global movements and stakes of the war. The language is rife with moral righteousness, referring to the United States (in Roosevelt's own earlier phrase) as the world's "arsenal of democracy"—an expression that has continued to reverberate—and indexing the Four Freedoms. First enunciated in the State of the Union address on January 6, 1941, the Four Freedoms have become, more than almost any Roosevelt text, part of his cultural and political heritage. This Fireside Chat shapes FDR as a *man*—a person as well as a masculinity—through Roosevelt's morally just military mission in the world. Roosevelt presents himself as the moral voice and commander in chief of the nation, and does so in a highly individual manner, suggesting that he is its savior. This speech successfully constructs a public image of a profoundly frank and morally upright man but is at no time really inward-looking.

Four days prior to this Fireside Chat, FDR issued Executive Order 9066, which ordered the internment of approximately 122,000 innocent Japanese Americans without due process or stated end date. The fact that FDR had taken this action just days before is wholly absent and irrelevant to this speech, a text that—unlike the executive order—reached the majority of Americans and was delivered to most of them in Roosevelt's own intimate radio voice. This Fireside Chat obscured one of the most immoral acts of his presidency and contributed to the framing of the Japanese internment as an event for which no one bore personal responsibility.

Autofabricating an Authentic Public Image

For a modern politician, projecting an appealing public image while concealing the less glorious parts of his story is essential to legitimizing political power. If this process of public image-making—which I term *autofabrication*—is skillfully carried out, it crafts a convincing sense of authenticity, an impression that private identity and public image have merged entirely. Autofabricating political leaders are acutely aware of both the force they use to impose limits on their constituents and the need to obscure this force. This chapter argues that efforts by FDR and his team to obscure his use of political power—distancing himself or distracting from certain political actions, or implying support without concretely giving it—were key to his autofabrication and thus to his rhetorical production as a cultural icon.

I build the notion of autofabrication on both literary historian Stephen Greenblatt's concept of self-fashioning, with its Foucauldian emphasis on the cultural forces that shape all individuals, and on historian Peter Burke's concept of fabrication, which emphasizes the power of a leader's public image to determine the collective imagination. In *Renaissance Self-Fashioning*, Greenblatt defines *self-fashioning* as the "cultural system of meanings that creates specific individuals by governing the passage from abstract potential to concrete historical embodiment."[2] I incorporate a part of this definition into my concept of autofabrication: political leaders working to project a particular public image are themselves shaped by a cultural system of meanings. However, autofabrication—unlike self-fashioning—is not about identity or the internal experience of selfhood but about public image. Although it is applicable in many contexts, Greenblatt locates the origins of self-fashioning as a concept historically in the sixteenth century, a time when there was "increased self-consciousness about the fashioning of human identity as a manipulable, artful process."[3] When Greenblatt writes about a "manipulable, artful process," he is referring to the process of creating identity, not to a performance that might be removed from the internal experience of selfhood. It is this performance that I call autofabrication.

Although Greenblatt intended self-fashioning to refer to all aspects of self-making, I argue that self-fashioning is too limited a concept to grasp the cultural production of FDR. What happens when an individual becomes the embodiment of authority and can thus produce texts that legally and practically perform power? To address the cultural production, representation and remembrance of political leaders, I expand Greenblatt's concept of self-fashioning by including a notion of practice through executive power. *Practice* is a notion I derived from Michel De Certeau's response to Foucault. De Certeau argued that however oppressive dominant authorities may be, there is always also a practice in which individuals autonomously negotiate the existing structural demands. In *The Practice of Everyday Life*, he shows how people *can* use the street differently than the design demands, referring to this practice as "tactics" from the subjugated.[4] This theory is helpful in considering FDR's negotiation of his disability. Initially he had to act as if he was not disabled in order to be able to remain a serious contender for political office, but later his individual practice was enabled by his political power. As president he could, for instance, always request that lecterns would be screwed to the floor, so he could lean heavily on them. But FDR could "redraw the street map" (to continue De Certeau's metaphor) in a much larger sense as well, not only for his own sake, but also to give disabled, elderly, or unemployed people whole new sets of options.[5] Thus, autofabrication is self-fashioning (the shaping of one's self by oneself and others) combined with executive power (which one can use to change the game for oneself and others).

In terming FDR's treatment of his disability a "splendid deception," Hugh Gallagher was implicitly reflecting on the "honesty" of FDR's autofabrication vis-à-vis his disability. Gallagher expressed both admiration for FDR's presidency and frustration with the extent to which FDR "concealed" his disability. FDR enjoyed unusual privilege, first "just" as a very wealthy and well-connected man, and later, to an even greater degree, as president. Therefore, he had the means to deny to himself and others the notion that his disability was a part of his identity. However, many polio survivors like Gallagher had no such choice and were forced—and in some cases were eventually proud—to embrace that identity. Since Gallagher wrote his watershed *FDR's Splendid Deception* in 1985, it has become common in disability studies to consider FDR's treatment of his disability not in terms of deception but as "disability passing." This term encompasses a broader range of agents and attributes less blame to the subject who is passing as nondisabled (or, for that matter, as disabled).

Passing was a concept first developed to describe racial passing, in which people who were black according to social and legal principles of racial classification at the time could often escape racial violence by passing for white. This concept was popularized, for instance, through Kate Chopin's short story "Désirée's Baby" (1893) and Nella Larsen's 1929 novel, *Passing*.[6] Over the course of the twentieth century, passing was also increasingly used to describe and analyze queer people's strategies to pass as straight or cis-gendered, as well as straight culture's inability to "read" queerness. Although the dynamics are different in the context of disability, and the possibilities for different kinds of passing differ dramatically between different disabilities, the concept of passing lends itself very well to the social dynamics of disability.

Jeffrey Brune and Daniel Wilson write in the introduction to *Disability and Passing*: "disability passing encompasses the ways that others impose, intentionally or not, a specific disability or non-disability identity on a person. It even provides a framework for understanding how the topic of disability is ignored in texts and conversations." Thus, they make very clear that passing is fundamentally different from lying about or hiding a disability; it can encompass a wide range of acts and is something that involves many more people than just the passing subject. Furthermore, Brune and Wilson point out that "passing is an act that blurs the lines between disability and normality, but those lines were not always sharp to begin with."[7] These observations help us to understand why disability studies offers a useful critical lens to study FDR as an American icon: "minds and bodies are better understood in terms of variance than as deviation from a fixed norm." Thinking of FDR's experience in terms of variance (rather than dismissing his disability as "deviation from a fixed norm") may help us see how his treatment of his disability and his broader autofabrication profoundly informed one another.

FDR seemed to adhere to nondisabled norms; he was nimble in how he framed and employed his deviation from the norm, and usually did so without directly lying. FDR's manner of allowing people to believe something that was not quite true fits in a much broader pattern in his autofabrication. It is entirely understandable that many disabled people were frustrated with FDR's bland manner of passing and his apparent rejection of a disability identity. He would regularly irk political opponents and critical journalists in a somewhat similar manner: he was often very slippery and elusive, while seeming open and straightforward. However, like autofabrication, passing is not simply a matter of one person deceiving or concealing. Rather, it is a much more complex construction by various agents, inevitably offering a narrative that is, like all narratives, reflexive of the narrator's needs and interests.

In a democratic context, a leader often also needs to hide the exercise of power, which in itself is a form of autofabrication. An autofabricating leader crafts a public image both by performing who he "really" is credibly and charismatically and by hiding any actions that might be perceived as problematic. Such image-making is crucial to the leader's ability to wield executive power, as Roosevelt did in the example given at the beginning of this chapter.

Autofabrication, a term reserved for those with political power, thus complements self-fashioning, with *auto* referring not to the self in a Freudian sense but to the independent making of one's public image. Fabrication, with its implication of falsity, may seem too tendentious a word to refer to image-making, especially in the case of an authoritative and seemingly authentic leader like FDR. I use this term following Peter Burke, author of the paradigmatic *The Fabrication of Louis XIV*, and Hannah Arendt, who theorized about the importance of artfully constructed narrative "fabrications" in representative democracies. For Arendt, a fabrication is not an indication or euphemism for lying, but a logical sine qua non of representative democracies.[8] As a representative politician, one simply needs a well-considered narrative for oneself and many other things. Such narratives artfully construct order and so they are fabrications. FDR's passing as nondisabled is an example of fabrication in this sense, possibly one that functioned as an instructive example for himself of how to carry out autofabrication. It is important to recognize here that the dialectical nature of passing, which depends heavily on the eagerness of audiences to treat disability as invisible, is very similar to the dialectical nature of autofabrication. The *auto* may suggest that the subject is the only agent here, but audiences, too, are crucial to successful autofabrication.

In *The Fabrication of Louis XIV*, Burke contemplates "the public image of the king," the "place of Louis XIV in the collective imagination."[9] Burke focuses on the making of Louis XIV's public image, the visual and textual performance of kingship produced for the sake of visibility. Burke does not engage with

Louis XIV as an individual or a product of his culture, but as a celebrity who needed an artistic and artful apparatus to create a public image that would determine the collective imagination. Fabricating a public image in the way Louis XIV's image was made—divorced from the king's personality— has become impossible with the advent of modern mass media. However, I do borrow from Burke the idea that a leader's (auto)fabrication creates a public image that can shape the public imagination.

Successful autofabrication in the modern context hinges on the idea that the public image is authentic, that is, in synchrony with the leader's "real" self. This is impossible for politicians in a democratic system, who, on the one hand, exercise more brutal power than they can sell to their electorate, and who, on the other hand, must represent their constituents, metaphorically em- bodying all of them. Nonetheless, it remains important to be perceived as authentic; authenticity becomes a rhetorical performance. In Roosevelt's case, a wide range of dependent, independent, sympathetic, and disapproving voices contributed to his public image, because virtually every individual or organ- ization was free to engage with it. Nonetheless, Roosevelt's own PR machine set the tone and provided a leading voice in the fabrication of the FDR icon.[10]

FDR is one of the most intensely examined of all American presidents: only George Washington and Abraham Lincoln have been written about more of- ten.[11] Most works on FDR explicitly set out to give a new interpretation of who he really was, what he ultimately felt or thought, or what he obscured and revealed through his enigmatic texts and behavior. This book does not primar- ily address the mysteries, enigmas, and unanswered questions the Roosevelt icon offers, but rather theorizes the mechanics of becoming such an icon. Ken Burns, creator of the TV series *The Roosevelts: An Intimate History*, refers to four aspects that I consider to be at the heart of this issue.[12] The first aspect is who FDR was "as [an] individual"; the second is the environment that he was a product of ("riches" as well as what he endured); the third aspect is what it is that makes him a relatable public icon (i.e., the fact that he is so easily un- derstood as wrestling "with issues familiar to everyone everywhere"); and the fourth aspect is the "great public questions" that he answered in a way that permanently changed the parameters of American government.[13] These four elements are, I will argue, key to producing a political leader as a cultural icon that people recognize as representative of themselves as a collective.

Mediating between these four aspects requires an iconic leader to be a skill- ful and manipulative politician. Whereas self-fashioning is a process every individual is engaged in, autofabrication is an extension of self-fashioning specific to the making of icons, particularly political leaders. Political leaders in democratic systems are bound to represent a far larger constituency than just themselves and, therefore, need a public image that is recognizable to an immense range of citizens. They possess and often use their ultimate power over subjects' life and death but need to seem benevolent and considerate to all those they purportedly represent. I argue that a successful autofabrication needs to encompass an extremely plastic public image, so as to appeal to a wide variety of audiences and address "issues familiar to everyone everywhere."

One of the best and most well-known analyses of Franklin Roosevelt's maneuvering between openness and slyness is Warren Kimball's *The Juggler: Franklin Roosevelt as Wartime Statesman*.[14] On the one hand, Kimball sets out to analyze the nature and construction of FDR's essential slipperiness—much like this book—and, on the other, wants to pin FDR down. The latter strategy works only to some extent: Kimball argues that FDR as a wartime statesman knew exactly what he was doing, even if contemporaries and later historians have not been able to figure out what that was. This argument is not always convincing with regard to concrete war policies, but Kimball does elegantly show how FDR's elusiveness was constructed. He shows that many of FDR's messages are transparent in form and impenetrable in content: a nimble pairing that was probably a part of a largely intuitive strategy.

FDR's Reshaping of Presidential Templates

Most of this chapter focuses on aspects of Franklin Roosevelt's autofabrication that pulled public attention away from potentially unpopular ways that he used power. First, however, I highlight a constitutive part of FDR's early autofabrication: the ways that he both modeled himself on and defined himself against Theodore Roosevelt, reshaping presidential "templates" in the process.

FDR aspired to the presidency from very early on and admired his distant relative Theodore Roosevelt, who became president when Franklin was nineteen. On the day of Franklin and Eleanor Roosevelt's wedding, President Theodore Roosevelt, brother of ER's deceased father, gave the bride away and was the guest of honor. FDR habitually addressed Theodore Roosevelt as "Uncle Theodore,"[15] and his political career mirrored Theodore Roosevelt's in striking detail: they both became assistant secretary of the navy, ran unsuccessfully for vice president, and became governor of New York. FDR strongly believed from the 1910s onward that he could follow Theodore Roosevelt's path to the presidency.[16]

Before FDR's election, several presidential "templates" had been in vogue, such as that of the Founding Father President, the Frontiersman President, and the Civil War Veteran President.[17] FDR was none of those but was lucky to be able to mold himself outwardly on the model of Theodore Roosevelt, who, after initially being hailed as a war hero, was the first of what would later come to be regarded as the "Governor Presidents," which is why it is important that both were governor of New York before their presidencies. Theodore Roosevelt had also autofabricated himself as a frontiersman and a cowboy; he had worked as a rancher and exuded enormous physical strength, exuberant health, and confidence.[18] Without claiming to have been born in a log cabin—as had been essential for instance in Andrew Jackson's and William Harrison's campaigns—he revived the presidential template of the Frontiersman President that had served them.[19]

After 1921, when Franklin Roosevelt became disabled, he could no longer match any of these templates entirely. However, he worked hard to develop his chest and arm muscles, so that his upper body was and looked very strong.[20] Where Theodore Roosevelt was often photographed on horseback, FDR had his photos taken in his car, presenting a modernized version of his uncle and predecessor. Moreover, since Theodore's precedent, more people had entered the presidency from governor positions, in particular, another iconic president and mentor of FDR, Woodrow Wilson. So when FDR ran for president, he was following a recent template that suited him better than earlier available models; simultaneously, he did what he could to live up to and modernize the existing templates.

If FDR's hypermasculine performance evoked Theodore Roosevelt, who was widely remembered as a war hero and a cowboy, it additionally may have served as a key component of his "disability passing." Passing as nondisabled for many men involves a performance of hypermasculinity, as Katherine Ott argues, or—especially if they use prostheses—then "passing" as nondisabled may be replaced by a hypermasculine performance involving the prosthesis.[21] As I discuss in chapters 5 and 6, FDR himself seemed to focus his autofabrication efforts on "passing" as nondisabled, but later portrayals of him that showcase his wheelchair often do so to foreground a hypermasculine performance.

Copying Theodore Roosevelt's career worked out well in part because he was a presidential model FDR could match up to, and someone who had himself also modernized the model of the US president. More than his predecessors, Theodore Roosevelt understood the importance of mass publicity, and he was more than an administrator.[22] It was not until FDR was president himself that it became advantageous to publicly stress his links with his uncle. By that time, he had truly acquired his own position and could advertise having voted for Theodore Roosevelt; he also could adopt the name "New Deal" for his major domestic change program, in reference to Theodore Roosevelt's 1906 Square Deal program.[23] Thus, his uncle probably shaped FDR's autofabrication by creating space for him to get away from cultural molds he would not have been able to fit into.

In an article about the impact of presidential personality in the transition from FDR to Truman in 1945, Frank Costigliola also stresses FDR's ability to be flexible within and across roles that traditionally were often narrowly defined. With regard to Roosevelt's performance of masculinity, Costigliola notes: "With an unknowable degree of intentionality, FDR sometimes acted in ways that his contemporaries described as feminine. His mellifluous voice, patrician air, and nonstop talk and gesture all connoted effeminacy. Yet his muscular upper torso, developed after contracting polio; his visible courage; and his aura of power also denoted masculinity as it was and is conventionally understood."[24]

This "androgynous tendency," as Costigliola calls it, was part and parcel of FDR's broader flexibility and resourcefulness in offering the performance that was needed in specific situations and was, Costigliola argues, understood as such by contemporaries.[25] FDR was, by all accounts, extremely self-confident, which allowed him to not just "fill in" the role that people and context expected but to revise and shift expectations. As previously noted, FDR may have developed this "nimbleness" in performing a particular image or range of images—ironically, both in the context of masculinity and in the context of being paralyzed—in part because he literally could not move around easily.

Emerging from an old Dutch family as a disabled but rich inheritor, FDR could not lay claim to being a self-made man, a proponent of America's success in achieving its Manifest Destiny, or an embodiment of the American Dream. Theodore Roosevelt had not had most of these characteristics either but had adapted himself—for instance, by working as a cowboy for some time—whereas FDR, partly because his uncle had leveled the path, could get away with being an outlier. By the time Franklin Roosevelt's political career was budding, shifts that were already occurring created more space for him to modernize the older ideals. The nineteenth-century notion of Manifest Destiny, for instance, took on a new, more metaphorical shape, after the literal frontier had been closed. FDR played into this change. Following his predecessor and one-time boss Woodrow Wilson, he offered a concrete new national project by arguing that it was America's duty to uphold international law and order[26] and to become the world's "arsenal of democracy."[27] Indeed, the implicit presence of the older rhetoric of America's Manifest Destiny and American Civil Religion enhanced his argument against isolationism in the late 1930s.[28] At the same time, FDR's move away from the Emersonian rhetoric of self-reliance and "rags-to-riches" interpretations of the American Dream was well-received against the background of the Depression, which rendered so many American dreams ridiculous and gave the lie to so many people's sense of self-reliance.[29] One presidential template that FDR could conform to, at least to some extent, was that of the president as benevolent parent to the nation; an American archetype that had existed since the Founding Fathers. That was not a role he could step into before he was president and also because of his relative youth. He did find an early entrance to it, via his role of informal friend or older brother, a role he mainly developed in radio addresses, as the many letters he received in response attest. Here again, he did not only adopt a modern medium but also updated a much older ideal, aptly responding to society's need to modernize cultural archetypes.

One reason that FDR has become an icon in American memory—as I will argue in chapter 6—is that he was president during World War II, the period in which the United States assumed the dominant position in the global order that it occupied at least until 2001 (and arguably until 2016).[30] Both of FDR's presidential role models, Theodore Roosevelt and Woodrow Wilson, were essential forebears in this specific respect. Theodore Roosevelt established and solidified the United States' role in the western hemisphere as—in his discourse—arbitrator and harbinger of civilization, while Woodrow Wilson's leadership during World War I—and vision for the League of Nations—shaped FDR's own vision for America's and the world's future. FDR effectively synthesized Theodore Roosevelt's progressivism and Wilson's liberal internationalism, although he never quite managed to reconcile the two approaches, particularly with regard to the often-exploitative territorialization of the US empire. After World War II, Eleanor Roosevelt, among others, promoted his vision and helped bring it into being, although her convictions, more than FDR's, had evolved, already in the 1930s, toward internationalism.[31]

Thus, FDR as an American icon forms part of a longer historical line: a Rooseveltian vision and practice of shaping the United States' role in the world. This overarching Rooseveltian narrative is treated in an extended form in various scholarly monographs (e.g., James MacGregor Burns and Susan Dunn's *The Three Roosevelts* and Elizabeth Borgwardt's *A New Deal for the World*), as well as in popular texts such as Ken Burns's fourteen-hour documentary, *The Roosevelts.*[32]

But, of course, such views about a presidency's transformative impact on global politics are only possible with the benefit of hindsight. Early on in his political career, FDR realized that, however much Theodore Roosevelt had helped him to establish his vision of the presidency and to gain control over his public image, the family connection with Theodore and the Roosevelt name also meant that he needed to appear independent from his wife's famous uncle. One way in which he did that was by joining the Democratic Party; Theodore had been a Republican president. This may, however, seem to be a greater difference than it really was. At least initially, neither Theodore nor Franklin were strongly attached to their parties, and both were known for being realists rather than idealists.[33] They essentially shared all main political beliefs, which were best summarized under the term *progressivism.*[34] Theodore Roosevelt, after his presidency, left the Republican Party and started his own new Progressive Party, thus splitting the Republican electorate and giving the 1912 election victory to the Democrat Woodrow Wilson.[35] FDR may indeed have chosen to join the Democratic ticket in New York State mainly because as a Republican he would always have been overshadowed by the then still much more famous Teddy Roosevelt and, therefore, would have had no chance of election as a Republican.[36]

FDR's tendency to define himself against others is part of a larger pattern in his autofabrication. During his presidency, FDR's declared enemies were first the Great Depression and then the Axis powers (Germany, Italy, and Japan). These opponents were crucial to the fabrication of FDR's public image, as his two still-popular nicknames, Dr. New Deal and Dr. Win the War, attest. Although FDR's ideals seem to have derived primarily from antitheses to politics he strongly opposed, he became increasingly associated with his own active agenda. "Dr. New Deal" and "Dr. Win-the-War" suggest as much: they stress FDR's actions against the Depression and fascism rather than the mere fact of his opposition. The public increasingly saw FDR as an emblem of democracy in the broadest sense. This was in part because FDR defined himself in opposition to the "isms" of the day—colonialism, fascism, and communism—rather than presenting himself as an ideologue himself. It was also in part because he had to represent a wide spectrum of Democratic party wings and members. FDR cast himself as representative of the ideals that all true Americans shared; this was initially probably not an intentional strategy, but later became an active tool. Indeed, his eminently practical, "try something, if it doesn't work, try something else" approach to the New Deal was relatively successful in fighting the national spirit of desperation, because it tapped into the quintessentially American conviction that acting is better than theorizing.[37]

Although FDR first took ownership of his own image during campaigns for political office, his more transformative acts of autofabrication could only happen when he acquired the power of the presidency. After all, once he had risen to a position in which he could command everything from nationwide radio time to facilities for his disability, he could do more to present the image of himself that the wanted. Increasingly, he could even change the presidency through the way he filled it. The Franklin D. Roosevelt Presidential Library—the first ever presidential library—was FDR's idea; its construction began in 1938 and it opened in 1941. Those dates bracket another key moment in his presidency: his unprecedented third term reelection in 1940. After that, and especially after the United States became officially engaged in World War II, FDR's executive power—now also as commander in chief during wartime—became almost limitless.

This extreme power conferred upon an elected president—in a democracy traditionally highly suspicious of the corrupting effect of power vested in a single individual, yet also in need of continuity because of the ongoing war—called for a great deal of autofabrication on FDR's part. In particular, FDR's autofabrication as a masculine yet mild and humane parental figure to a country in wartime became necessary to create a sense of self-confidence and unity in the war, and to occlude the less heroic, or indeed criminal, elements of his presidency. As a war president in his unprecedented third and fourth terms, FDR acquired more room for autofabrication. He had more space to set his own conditions and to shape the circumstances under which people saw or heard him. After eight years, he was a very familiar figure to most constituents. At the same time, there was more work to do in hiding or spinning acts of his administration during the war. The novelty and uniqueness of the situation allowed him to shape expectations of what his legacy would be.

FDR Distancing Himself from the Atlantic Charter

Autofabrication, as I have argued, is inspired by the need both to put forward an iconic public image and to obscure evidence of power-mongering. Roosevelt himself acknowledged—albeit in the context of commenting on wartime international relations—that he was prepared to strategically tell "untruths." Roosevelt on May 15, 1942, famously commented in a conversation with Henry

Morgenthau: "You know I am a juggler, and I never let my right hand know what my left hand does . . . I may have one policy for Europe and one diametrically opposite for North and South America. I may be entirely inconsistent, and furthermore I am perfectly willing to mislead and tell untruths if it will help win the war."[38]

FDR is honest and open here about his duplicity in his war practice. "You know" stresses the addressee's awareness of the trickery while it is happening. The reference to his left and right hands primarily fits in with the juggler metaphor, but on a secondary level refers to his tendency to tell different cabinet members, officers, and other close assistants ("right hands") different and conflicting things.[39] It may even be read as referring to the left and right wings of the political spectrum, to which he provided contradictory narratives. The juggler performs a perplexing and confusing act that may seem impromptu but which can only be pulled off because of the juggler's practiced skill.

The juggling Roosevelt does in this now epigrammatic statement puts a bewildering and falsely reassuring spin on his actual behavior as a wartime president. The statement puzzles while claiming to be revealing. Its skillful use of language shows FDR to be a nimble figure and draws attention away from his physical inability to move independently. This nimbleness distracts from what it is that he misleads and tells untruths about. Thus FDR engages in autofabrication primarily through textual rhetoric. He did very real things; indeed, he exerted his presidential power in unprecedented ways and to extreme extents, sending more than twelve million American soldiers into combat and incarcerating nearly 122,000 Japanese Americans without proof of disloyalty. Such acts were made possible primarily through his texts, which I consider to have been performative in several ways.

I use *performative* here in J. L. Austin's sense—that is, meaning that the texts perform, or *do* something—but are not necessarily a rhetorical expression of the signatory. Roosevelt issued executive orders—texts with legal status—commanding the execution of specified acts, such as the internment of potentially disloyal citizens on the West Coast, Executive Order 9066 (February 19, 1942). With over 290 executive orders per year in office, FDR issued far more of them than any president before or after him.[40] Herbert Hoover saw this as a dictatorial tendency: "Roosevelt frequently denied any dictatorial tastes, but a small side evidence is indicative. That was the daily issuance of executive orders in peacetime."[41] Generally, political scientists agree that "beginning with Roosevelt, chief executives started to use executive orders to establish major policy," a notion first popularized by Arthur Schlesinger in

The Imperial Presidency.[42] Thus, in the face of the Great Depression and World War II, FDR through an avalanche of executive orders unilaterally made and implemented policy at unprecedented speed. This was to a large extent necessary and part of a trend (President Hoover himself had issued more executive orders than any president before him, and presidents since have also used them extensively for policymaking).

But exerting power in this way, through texts that are impersonal yet have a great impact, was, in FDR's case, also part of his autofabrication, precisely because executive orders made him invisible. Their texts are explicitly performative—"by virtue of the power vested in me as president," as Executive Order 9066 (EO9066) has it—and avoid fabricating FDR as a public icon or an individual. Instead, the language puts distance between the executive order and the president. "By virtue of the power vested in me" is a passive formulation: "by virtue of the power" suggests that FDR is not personally doing anything. Rather, the depersonalized "power" is acting and not of its own accord but "by virtue," a phrase that implicitly signals that there is a moral justification involved. Moreover, "vested in me" suggests that anyone (given the democratic structure, perhaps everyone) did the vesting except for FDR himself. This glosses over the fact that FDR actually exerted "the power" personally, when he had a choice to do otherwise. EO9066 is a very specific and much debated example. Its wording is formulaic and not typical of FDR. However, my point here is that FDR did not shun the execution of extreme power, including the suspension of the writ of habeas corpus for particular ethnic groups, but used his power through extremely impersonal means and language. EO9066 was held up by the Supreme Court during FDR's presidency— it was only rescinded decades later by Gerald Ford in 1976—so it was a decision supported by the system of checks and balances, perhaps hardly actually linked to FDR personally. Still, while EO9066 was a text FDR issued that had great practical impact on the lives of people, its impersonal framing avoids shaping FDR's public image as a person, although he had a personal role in its drafting, and planning, based on long-held prejudices about Japanese people.[43] I see it as an act of autofabrication in its near-denial of the fact that there was an individual exercising tremendous power (although, clearly, Hoover was onto his game).

A crucial pair of moments in FDR's autofabrication was his Four Freedoms speech—the traditional State of the Union address he gave on January 6, 1941, before official American involvement in World War II—and his meeting off the coast of Newfoundland with British Prime Minister Winston Churchill on

August 14, 1941, that produced the Atlantic Charter.[44] The latter is an example of FDR's "juggling" to distance himself from an agreement that may have been politically unpopular. In the Four Freedoms Speech, Roosevelt formulated his definition of freedom ("the supremacy of human rights everywhere") and specified the Four Freedoms at the heart of human rights:

> In the future days, which we seek to make secure, we look forward to a world founded upon four essential human freedoms. The first is freedom of speech and expression—everywhere in the world. The second is freedom of every person to worship God in his own way—everywhere in the world. The third is freedom from want—which, translated into world terms, means economic understandings which will secure to every nation a healthy peacetime life for its inhabitants—everywhere in the world. The fourth is freedom from fear—which, translated into world terms, means a world-wide reduction of armaments to such a point and in such a thorough fashion that no nation will be in a position to commit an act of physical aggression against any neighbor—anywhere in the world.
>
> That is no vision of a distant millennium. It is a definite basis for a kind of world attainable in our own time and generation. That kind of world is the very antithesis of the so called new order of tyranny which the dictators seek to create with the crash of a bomb. To that new order we oppose the greater conception—the moral order. A good society is able to face schemes of world domination and foreign revolutions alike without fear. Since the beginning of our American history, we have been engaged in change—in a perpetual peaceful revolution—a revolution which goes on steadily, quietly adjusting itself to changing conditions—without the concentration camp or the quick lime in the ditch. The world order which we seek is the cooperation of free countries, working together in a friendly, civilized society.
>
> This nation has placed its destiny in the hands and heads and hearts of its millions of free men and women; and its faith in freedom under the guidance of God. Freedom means the supremacy of human rights everywhere. Our support goes to those who struggle to gain those rights or keep them. Our strength is our unity of purpose. To that high concept there can be no end save victory.[45]

The most frequently quoted lines are the ones in which FDR names the Four Freedoms. Because they are usually quoted in isolation, this seems a purely idealistic text, largely or entirely divorced from its historical circumstances and practical impact.[46] They did, however, have great impact, not only rhetorically at the time of the address's delivery, but also in the formulation of the United Nations' aims. These lines are some of the most central and best remembered statements of FDR's principles. But this long excerpt also shows how the speech functioned as a whole. It was in the first place a war message at a time the United States was not yet involved directly in the war and when public opinion largely opposed involvement. Roosevelt explicitly stated his opposition to "the so-called new order of tyranny which the dictators seek to create with the crash of a bomb." He used clearly belligerent words—supremacy, struggle, strength, victory—in a more or less metaphorical context, but the pointed theme of all these metaphors was war.

While the speech seems to be, and tends to be remembered as, a plea for freedom and human rights and against violence, Roosevelt invoked those high principles to ready the nation for war. At the same time, his formulation of the Four Freedoms was a constitutive part of his autofabrication, presenting his character as kind, fatherly, and morally firm while also linking his principles directly to the ideological foundations of the United States. Jeffrey Engel and others have pointed out that FDR tapped into and cemented an American ethos and discourse that had existed before and that through this speech only became more important in presidential rhetoric across the political spectrum.[47] The speech thus contributed to FDR's making and remembrance as an American icon.

When saying, "Since the beginning of our American history, we have been engaged in change—in a perpetual peaceful revolution," he used "we" to ostentatiously place himself and his contemporaries in the same glorious historical context of peaceful change. To say simultaneously that "there can be no end save victory" implied that there would be war. Thus, the autofabrication lay in FDR's proposition of a public image that stressed his uniquely American peacefulness, morality, and zeal for freedom. The latent message that was insinuated in passive terms, and which the assertive autofabrication covered up, was that, under FDR, the United States would go to war.

The first key and most direct reconfiguration of the Four Freedoms speech was in the Atlantic Charter, issued on August 14, 1941. The meeting between FDR and Winston Churchill that produced the Atlantic Charter, a pivotal policy statement which officially formulated their shared aims for the postwar world, was held in secret on the HMS *Prince of Wales* in Placentia Bay, off the coast of Newfoundland. This secrecy is in itself worthy of note: while there were, of course, security issues involved, FDR and his staff went out of their way to present alternative narratives about FDR's whereabouts.[48] The Atlantic Charter itself is a key document in its statement of agreed principles between the United States and Great Britain, including the projected end of

European/British colonialism, the envisioning of the United Nations as a global body to assert the Four Freedoms as central aims for humanity, and the statement that "the Nazi tyranny" must be destroyed. Its sixth point illustrates this all-encompassing quality very well: "After the final destruction of Nazi tyranny, they hope to see established a peace which will afford to all nations the means of dwelling in safety within their own boundaries, and which will afford assurance that all the men in all the lands may live out their lives in freedom from fear and want."

Apart from the principles Churchill and Roosevelt formulate for the entire world here, including refraining from national expansion and explicating "freedom from fear and want" as ambitions every nation ought to have, this point became especially important because of the opening subclause. Hitler read the Atlantic Charter days after Roosevelt and Churchill drafted it—diplomatic relations between the United States and Germany were still intact and functioned—and he allegedly and understandably interpreted it as a declaration of war.[49]

The first meeting between Roosevelt and Churchill, and the Atlantic Charter they produced, formed a key turning point in World War II, even before the United States was officially engaged. However, while this was one of the moments in which Roosevelt used the presidential power at his discretion most forcefully and influentially, the meeting was clouded in secrecy, and the text of the Atlantic Charter was extremely impersonal. Although the Atlantic Charter formulated some of Roosevelt's most favored principles, its text refers to him twice as "the President of the United States" and never uses his name. This is all the more striking since "the President of the United States" is on both occasions mentioned alongside "the Prime Minister, Mr. Churchill." The Atlantic Charter was for Churchill a more problematic message to bring home, because it stated the vision of a world without colonialism, obviously a sacrifice for Great Britain, but gave no clear guarantees of American help in fighting the war. Nevertheless, Churchill owned the message personally, whereas Roosevelt ostensibly acted only through the power invested in the president. Indeed, there was no official signed version of the Atlantic Charter; the text was telegraphed to London and Washington. Roosevelt at a press conference in 1944 said about this: "There isn't any copy of the Atlantic Charter, so far as I know. I haven't got one. The British haven't got one. The nearest thing you will get is the [message of the] radio operator on *Augusta* and *Prince of Wales*. That's the nearest thing you will come to it . . . There was no formal document."[50]

Statements like the one above—with their bantering tone, tendency to draw up smokescreens, and denial of the existence of the Atlantic Charter in official document form—call to mind the "I'm a juggler" epigram. Churchill was also a very strong autofabricator, but he played this particular game differently, using his name and persona to sell the deal at home. Roosevelt openly and in a personable manner stated that he had acted presidentially at his discretion on behalf of the nation, without attaching his name to any document. The Atlantic Charter was a pivotal policy statement and a product of Roosevelt's personal interaction with Churchill and with the country he represented, yet his name was as far away from it as possible, a fact he cared to stress explicitly. His active autofabrication of his iconic image lay elsewhere: it was part of his public addresses such as the Four Freedoms speech. The autofabrication involved in Roosevelt's treatment of the Atlantic Charter was its passive counterpart: the secrecy surrounding the meeting and explicit denial of the existence of a formal document themselves contributed to the image of FDR as a compelling but elusive icon.

Eleanor Roosevelt Deflecting Attention through Soft Power

Eleanor Roosevelt was a crucial agent in FDR's autofabrication and, because she survived him and remained publicly active and visible, of his legacy. This is not to suggest that ER was only instrumental to her husband's policies. She had her own strong political convictions (often very different from FDR's) and successfully, though even more covertly, carried out her own autofabrication. While often helpful to the Roosevelt administration, she also assumed a great deal of autonomy and, at times, disregarded FDR's ideas and political interests entirely.[51] However, ER's role is discussed here only to the extent that it is immediately relevant to Franklin Roosevelt's autofabrication. What made ER particularly important in the context of FDR's autofabrication was her faculty to informally and indirectly expand his influence into areas such as the domestic sphere and the entertainment sector of mass media. ER made FDR's autofabrication more powerful, because she mitigated his influence into areas not habitually considered the realm of presidential leadership. By providing disadvantaged or aggrieved groups with "soft" recognition, she deflected attention from the fact that FDR was providing little in the way of "hard" political measures or financial compensation.

Eleanor Roosevelt often depoliticized issues for her husband, deftly drawing them out of the realm of executive power. Her ability to do so offered his administration an extra pathway, for instance, to keep the more radical left wing of the party in the Democratic fold; this, in turn, gave her unusual political clout for a First Lady. ER resided in the White House, in the sense that she lived there, but she effectively also had an important political role there, despite not being elected for political office. She was very important to the Roosevelt administration as a channel of communication with groups and spheres traditionally outside of the political arena, both through writing for many lady's magazines and appearing in radio shows aimed at women, and through lending her ear to representatives of marginalized groups, most importantly to civil rights leaders.[52] Through these roles, ER was able to help many groups via traditionally nonpolitical or disenfranchised spaces in ways that had impact, not on a formal political level, but in terms of civic empowerment.

For instance, Eleanor Roosevelt gave her own White House press conferences and made them accessible to women only, in order to force the press to employ female White House correspondents—a plan that originated with her close friend Lorena Hickok.[53] These conferences were often engaged with topics that were traditionally associated with femininity (youth, the elderly, poverty, the decision to start serving alcoholic beverages in the White House after the end of Prohibition) and that did not carry high political stakes. Nevertheless, the conferences were very successful; she held 348 between March 1933 and April 1945 (mostly women only), next to her husband's 998 in the same period.

Particularly with regard to racial oppression, Eleanor Roosevelt had a crucial role in FDR's administration. Because the Democratic Party still included a key block of states in the Jim Crow South, it was politically risky for FDR to support legislation that might "disturb" the uneasy equilibrium within the party. As Ira Katznelson, Kim Geiger, and Daniel Kryder put it:

> Roosevelt and congressional leaders tailored New Deal legislation to southern preferences. They reached an implicit modus vivendi: southern civil society would remain intact and southern representatives would support the key elements of the administration's program. There would be no attempt to build a mass biracial base in the South; nor would even the most heinous aspects of regional repression, such as lynching, be brought under the rule of law. Further, sponsors fashioned key bills to avoid disturbing the region's racial civilization by employing two main policy instruments: the exclusion of agricultural and domestic labor, the principal occupational categories of blacks, from legislation, including the National Recovery Act, the Wagner Act, Social Security, and the Fair Labor Standards Act, and decentralized administration.[54]

This implicit agreement set the stage for the New Deal's blatant and well-remembered neglect of Black Americans' destitution. Some historians have argued that through the Supreme Court, FDR did eventually lay the groundwork for watershed cases like Brown v. Board of Education, but on the whole, FDR did little to concretely support or empower the budding Civil Rights Movement.[55] Nevertheless, he was generally popular among African Americans (as he was among American Jews, whom he equally could have supported more concretely but didn't out of political carefulness or opportunism). This was the kind of situation in which Eleanor Roosevelt was able to play an important, if somewhat ambivalent, role.

Perhaps the most famous instance of this was Eleanor Roosevelt's resignation as a member of the Daughters of the American Revolution, following the club's racist refusal to allow Black opera star Marian Anderson to perform in its auditorium.[56] Instead, ER invited Marian Anderson to perform at the Lincoln Memorial in Washington, DC, an iconic moment in civil rights history, although also an ambivalent one. ER's acts were crucial for the careers of those directly involved—Marian Anderson as well as the female journalists to whom she gave exclusive access to her press conferences—and symbolically important for the groups they represented. At the same time, she attended to these issues in realms where they would not immediately lead to demands that FDR address head-on political hornets' nests. Marian Anderson's performance at the Lincoln Memorial in 1939 was important civically and as a media event but did not give the vote to disfranchised African Americans. Although the event can be regarded as premediating the Civil Rights Movement of the 1950s and 1960s, on another level, it may have canalized feelings in the African American community, thus helping the administration in sustaining the inequality. In terms of autofabrication, such mediagenic actions by ER, for instance, may have obscured or counterweighted painful race issues, such as FDR's refusal to speak out in favor of the anti-lynching Costigan–Wagner Act, which was subsequently narrowly defeated as a result of Southern Democratic opposition in Congress.[57] Thus, ER's public and widely publicized civil rights activism helped give FDR the political leeway to retain his popularity with African Americans, even though he refused to actually use his political sway to act in their support.

Thus, Eleanor Roosevelt's activism could address problems experienced by marginalized groups by seeming to allow them entrance to the traditional political arena without actually doing so. The recognition and solutions offered through her interference existed in the public sphere but not in the heart of power politics. This benefited both those involved and FDR's administrations (by precluding more pervasive demands), also giving an important measure of informal power to ER. In fact, for someone who was not elected, she arguably had an inordinate amount of political clout within the White House precisely because she could keep so many issues out of it.

Eleanor Roosevelt unofficially addressed issues the administration could not officially say anything about. FDR often spoke to journalists off the record, but even then, he was limited by political constraints; ER supplemented FDR's public image with an unofficial, radical voice. Together FDR and ER could decide, whether or not they actually discussed such things explicitly, that ER would address an issue—always *á titre personnel*—providing those involved with a kind of "soft" acknowledgement by the president. One frequent motive for this, from the FDR administration's perspective, was to deflect demands for "hard" political measures or financial compensation. ER's treatment of issues as an unofficial mouthpiece for FDR could obscure what the president was doing elsewhere; she contributed to the public icon by eliding the exercise of power. At the same time, her treatment of issues carried its own form of soft power.

The story of Eleanor Roosevelt's 1933 visit to the Bonus Army, which led one veteran to say, "Hoover sent the Army, Roosevelt sent his wife," is exemplary here. The veteran's comment was echoed by innumerable journalists at the time and by historians, schoolbooks, documentaries, and websites since. Although the visit was an important and intentional affirmation, it was not an official government statement. As such, it was a classic Rooseveltian example of symbol politics. ER was kind, compassionate, and good at making the veterans feel they were being seen and heard, but their demand for money was not granted or even seriously considered.

The Private Arena as a Means to Distract

Through her writings, Eleanor Roosevelt could introduce carefully selected aspects of the Roosevelts' private life into the public view. During the war, for instance, she regularly stressed that all four Roosevelt sons had commissions in the US army. This helped to deflect accusations that FDR had—against his promises, some felt— sent other people's sons into war and selfishly abused his power to keep his own safe, and it profiled the presidential family as dedicated and patriotic on a personal level.

Eleanor Roosevelt introduced their private family sphere as a means to depoliticize issues. FDR himself applied the same tactics, drawing issues out of
the realm of serious political debate; for instance, in 1944, he attacked Republicans who had accused him of using public means for his private needs. In a
Radio News campaign speech on September 23, 1944, he said:

> These Republican leaders have not been content with attacks on me, or my wife,
> or on my sons. No, not content with that, they now include my little dog, Fala.
> Well, of course, I don't resent attacks, and my family don't resent attacks, but Fala
> does resent them. You know, Fala is Scotch, and being a Scottie, as soon as he
> learned that the Republican fiction writers in Congress and out had concocted
> a story that I'd left him behind on an Aleutian island and had sent a destroyer
> back to find him—at a cost to the taxpayers of two or three, or eight or twenty
> million dollars—his Scotch soul was furious. He has not been the same dog
> since. I am accustomed to hearing malicious falsehoods about myself . . . But I
> think I have a right to resent, to object, to libelous statements about my dog.[58]

Not only did this turn serious—and probably to some extent justified—charges
into a joke, it also removed the issue from the locus of political debate about
governmental expenditure to the homely, cute, and obviously nonpolitical site
of the Roosevelts' family dog. The rhetorical deftness lay in the fact that Roosevelt was accused of spending public money on his dog, thus drawing Fala
into the political sphere, and deflected the attack through the same movement
that the accusers objected to. Rather than defending his spending, or even answering the charges made, he switched to discussing the accusations' supposed effects on Fala. Relocating the discussion to the private sphere, he depoliticized the issue and ironically, in doing so, objected to that very movement.
In a broad paraphrase, he asked that Fala be left out of the game, while at the
same time bringing Fala into it himself. This rhetorically invalidated the
charges by displacing them into the private sphere, which was all the more
ironic because the actual displacement of the dog and its alleged rescue with
government means was what led to the discussion in the first place.

This use of Fala and persons from his private sphere was also characteristic of the manner in which FDR's associates depoliticized his remembrance.
Fala survived FDR by seven years, and thus, in mass media, moved from
being one of FDR's often photographed and described attributes to one of
Eleanor Roosevelt's, one of the most publicly visible assets to pass from him
to her in 1945. Even the earliest exhibitions in the Franklin D. Roosevelt Library and Museum included a "Fala corner" dedicated to the remembrance

of the family dog. Although the Fala speech was an important element in it, this remembrance was almost ostentatiously nonpolitical.

Like everybody, a political leader is shaped by environment and circumstances and must, in order to be successful, perform to the standards of authorities. This is self-fashioning. However, when this is successful and the leader acquires a position of power, space becomes available to autofabricate by projecting a particular public image and even changing the rules of the game. In a representative democracy, the position of power also brings with it a need to keep certain things out of the public view. Roosevelt, initially, was shaped largely by his wealthy upstate New York upbringing and by the presidency of his uncle Theodore Roosevelt, on whose example he molded his own political career. The disease episode in 1921 that paralyzed his legs almost prevented him from taking on a public role, but eventually, his inability to conform to previous standards also helped him fill the job in his own manner.

In Franklin Roosevelt's autofabrication, one key element was his strong inclination to pose as apolitical and to suggest that issues were not points of political contestation but rather of "finding the best solution." Thus, he deflected attention away from politically controversial issues, such as United States involvement in World War II or the internment of Japanese Americans on the West coast (the latter only became politically problematic years later). At the same time, he drew specific attention to his personal life through, for example, his intimate radio addresses and his dog Fala. His wife Eleanor Roosevelt played a special role in this, in the sense that she often "solved" issues the White House was confronted with but in areas of public life outside of politics. Her involvement could both depoliticize issues and make the presidency seem more personal, often without leading to actual political action. Through such means, FDR managed to create a public image that made him seem kind and transparent, while he exerted life-and-death power over his subjects.

Of course, FDR's autofabrication did not come about in a vacuum. The 1920s and 1930s were decades that—because of profound changes in the media landscape and broader culture—allowed for new kinds of performance of one's persona. This was the era in which literary and other celebrities such as F. Scott Fitzgerald came to occupy their positions as highly visible and celebrated society figures. Moreover, this was the era in which branding and advertising came into vogue.[59] FDR seems to have caught on to the idea of personal branding at an early stage and continues to be associated with visual props denoting his patrician air of easy self-confidence, such as his cigarette pipe and fedora hat.

The rise of radio was a primarily technological development that Roosevelt was among the first to be able to utilize on his path to the presidency. His use of radio will be discussed in detail in chapter 2, but it is important to point out here that radio gave him a new and unusual opportunity for autofabrication. Roosevelt could not only advertise himself via the radio but could also jump onto the bandwagon of the United States' evolution toward what Benedict Anderson has called an "imagined community."[60] Anderson explains that the nation is "imagined as a community, because regardless of the actual inequality and exploitation that may prevail in each, the nation is always perceived as a deep horizontal comradeship."[61] Thus, Anderson uses "imagined community" to denote a nation as a collective of people who can never all know one another, but still conceive of themselves as a community. Anderson locates the origins of imagined communities in the nineteenth century with the rise of newspapers and novels.

In the United States (a much larger and more diverse nation in the first place than the European countries, Anderson examines), radio was arguably a much more powerful medium for creating a "deep horizontal comradeship" across the entire nation. FDR's radio addresses were scheduled to be more or less prime time radio for Americans across all time zones, and they were broadcast live, so that everyone—at times more than 80 percent of American citizens—could hear the president live at the same time.[62] Thus, Roosevelt managed his own autofabrication through his use of radio and also profoundly influenced and strengthened the imagined community that had practically and ideologically created him.

CHAPTER TWO

The Collective Rhetorical Production
of FDR, 1932–1945

Louis McHenry Howe was Roosevelt's closest friend and most devoted political adviser; together with a host of other advisers, cabinet members, and ghostwriters, he helped to produce the public FDR voice. He was the political first
adviser to FDR who was not family and kept his role until his death in 1936.
Although generally invisible to the public, Howe was a colorful figure, and certainly among Roosevelt biographers, he remains understandably beloved:

> Eleven years older than FDR, Louis Howe . . . was barely five feet tall, emaciated,
> his face scarred by a childhood bicycle accident, a malodorous Sweet Caporal
> cigarette dangled perpetually from his lips, the ashes falling randomly on his
> rumpled three-piece suit. Even when freshly scrubbed, which was not often, he
> looked dirty and unkempt. Howe took perverse pride in his appearance, claim-
> ing to be one of the four ugliest men in New York. "Children take one look at
> me on the street and run." A fellow reporter one called him a "medieval gnome,"
> and Howe accepted the designation with delight. His cynical view of human
> nature rarely left him disappointed. And he was always broke.[1]

From the very first moment, Howe saw in FDR a future president and was
undeterred by the setbacks Roosevelt encountered on his path to the presidency. Howe completely dedicated himself to assisting FDR and helping him
to strategically shape his public image and voice. He himself was not, as he realized all too well, a mediagenic character, but he considered himself—and
was—an excellent kingmaker. Descriptions of Howe, both by himself and by
later commentators (including Jean Edward Smith in the quotation above),
have imagined him as a kind of court jester. A critical and incisive sidekick in
FDR's presence, Howe was extremely loyal to FDR in public settings. Indeed,
Howe was one of the main authors of Roosevelt's speeches and a personal
coach guiding his performances.

Howe was an important member of a larger team of people who helped
FDR craft his public voice. As with all political leaders, FDR had a number of

people who worked for him as speech writers and who otherwise helped him to formulate a vision on all kinds of topics and express this vision in many different contexts and media. Audiences knew that the public FDR voice was in a sense a collective production and yet, seemingly paradoxically, they still perceived it as authentic. This chapter sets out to understand the collective rhetorical production of that authentic voice.

I consider two rhetorical modes of Roosevelt's voice. First is his *synecdochic* voice, contained in his body and representing him as an individual. This includes his voice in the narrow, literal sense of sound waves emanating from his chest, encompassing aspects such as elocution, tone, and accent. It also includes other instances in which FDR was physically involved in producing a message, for example, writing out texts in his own hand. Second, I distinguish his voice in a *metonymic* sense: FDR as the voice of the nation, viewed as representing the collective of all Americans. This was the mass-mediated (yet personal) voice, the "narrator" of what was then the current state of the nation. This voice was most often heard via radio, thus intermingling with the synecdochic voice. FDR deftly utilized both rhetorical modes. He would alternately position himself as speaking "as himself"—a "random" American who could stand in for any individual American—or as embodying the nation as a whole. Through this intermingling, he autofabricated (with others' help) his larger-than-life public image.

Speechwriters and other members of FDR's team helped craft his metonymic voice; the team also had at least some influence on his synecdochic voice. FDR's use of a fake tooth during radio addresses, thus aesthetically improving his synecdochic voice, was a conscious and considered choice made by his team.[2] This points to a key aspect of FDR's autofabrication: the use of prosthetics. Roosevelt involved many specifically designed devices and artifacts in his autofabrication. Purely functional prosthetics were as invisible as possible (one element of autofabrication). Others—like the gentlemanly cane he often used—were more visible, because in addition to serving a concrete physical purpose, they also helped FDR to perform a particular kind of masculinity that was integral to his passing as nondisabled. In a similar manner, FDR's many aides both physically helped him and assisted him in passing as nondisabled, as well as contributing to his broader autofabrication effort.

Many scholars have tried to analyze to what extent Roosevelt authored his speeches, often analyzing manuscript versions with scribbled additions and deletions in Roosevelt's hand.[3] Although I am interested in the dynamic that produced them, I do not contribute to the debate about to what extent Roosevelt really authored his speeches, because I regard any help Roosevelt had from ghostwriters as part of his autofabrication. Instead of trying to establish precisely what was authored by FDR personally, I propose that we consider all of his public expressions as forms of autofabrication. He was not the sole author of the speeches but definitely endorsed the texts he spoke. He owned the voice, both in the sense that he chose what texts to speak or sign, and in the sense that nobody else could assume his metonymic or synecdochic voice.

It is important to mention that Roosevelt's passing as nondisabled was a collective effort, part and parcel of the autofabrication effort. Dealing with FDR's disability probably even set the stage for a more wide-ranging autofabrication effort by his staff and aides than would have otherwise happened. For example, as "passer-in-chief" FDR employed an elaborate practice with two of his bodyguards who would carry him up the stairs in a standing position, and secretary Grace Tully recalls incidents of staff members having to run and find FDR's "fake tooth" (which prevented him from whistling between his teeth) before radio addresses. Thus, it may well be that such collective negotiation of FDR's passing efforts created an atmosphere around him that inspired staff to conceive of themselves as FDR's extended body parts. In the course of practicing the "walk" to the rostrum that FDR often performed on the arm of his son James—a laborious and risky effort—Roosevelt told his son to "look around, smile, make it look easy." This seems illustrative for practically everything that Roosevelt did as president: the smile and show of self-confidence were initially a performance but became performative in a broader sense, for instance, when FDR reassured people about leaving their money in bank accounts of banks that would otherwise fail.

I focus in this chapter on the concrete autofabrication strategies Roosevelt used to create his public voice and image as president. The chapter is divided in three subsections. In the first, I discuss Eleanor Roosevelt, who narrated FDR's person and presidency and at various moments served as FDR's most important proxy, and I turn to the other people—spin doctors, staff, ghostwriters—who helped Roosevelt to create his public voice and, thus, image, mostly by contributing to the metonymic voice. Second, I examine the ways that Roosevelt employed media to project himself (both his voice and his image) as a metonym for the nation. Finally, I look at the press and public opinion polls that kept Roosevelt in touch with the electorate, metonymically but also symbolically.

Most of the evidence in this chapter consists of well-known facts and quotations from public speeches. Roosevelt's—and others'—private words in conversation, letters, or elsewhere are no direct part of his creation of his own public image unless published or used publicly. These are nonetheless sometimes important sources for this chapter, because Roosevelt and his correspondents do refer in private to their efforts in making and influencing Roosevelt's public image.

Eleanor Roosevelt, Spin Doctors, Advisers, Staff, and Ghostwriters

Both before and during FDR's presidency, Eleanor Roosevelt regularly functioned as a narrative proxy for her husband's political work, primarily by attending ceremonies, giving speeches, and writing letters on his behalf. Of course, she was her own person, with her own relatively radical political convictions, compared to Franklin's. She did not refrain from using her position to advance her own agenda and autofabrication, often while claiming modesty or suggesting she was speaking for her husband. However, at the risk of seeming to project ER as more of a supportive helpmeet and soft power to back up her husband, this chapter will only highlight how she played a role in his autofabrication (and not how she often did other things or carried forward her own autofabrication). Certainly, early in the 1920s, ER did first find her voice as a public speaker and political agent while substituting for her husband.[4]

After FDR became ill with polio in 1921, he needed about seven years to recover enough to be able to appear in public again; ER acted as his proxy in political campaigns, traveling around and speaking on his behalf. After 1921, Louis Howe—deeply convinced of the need to have a nondisabled Roosevelt operate alongside FDR and literally in his name—is often credited by ER and by biographers as crucial in coaching her to occupy a mature position as an independent agent beside FDR. As mentioned in the previous chapter, ER was able to attend to political issues as if they were outside of the political sphere, broadening the scope of politics in terms of gender and in relation to social issues. ER enabled the creation of a more personal public image of the president.

Next to Eleanor Roosevelt, the most important of the people representing FDR to the public in the years leading up to his first election as president was Louis Howe.[5] Howe and Roosevelt first met in 1911, when Howe was covering Roosevelt's campaign for state senator as a journalist. Howe became a key figure, both in repairing the break between Franklin and Eleanor following Eleanor's discovery of her husband's affair with her secretary Lucy Mercer in 1918 and in getting FDR back into politics after his bout of poliomyelitis in

1921. Howe was, above everything else, a political strategist who, from the very first, believed that Roosevelt could and should become US president, and he made it his personal crusade to get Roosevelt there.[6] Though Howe did not at all aspire to being in the limelight, he has become something of a celebrity in his own right—enigmatic, cunning, and powerful—but physically slight, whose endlessly recurring epithets are "ghoulish" and "gnome-like."[7] This is relevant because he did more than produce the metonymic Roosevelt voice; he even, on occasion, replaced Roosevelt physically, a tradition started in 1912, when FDR was ill in bed throughout his campaign for the State Senate.[8]

In early 1933, Howe was made chief of Roosevelt's White House secretarial staff and main adviser, especially on matters of public opinion, until his death in 1936. Alongside Howe, Roosevelt employed two secretaries, Marvin McIntyre and Steve Early, both also personal friends of the president who had also performed important roles in Roosevelt's 1932 campaign. McIntyre was appointments secretary until 1938, when he became ill; he later returned as correspondence secretary. Early was press secretary throughout the Roosevelt presidency.[9] With the growth of the media landscape and the development of modern communication, public relations and marketing, the presidential secretariat had also grown, and under Roosevelt became larger and more professionalized than ever before. Howe, McIntyre, and Early were not only clerks, but important political figures in the administration, making wide-ranging policies in their areas of expertise.[10]

Samuel Rosenman was Roosevelt's main speechwriter. He was also editor of his *Public Papers and Addresses*; as such, he was consciously occupied with representing Roosevelt to future generations.[11] Other important figures were his private secretaries, Grace Tully and Marguerite LeHand, and the ghostwriter of Roosevelt's first inaugural address, Raymond Moley. All these people, and indeed many more, were occupied daily with aspects of FDR's autofabrication, each at least for part of his long presidency. Many of these figures also furthered Roosevelt's posthumous status as a cultural icon by publishing their memories of Roosevelt in diaries, memoirs, or Roosevelt biographies, and by remaining active in other ways, for instance, in commissions to create Roosevelt memorials.[12]

Roosevelt started to seriously expand the apparatus of his autofabrication in the months leading up to the Democratic National Convention in Chicago in January 1932, gathering around himself two more or less separate teams. The first was a group of political campaign managers, headed by Howe and James Farley, chairman of the New York State Democratic Committee. The second was a group of intellectuals occupied not with the campaign itself but primarily with developing Roosevelt's policies.[13] This second group was headed by Samuel Rosenman and Raymond Moley.[14] Journalist James Kieran referred to the group as "FDR's brains trust" in the *New York Times* for the first time in April 1932, and that has since been its nickname.[15] As part of developing and articulating Roosevelt's policies, they wrote his speeches, and in doing so, eventually metonymically represented FDR's mind. The only one who was really involved in both teams was Louis Howe—sometimes to the chagrin of the brain trust. Howe, a former editor, was wont to rewrite speeches at the very last minute and to use the power he derived from having more information than the others.[16]

Howe orchestrated Roosevelt's first nomination and campaign.[17] Examples abound of his intuitive brilliance as a political image-maker. For example, following John Mack's speech nominating Roosevelt in Chicago—while the candidate himself was at home in Albany—the organ played "Anchors Aweigh," Roosevelt's own choice. When Howe sensed the effect of this mournful song, he gave orders to switch immediately to "Happy Days Are Here Again," which was the standard Roosevelt campaign song from then on.[18] Once Roosevelt was nominated, he famously took an airplane to the convention immediately to accept his nomination in person—an entirely new feat, technologically and otherwise, arranged by Howe. It formed a dramatic break with the tradition that a candidate would receive his formal nomination at home, weeks after the event, and officially accept it from there. In his acceptance speech, Roosevelt addressed these "foolish traditions," making clear that he was not only the Democratic presidential candidate but also a party reformer. As Raymond Moley wrote to Louis Howe on November 12, 1932: "You and Jim [Farley] have done more than elect a President. You have created a new party that ought to hold power for twenty-five years."[19] Although the acceptance speech—including such climactic policy promises as "I pledge you, I pledge myself to a new deal for the American people"—was a collective product of the brain trust, the show as a whole was devised by Louis Howe.

One of Howe and Farley's key campaign strategies was to write thousands of letters to Democrats all over the country, keeping in close touch with campaigning party members at the local level, and requesting that they write to them about the issues most important to their constituents. This letter writing strategy had been Roosevelt and Howe's favorite before. It remained useful later, when Roosevelt as president wanted to appear to stay personally in touch with American citizens: he thought of it as offering insight into public opinion and it created a sense of proximity between the president and the people.[20] Moreover, Howe commissioned and oversaw the writing of various campaign biographies focusing on FDR's life story. The most serious of these was Ernest Lindley's *Franklin D. Roosevelt: A Career in Progressive Politics* (1931), but Howe and his staff also helped FDR's mother Sara Delano Roosevelt to write her memoir, *My Boy Franklin*.[21]

The most notable campaign biography was Earle Looker's book *This Man Roosevelt* (1932). Looker was a Republican journalist who wrote celebratory biographies about FDR from that vantage point, including a now-famous investigation into FDR's physical health, proving his physical fitness for the presidency. Biographer Alfred B. Rollins speculates that Howe—who was deeply convinced that it was critical for FDR to pass as nondisabled—may have set Looker up to start this investigation. In any case, "Louis [Howe] ordered 50,000 reprints of Looker's dramatic article in *Liberty*. This led to a quiet arrangement among Roosevelt, Howe, Looker, and the magazine. *Liberty* would buy a 400-word article, every two weeks over Roosevelt's signature; Looker would write them."[22] Thus, Looker turned from a contributor to FDR's public image—indexing him as a relatable individual across an unusually large political rift for a campaign biographer—into a writer of his metonymic voice. (Considerable falsification was needed to achieve this, given that Looker's columns were supposedly signed by FDR.) It seems likely that Looker was never really opposed to Roosevelt's candidacy—he was rather too easily "converted"— but the shift from opponent to ventriloquist typifies the building and consolidation of Roosevelt's autofabrication apparatus.

Drafting the First Inaugural Address and Other Speeches

Roosevelt's first inaugural address—delivered on March 4, 1933, at a time of national despair—was a defining moment in shaping his public persona and image. Roosevelt began by establishing explicitly the mutual expectations between himself and the American public.

> My friends, this is a day of national consecration. And I am certain that on this day my fellow Americans expect that on my induction into the Presidency I will address them with a candor and a decision which the present situation of our people impels. This is preeminently the time to speak the truth, the whole truth, frankly and boldly. This great Nation will endure as it has endured, will revive and will prosper. So, first of all, let me assert my firm belief that the only thing

we have to fear is fear itself—nameless, unreasoning, unjustified terror which paralyzes needed efforts to convert retreat into advance. In every dark hour of our national life a leadership of frankness and vigor has met with that understanding and support of the people themselves which is essential to victory.

By far the most famous phrase of this passage—quoted and otherwise invoked by the majority of later Roosevelt representations—is "the only thing we have to fear is fear itself." Most Americans have come across this phrase in various forms of public history or popular culture. If any single phrase supports the hypothesis that Roosevelt's own attempts to manage his public image have a continuing influence on Roosevelt representations, it is this one.

In this inaugural address, the quintessential first impression for a newly elected president, Roosevelt clearly casts himself as a friend of the people—"my friends," "my fellow Americans"—and a brave and honest leader in hard times. He stresses the word *frank*, using it twice ("frankly," "frankness") in his first few sentences as president, associating himself implicitly with the characteristics that name suggests. *Frank* works metonymically and by means of association; it forges a link between text and person, and is constative as well as performative. "I am Frank" could, on the one hand, be paraphrased as "I am forthright." On the other hand, it suggests informal intimacy and personal contact— FDR's actual friends called him Frank. This new suggestion of intimacy was further strengthened by the fact that, for the first time ever, Americans listened to an incoming president's inaugural address gathered around their radios.[23] Another element contributing to this intimacy is perhaps that FDR obliquely referred to his disability to project himself as vulnerable and thus "safe" for intimacy. In his reference to metaphorical "paralysis," he extended implicitly to those in the know about his polio history (presumably by this time most Americans, although they did not know the extent of his disability) a bond of mutual sympathy.

At the same time, the first inaugural address broadly outlines the New Deal and all but threatens Congress into granting FDR "broad executive power to wage a war against the emergency." The address outlines the New Deal through metaphors and imagery—"the unscrupulous money-changers stand indicted in the court of public opinion," "we must move as a trained and loyal army"—as well as relatively concrete statements. The leading metaphor is that of a nation at war, implying that an unusual level of unity, discipline, and personal sacrifice will be asked of the people, and that Roosevelt will have to be granted unusual executive power. At the same time, the metaphor gives the general impression of a courageous president while avoiding the impression of a dictatorial one.

The address contains a number of fairly direct attacks on Hoover such as, "Stripped of the lure of profit, by which to induce our people to follow their false leadership, they have resorted to exhortations, pleading tearfully for restored confidence."[24] To be sure, Roosevelt's inaugural address did restore public confidence much more than any of Hoover's recent efforts had done.[25] Thus, the first inaugural address casts Roosevelt as a strong, frank, and fearless man, sensitive to his fellow Americans' hardship and ready to take action against it, at the expense of a largely unidentified group of "money-changers," with Hoover as the only individually recognizable outsider. This rhetoric worked all the better because between his election and inauguration, Roosevelt had been pointedly silent, while the crisis rapidly deepened.[26]

Roosevelt did not write the first inaugural address alone. Unlike most of his addresses, however, this one was not circulated widely before it was delivered. Davis Houck relates in his book, *FDR and Fear Itself: The First Inaugural Address*, how Roosevelt commissioned Columbia University professor Raymond Moley to draft the address.[27] Moley—selected for the job by Louis Howe—had previously written speeches for Roosevelt and traveled with Roosevelt throughout the presidential campaign to write and adapt speeches for him. On a few occasions, they brainstormed together; Roosevelt gave his ideas for the inaugural address and possible metaphors to use in it. Moley, however, came up with the first draft, which they discussed again on the night of February 27.[28] This discussion changed the draft extensively; Louis Howe changed it further.

Despite the fact that Moley wrote the main drafts for the inaugural address, he remained relatively unknown. According to Houck, this was by specific design of Roosevelt, who copied Moley's draft of the address in his own hand in order to "own" the speech in the eyes of history. Any signs of the texts being a team product had to be erased in order to achieve this effect. Copying the speech made it seem to belong to FDR, the voice of the nation, more fully; thus, we can see the act of copying as part of his metonymic voice. Copying it in his own hand made it part of FDR's synecdochic voice as well.[29] Houck goes to great lengths to explain that Moley understood the transcription to be necessary. He even, in a dramatic gesture, threw the draft in his own typescript in the fire at the end of his last discussion of it with Roosevelt on the night of February 28, keeping, however, his notes and diary, so that Houck could still write his book. While some of Houck's claims seem somewhat speculative, especially given the fact that he largely based himself on Moley's archive and ego-documents (diaries, calendars, and the like), *FDR and Fear Itself* is a minute reading and discussion of the various remaining drafts of the inaugural address. Perhaps Moley exaggerated his own role in devising the speech as much as Roosevelt later tried to understate Moley's importance. However, the inaugural address was clearly not widely disseminated before it was held and comparatively few people worked on it.

More speech writers were involved in drafting Roosevelt's famous radio addresses. He was aided in writing the Fireside Chats by about twenty people over the years, though usually not more than five to seven at the same time.[30] Roosevelt usually made changes and additions to their drafts, in his own hand on paper as well as during his live radio delivery. Indeed, he seems often to have asked various speechwriters to draft one Fireside Chat for him, eventually combining their drafts, borrowing various ideas and phrases.[31] One speechwriter, Charles Michelson, remembered that Roosevelt had asked him and two others to prepare a speech. Roosevelt listened to all three of their drafts and then, "stretched himself on a couch and with his eyes on the ceiling dictated his own version, occasionally using one of our phrases but generally culling the best ideas that had been submitted and putting them in his own way. So far as I know, this was the practice with every speech . . . Take it from one rather experienced in the formation and presentation of speeches: Franklin Roosevelt is a better phrase maker than anybody he ever had around him."[32]

Whether Roosevelt was as good a phrasemaker as Michelson would have him, he was certainly extremely good at recognizing potentially great phrases. Through this collective process of writing, followed by Roosevelt's vocal dictation, the synecdochic voice was intermingled with the metonymic—FDR "tried on" the text to see if speaking it would fit him. Michelson's emphasis on Roosevelt's bodily positioning and "his eyes [focused] on the ceiling" help readers experience the corporeality of Roosevelt's voice, even as it was collectively produced. Rosenman even goes so far as to argue that "the speeches as finally delivered were his—and his alone—no matter who the collaborators were . . . No matter how frequently the speech assistants were changed through the years, the speeches were always Roosevelt's. They all expressed the personality, the convictions, the spirit, the mood of Roosevelt. No matter who worked with him in the preparation, the finished product was always the same—it was Roosevelt himself."[33]

The assertion that "the finished product . . . was Roosevelt himself," and the idea that the speeches "expressed the personality, the convictions, the spirit, the mood of Roosevelt," implies that the speeches were entirely metonymic, to the point of erasing the professional speechwriters around FDR, whom he suggests are entirely interchangeable. Indeed, it is part of the professionalism of a speechwriter to deny that he did any work at all, and the eradication of his own voice is necessary to enable ventriloquism. At the same time, Roosevelt as an individual was very receptive to autofabrication for a large audience by a team, because he could transform a collectively produced voice to a metonymic and synecdochic one that seemed to come entirely from himself. FDR contributed his unique physical voice, presentation and improvisation talent when he spoke carefully and collectively produced texts, particularly over the radio. At the same time, the speech writers' work was not just to produce FDR's voice but also to help him pretend that he had never had any help.

Creating an Iconic Image: FDR's Use of Radio, Photography, and Film

I never saw him—
But I *knew* him. Can you have forgotten
How, with his voice, he came into our house,
The President of the United States,
Calling us friends[34]

Author and poet Carl Lamson Carmer here refers to a sentiment that seems to have been extremely widespread in the United States between 1933 and 1945: the sense that Americans knew President Roosevelt well on a personal basis, as a result of his "coming into their houses" as a family friend through the radio. This poem, published two days after Roosevelt's death, refers to the Fireside Chats, Roosevelt's most famous and most puzzling media expressions. Between March 12, 1933, and June 12, 1944, Roosevelt addressed the American people in thirty one radio speeches. The term "Fireside Chat" was coined by CBS's Harry Butcher in 1933 and was picked up immediately by the rest of the press.[35] Roosevelt himself soon also adopted the name, particularly liking the informality suggested by "chats" or "talks" rather than "addresses," though he did stress that the coinage was not his own invention. The Fireside Chat of June 24, 1938, begins: "I think the American public and the American newspapers are certainly creatures of habit. This is one of the warmest evenings that I have ever felt in Washington, D. C., and yet this talk tonight will be referred to as a fireside talk."[36]

This beginning is, of course, a joke, but the joke is on the American public and newspapers; FDR seems to deny that *fireside talk* is a term his own

FDR at his home in Hyde Park, New York, delivering a national radio address, December 24, 1943. Courtesy of the Franklin D. Roosevelt Library and Museum, Hyde Park, New York

administration endorsed. Roosevelt was known as and admired for being an easy jester, and this joke is particularly successful: through its benignant mockery, it attributes the association with the fireside to the public and press, rather than to himself. Roosevelt implies he is not speaking by his own fireside, although his fellow Americans may be by their firesides, or by the modern replacement of a fireside as the center of familial gathering—the radio. Roosevelt's quip stresses various implicit assumptions: first, that Roosevelt, through his synecdochic and metonymic voice, visits Americans in their family homes, and second, that it is the people's own feeling that the heart of the family home is the most appropriate place for talks with the president. In jokingly distancing himself from the term, Roosevelt transfers responsibility for using it to his audience. Successfully so: it has remained one of the most popular phrases in relation to Roosevelt and his presidency. There are many widespread conceptions and misconceptions about the speeches—that they were held weekly, that they were intimate—which seem to have been inspired or supported more by the name Fireside Chats and other aspects of form than by their content. As Henry Fairlie described it in *The New Republic*: "Radio sets were not then very powerful, and there was always static. Families had to sit near the set, with someone always fiddling with the knobs. It was like sitting around a hearth, with someone poking the fire; and to that hearth came the crackling voices of Winston Churchill, or George Burns and Gracie Allen, and of FDR. It was not FDR who was at his fireside . . . it was we who were at our firesides."[37]

While focusing on the reception of the Fireside Chats—families had to sit near the radio, fiddling with it was like poking the fire—Fairlie here also stresses the metonymic quality of a radio voice. Realizing that FDR was not the one at his fireside, Fairlie nonetheless shows how FDR's radio voice brought others to stoke their fires in a metaphorical sense.

There is some discussion as to the number of Fireside Chats, caused by the fact that Roosevelt used the radio to address the nation more often than the thirty or so addresses that are counted as Fireside Chats. *The Public Papers and Addresses of Franklin D. Roosevelt* lists eighty-three radioed addresses, of which twenty-seven are considered Fireside Chats. However, in 1973, tape recordings of all but three of the Fireside Chats were issued by Mass Communications, Inc., which asserted that there were actually thirty-one of Roosevelt's radio addresses that should be considered Fireside Chats.[38] These were defined as informal presidential addresses of fifteen to forty-five minutes, not only broadcast via the radio, but expressly written to be presidential radio addresses, and broadcast throughout the United States at the same time, as close to prime time as possible.

Radio was the first mass medium that could achieve temporal simultaneity in that way, and, therefore, a strong force in creating an imagined community. It created what Hadley Cantril called "the largest grouping of people ever known." In a series of articles that political correspondent Anne O'Hare McCormick wrote about radio for the *New York Times Magazine* in the spring of 1932, she spoke of "the incredible audience," "millions of ears contracted into one ear and cocked at the same moment to the same sound."[39] Here, McCormick's description of synecdochic "ears" contracted into one metonymic national "ear" elides the differences between countless physical ears, the listeners they belong to, and the collective of a nation listening together to the same voice. This voice, in turn, is both synecdochic of the corporeal FDR and metonymic of his radio presence and message.

Roosevelt was not the first president to be broadcast on the radio, nor was he the first president to foster a patriotic sense of imagined community across the nation. Both Warren Harding and Herbert Hoover had the technology available and used it, though neither with much awareness of the specific needs and qualities of the medium, nor with much measurable impact. The first serious effort at a federal level to forge an American imagined community in the United States—geared strongly toward creating a nationwide sense of collectivity—was carried out by Wilson's Committee for Public Information during the United States' engagement in the First World War. This effort—which worked primarily through a News Division, but also via posters (generating, for instance, the famous Uncle Sam "I want YOU, for US Army" poster)—was highly successful but did not yet employ radio.[40]

Other contemporary leaders, such as Hitler or Stalin, were broadcast on radio but did not have a specific radio style. Their speeches were aimed primarily at large gatherings of their party members. While these addresses also work to some extent when heard over the radio, they had none of the specific intimacy and awareness of the private sphere that Roosevelt's speeches had and did not work on synecdochic and metonymic levels at once. Winston Churchill did develop a radio broadcasting style that worked somewhat similarly but only later, during World War II. Roosevelt was among the first generation of successful radio speakers, together with figures such as W. K. Henderson, Father Coughlin, and Walter Winchell.

Radio in the 1930s became by far the most accessible and most widely used mass medium in the United States. In the course of the 1930s, more than 80 percent of American households acquired a radio set; some Fireside Chats are estimated to have been heard by more than 85 percent of the adult population.[41] Hadley Cantril and Gordon Allport estimated in the mid-thirties that "our countrymen spend approximately 150,000,000 hours a week before the [movie]screen, but nearly 1,000,000,000 hours before the [radio] loudspeaker." It is striking that they and other commentators in the 1930s thought of radio in particular as a means of mass education and as a strong agent in further democratization. As Levine and Levine note: "Lew Sarett and William Trufant Foster compared radio to the ancient Greek Acropolis: 'a place from which the Elders might speak to all the citizens at once.'"[42] The perception of radio as "a place from which the Elders . . . speak to all the citizens at once" prefigures Jacques Lacan's theory of radio: Lacan understood radio as a "superegoic voice." "Radio transforms the voice into aural material that shakes us up because it seems to be audible everywhere, all at once."[43] Thus, in Lacan's view, radio divorces the synecdochic voice from the body, transforming it into not just a metonymic but also a symbolic force, a kind of superego, coming both from outside and from within the listener.

This is at odds with the supposedly innate democratizing effects of the radio. That is also the case with Hitler's inflammatory speeches, which, though not primarily meant for the radio, were also effective as radio broadcasts. German theorists such as Bertolt Brecht and Walter Benjamin have both argued in the 1930s that radio was too one-sided a medium to be democratic or to establish meaningful contact between speaker and audience. Brecht particularly focused on how the unilateral quality of radio closed off any possibility of audience response or debate between sender and receivers; as he framed it, "The radio has one side, where it ought to have two."[44] Benjamin equally felt that radio did not allow for real contact to be established between performer and audience. He stressed that it was impossible for the sender to receive feedback from the audience, having instead to indiscriminately reach out to "the consumers who constitute the market." However, "this market, where he offers not only his labor but also his whole self, his heart and soul, is beyond his reach."[45] While Benjamin might have been surprised by FDR's success in reaching his "market," he evidently did grasp the metonymic and synecdochic potential of radio.

Roosevelt partly evaded these problems of radio's one-sided quality by inviting his listeners to respond to his Fireside Chats in writing. He consequently received an unprecedented amount of mail from American citizens. This combination of a new medium and an old one contributed to the democratic image of radio in America; the correspondence had the advantage of seeming extremely personal.[46] Although Roosevelt did not answer most letters personally, many letter writers—at least those who were positive about the administration and its policies, or at a minimum friendly in tone—did receive a response from the White House. These responses were often short and mostly formally acknowledged the letter rather than answering it, but a great effort was nonetheless made to give the letter writers the feeling they were being heard. Bunches of the letters were selected by the staff and Eleanor Roosevelt for FDR to read, and both Roosevelts did also respond personally to some letters.[47]

In many of his radio addresses, Roosevelt explicitly invited particular groups of listeners to write to him to share their thoughts or to fill out and return government surveys.[48] This strategy helped to create a sense of intimacy and personal contact between Roosevelt and his listeners; it also provided information about public opinion. Radio networks often invited audiences to send in written responses—indeed, in the early days of radio, this was the only way available to radio stations to glean the listeners' reactions to their programs. So while Roosevelt was not the only radio speaker who did this, his requests built on a custom that he made "a central part of this process."[49] Indeed, "Roosevelt's radio speeches helped to make participants—even activists—out of his audience." This led to an unprecedented flow of letters to the president; in some weeks following Fireside Chats, more than 450,000 letters would be delivered to the White House. As Ira Smith, the White House chief of mails, remembered, especially after the first few Fireside Chats people "believed that he was speaking to them personally and immediately wrote him a letter. It was months before we managed to swim out of that flood of mail."[50] When, however, the volume of the mail to the White House decreased, Smith recalls, "We could expect to hear from him or one of his secretaries, who wanted to know what was the matter—was the President losing his grip on the public?"[51]

Yet, despite the democratic image of radio, Roosevelt could also be argued to have used it to sidestep Congress, traditionally regarded as the most democratic body in the federal government and the most immediate representative of the people. Journalist Stanley High noted about the Fireside Chats: "The spirit, even more than the content, of his "My Friends" speeches was something new in the annals of our democracy. There is a latch-string-is-always-out quality about them. They invite familiarity. [The nation] sends its orders to its Congressmen. But it talks things over with its President."[52]

This sense that radio, and the Fireside Chats in particular, could contribute to a more direct democracy was especially useful to Roosevelt, since he was often unhappy with the way he and his policies were mediated by the press. Roosevelt had a good relationship with many journalists, but he also strongly believed that most newspaper owners disliked him and unfairly accused him of trying to manipulate them.[53]

In that light, it makes sense that Roosevelt felt the need to address the public directly, unmediated by a radio program or by the possibly hostile newspaper press. The way the Fireside Chats were broadcast—simultaneously by the two competing nationwide radio broadcasters at the time, NBC and CBS—ensured that FDR had great power over the broadcast. The medium gave credence to the message: it was on the radio, so it must be true, especially given that the two nationwide radio broadcasters both carried it, suggesting that FDR was "above the parties." The medium amplified, metaphorically as well as literally, Roosevelt's voice as a leader who stood above partisan politics. He felt that he was "able to accomplish reform and progress only because the public was ready for them, wanted them, and was willing to help me carry out the people's will." Because of this, he could go "over the heads of the Legislature and sometimes over the almost united opposition of the newspapers of the State."[54] This means that already as governor of New York, Roosevelt was convinced that radio was an important medium of communication for him, explaining that it was "invaluable as a means of public approach."[55] Roosevelt was clearly aware of the agency radio gave him in his autofabrication, not only in terms of how the public viewed him, but also in the sense that it effectively helped him to strengthen the presidency at the expense of legislative power.

It is difficult to gauge how conscious Roosevelt and his staff were of the autofabricating qualities of the Fireside Chats. Did they deliberately merge metonymic and synecdochic modes of Roosevelt's voice to enhance its rhetorical force? Although only a few direct clues provide evidence that Roosevelt and his staff were acutely conscious of the need to autofabricate, the extreme care with which the addresses were made and broadcast does suggest a great awareness of and interest in their effect on Roosevelt's public image. Despite the consistent impression that Roosevelt held his Fireside Chats weekly, or otherwise frequently and regularly, he was, for instance, aware of the need not to appear on the radio too often. Many letters in reaction to the Fireside Chats asked and advised the president to address the nation in this way more often, but as Roosevelt wrote in a letter in March 1942: "Sometimes I wish I could carry out your thought of more frequent talking on the air on my part, but the one thing I dread is that my talks should be so frequent as to lose their effectiveness." A week later, he wrote in another letter that "in England, Churchill, for a while, talked too much, and I don't want to do that."[56] Both of these statements suggest that Roosevelt was consciously orchestrating the effects of his radio addresses on his public image.

The texts of the Fireside Chats come across as content heavy: they seem to concentrate more on policies, programs, and problems that Roosevelt and the nation encountered than on Roosevelt's person or the relationship between him and the Americans. However, in terms of form, the Fireside Chats were extremely carefully set up and organized. Roosevelt's Secretary of Labor Frances Perkins has suggested that Roosevelt relished the ease with which he could manipulate his radio appearance, presumably because it synecdochically represented him, without any risk of unduly exposing his wheelchair. His synecdochic voice was clearly that of a patrician but that seems not to have alienated the listeners—many probably felt that that was entirely suitable for a president. Most Fireside Chats were broadcast from a professional studio in the White House, where he did have a small audience present to create an atmosphere of intimacy.[57]

Although the content and tone of most of the Fireside Chats were businesslike and even castigatory, Roosevelt famously began almost every Fireside Chat with "My friends" or "My fellow Americans." From the enormous number of letters and telegrams Roosevelt received from "ordinary Americans" (his phrase) after each Fireside Chat was broadcast, the impression arises that he was regarded by many of the letter writers as a kind of older brother or friend. This was perhaps most clear when, after the first Fireside Chat—about the Banking Crisis on March 12, 1933—people effectively were prepared again to leave their money in the banks. Many letter writers stressed that they had never felt inclined to write to their president, but now did because Roosevelt in his address had taken them so seriously and addressed so exactly their most pressing worries.[58] In 1933, the radio audience was still "young"—the medium was relatively new—and, therefore, perhaps naive in its perception of radio as a medium approaching personal communication. However, listening to the Fireside Chats was not listeners' first or only experience of radio entering the private sphere, and the Fireside Chats clearly stood out to many listeners as particularly intimate and moving.

Intimate has ever since remained one of the most popular qualifications for the Fireside Chats, even though this qualification does not really do justice to the content of the texts. Many have argued that the Fireside Chats were more accessible than other presidential speeches, and that this has contributed to the sense of intimacy and contact between Roosevelt and "the common man."[59] Rhetorician Elvin Lim, however, uses content analysis to argue in "The Lion and the Lamb: De-mythologizing Franklin Roosevelt's Fireside Chats" that this is a misconception. According to his analysis, the Fireside Chats are not easier to understand or more intimate than other presidential speeches. However, whether a misconception or not, the idea that the Fireside Chats are intimate and easy is overwhelmingly present in films, documentaries, popular biographies, and more general academic writing about Roosevelt. Lim spends a great deal of attention addressing and defusing the misconceptions he sees, aiming to assess how the Fireside Chats should really be understood, rather than to understand how the alleged or real misconception evolved.

Lim's convincing use of content analysis and other quantitative techniques demonstrates that the Fireside Chats were neither intimate on a textual level nor particularly accessible in their discourse to a general audience. As Lim shows, in the Fireside Chats Roosevelt used more words like "prices," "banks," "money," "recovery," "wages," and "coal," and other economic terms than he did in other public addresses, or than presidents before and after him did. He also used many multisyllabic words of Latin origin, long sentences, and unusual style figures. Lim also convincingly argues that the Fireside Chats are not the entirely novel media performances they were, and are sometimes taken to be, but are actually built on a long tradition of presidential soapbox oratory. It is true that the Fireside Chats are both in tone and content more confrontational and castigatory than one might expect on the basis of their informal-sounding name and their reputation. Roosevelt repeatedly refers to political opponents as "a few selfish men,"[60] "money changers," "prophets of evil," "petty chisel-ers,"[61] "self-seekers," "theoretical die-hards," "doubting Thomases,"[62] "ene-mies of American peace,"[63] "rumor mongers,"[64] "noisy traitors," "betrayers of America," and "would-be dictators."[65] The comparison with stump speeches is justified—indeed, Roosevelt seems at times to emulate his uncle, an expert in the genre. It is, however, not enough to simply state that the Fireside Chats were not intimate. They were perceived as such by their listeners, as phrases in letters to Roosevelt like "Having just heard your most loving, clear voice . . . I cannot help, but to try and express my feeling" attest.[66] If the public reaction to the Fireside Chats was not a straightforwardly "correct" assessment of them, where does this supposed miscommunication come from?

The Fireside Chats may have been perceived as intimate because they were listened to in the private sphere. Of course, this is true of all radio, but Roo-sevelt's special success lay in his ability to transform a collectively produced voice into metonymic and synecdochic voices unique to himself. These voices represented him on the one hand as an embodiment of the nation, and on the other, as a relatable individual who could represent it; the letter writer's refer-ence to "your most loving clear voice" attests to FDR's relatability. Despite their often-aggressive tone, stump speeches also had an intimate quality, deriving from the fact that speaker and audience were in the same space. Thus, they gave room for audience reaction; the letters to the president may be seen as a (mostly symbolic) substitute for audience response. FDR's intimate Fireside Chats were the radio equivalent of stump speeches, and an equivalent that al-lowed FDR to work on his own terms (as he could not have stood on a "stump").

Roosevelt's name calling within the Fireside Chats was always aimed at "a few selfish/scared/evil people," who were of course not the "fellow Americans" that the Fireside Chats addressed, thus defining an outgroup.[67] The outgroup functioned as the *other* to be distinguished from Roosevelt and his audience—"my friends"—strengthening the ingroup sentiment of fellow Americans, who were all listening to their president on the radio at the same time. Roosevelt's name-calling was not in itself intimate but may have helped to create a sense of connection between those who did not consider themselves to be one of the "few selfish people," presumably, most of the listeners. Roosevelt cleverly played to the wish of his listeners to belong to the ingroup of his fellow Americans.

Using that phrase over and over throughout the twelve years that he held Fireside Chats rhetorically helped to rid him of partisanship and create a sense that the dissenters were only very few. That was, of course, not the case—indeed, he needed to create that idea probably because he encountered so much political resistance—but the strategy worked to a large extent.

Stanley High's argument that the strength of the Fireside Chats was in "the spirit, even more than the content" is thus more relevant than Lim's analysis of the contents. Although Lim's argument that the Fireside Chats were in terms of content anything but intimate holds true, the form was intimate in a number of ways: the setting in which they were heard, Roosevelt's voice and presentation, his creation of a sense of community through phrases like "my friends," and his efforts to stimulate response and to take it seriously. Roosevelt seems to have been especially astute at creating a sense of intimacy and personal contact, not by being soft-hearted or personal in what he said, but rather in his manner of speaking. Frances Perkins, Roosevelt's secretary of labor, remembered being present in the room while Roosevelt gave some of his Fireside Chats live on air:

> His voice and his facial expression as he spoke were those of an intimate friend. After he became President, I often was at the White House when he broadcast, and I realized how unconscious he was of the twenty or thirty of us in that room and how clearly his mind was focused on the people listening at the other end. As he talked his head would nod and his hands would move in simple, natural, comfortable gestures. His face would smile and light up as though he were actually sitting on the front porch or in the parlor with them. People felt this, and it bound them to him in affection.[68]

Perkins stresses the intimacy upfront. The situation she describes is somewhat odd: she heard these performances as a member of a small audience of people, all engaged in FDR's autofabrication. One might think these people were called up to act as a live audience to help FDR talk more naturally, but the live audience seems to have been an almost ghostly presence. This makes sense in that they were coproducers of FDR's content and voice, but the act he performed here was to transform the collectively written text to a synecdochic voice, helped by the gestures and smiles, and a metonymic one, through his "focus on the people listening at the other end." Speaking to a small group of actual people helped FDR sound like he was talking to families gathered around their fireplace. The "almost ghostly" effect results from the fact that most of the people there actually produced the text that he was, in a sense, playing back to them.

Another medium through which Roosevelt could present himself as an articulate, frank, informal, and energetic leader was photography. The issue of what does and does not constitute autofabrication in photography is complex. Scholars who are analyzing texts must figure out who literally wrote what, and who had the final say over a text; in this case, the answer is Roosevelt. Photographs have a congruent, though less manageable dynamic. Who posed for a photograph? Who composed the picture as a whole? Whose idea was it to take a particular photo? What are its implications? Who can choose to publish particular photos and not others?

Roosevelt often took time to pose for press photographs, and Stephen Early made many photos available to the press and others; in both cases, the photographs may be considered part of Roosevelt's autofabrication. However, many pictures were also taken by press photographers without Roosevelt's active awareness or participation, just as there appeared articles about him. Even then, Roosevelt did have a hand in what pictures were taken and which could be published, as his famous 1932 words attest, "No pictures of me getting out of the car, boys."[69] Roosevelt, thus, autofabricated via photography in two central ways: first, through his staff taking and publicizing official photographs, and second, by posing for press photographers and trying to manage which pictures they would and would not shoot or publish.[70] He did not, however, have anything approaching real control over which pictures of him were published. In most cases, it is impossible to know precisely to what extent he or his advisers managed to oversee this process, although it is clear that they did to some extent. It is also clear that hardly any photos of FDR in his wheelchair ended up being published.[71]

Previous presidents had dealt in relatively haphazard ways with journalists wishing to photograph them. Wilson disliked being photographed and thought it the duty of photographers to stay away from him. Coolidge, on the other hand, felt he ought to make himself available to be photographed and was, as a result, sometimes used by photographers who wanted to picture him in silly or embarrassing situations.[72] Both Wilson and Coolidge had presidential secretaries who were primarily clerks; no one actively managed how the president would or might be photographed, other than the president himself. Steve Early, on the other hand—like secretaries Howe and McIntyre, a former newspaperman—did not only manage Roosevelt's press relations and organize press conferences but also made and guarded policies surrounding Roosevelt's radio and camera appearances.[73] Roosevelt no doubt employed a more extensive staff in part because he took himself more seriously as a mass media figure than his predecessors had. However, the additional staff were also necessitated by his disability, and the labor involved in the collective effort to pass FDR off as nondisabled.

Photography had, by the 1930s, gained considerable impact, mainly through magazines such as *Time* and *Life*, which printed many photos and were distributed nationwide. Roosevelt was a photogenic man, keen to give the press photographers surrounding him "something to shoot."[74] His informality and vivid facial expressions made for striking pictures in a period when technology had advanced far enough to allow photographers to take pictures with short exposure times and little preparation and to allow papers to print these quickly in high quality. Roosevelt was more conscious than Coolidge of the impression particular photos might make and was more restrictive toward photographers, who did, however, know that they could always take engaging pictures of him. There are counterexamples to the statement that Franklin Roosevelt was the first US president to smile in photos, but these are few; he seems to have been the first to make it a habit. Exposure times for pictures had been very short for some decades already, so that it was physically easy to appear smiling or laughing in a photograph, but for a long time it was hardly considered appropriate for the president to be photographed smiling. FDR, however, seems to have been aware of his own ability to appear confident and congenial through his photos. Roosevelt was the first president to be photographed with a cigarette holder—often described as being "at a jaunty angle"—a cocktail, his fedora hat, and his car, all visual elements that have stuck to his image in the long-term. His association with "Happy Days Are Here Again," enhanced by his ending of Prohibition, is another example of a metonymic link between Roosevelt and a particular atmosphere of relaxed confidence that contributed to the image of a confident, modern, and informal man. Roosevelt embodied the atmosphere of relaxed confidence. Using this song as his campaign song produced and strengthened that link.

Steve Early's role in regulating the press created the circumstances in which Roosevelt could easily be pleasant with journalists and photographers. Early set the conditions for journalists to be around the president or to attend press conferences, giving them detailed rules about photographing. While he did not forbid members of White House staff to take informal pictures, he required those to remain private. After a birthday party for Roosevelt in 1934, he sent around pictures taken by a White House photographer, asking that they "be safeguarded against duplication" so that they would not "be discovered by an outsider."[75]

Such attempts to control the dissemination and publication of pictures of Roosevelt were extremely successful, partly because Early was resolute in punishing offending members of the press, for instance, by exclusion from the presidential press conferences. Other reasons why candid photos were not often published were that it was still relatively hard technologically to take real snapshots, and that photographers themselves were respectful of the president's privacy. For instance, in one oft-cited case, when a Republican newspaper cameraman tried to photograph Roosevelt being carried, colleagues blocked his view and moved his camera, so that the picture could not be taken.[76]

Roosevelt seems to have been relatively reticent in using film to have himself portrayed. That he was aware of the potential of cinema, and used it to get across his aims and accomplishments, becomes clear from Pare Lorentz's films about New Deal projects, which Roosevelt commissioned. Lorentz made films which—in Roosevelt's words—"show America as it really is."[77] After seeing Lorentz's film *The River* about the southern states, Roosevelt put Lorentz on the payroll of the Works Progress Administration (WPA)—one of the largest public works programs—and made sure that his film was distributed on a large scale to movie theaters. Later, Roosevelt commissioned Lorentz to make thirty, three-to-five-minute films about pending New Deal public works programs. These reached an enormous audience at the time, and some of them are still available in the educational section of the Franklin D. Roosevelt Presidential Library, aptly called the Pare Lorentz Center. At a public dinner, Roosevelt introduced Lorentz as "my shooter."[78] Thus, while Lorentz did not directly make propaganda for Roosevelt, it is clear that Roosevelt realized that Lorentz's work promoted his public image. It is striking, in this context, that FDR did not engage a "shooter" or film crew to film himself, his speeches, or other public performances. He was clearly aware of the potential of cinema but did not think of it as an appropriate medium for presenting himself in the body. It is tempting to assume that Roosevelt did not use cinema to assert himself as an iconic figure because of his keenness not to expose his disability through the moving image.

However, there were newsreels which showed Roosevelt. Newsreels blur the boundary between autofabrication and portrayal by others in ways comparable to photography. The Roosevelt clips in newsreels are practically all or parts of public addresses or other public appearances, situations in which Roosevelt was well aware that he was being watched and filmed. In that sense, they are visual registrations of Roosevelt's well-considered performances. However, the editing of the reels—which is where the storytelling happens—was not monitored.

Roosevelt had no hand in which parts of his performances were eventually shown, in whether, how, and from what angles they would be filmed, what the voiceover comments would be, or how the news story would be framed in general. Therefore, the newsreels do not add substantially to Roosevelt's autofabrication, beyond the texts that he spoke in them and acts like his "walking" to the rostrum.

FDR's Approach to the Press and Polls

Roosevelt is famous for his excellent contact with journalists and the press. Historian John Tebbel writes that "he understood the press as no president has before or since."[79] Betty Winfield, in *FDR and the News Media*, conjectures that Roosevelt "may have publicly personalized the presidency so much through his astute use of the existing mass media that he created unreasonable expectations for those less personable and less talented presidents who followed him."[80] "Publicly personalizing the presidency" through the use of mass media was clearly essential in Roosevelt's public expressions in general and particularly important for his dealings with the news media. Roosevelt's easy bantering with the press was perhaps more a part of his public image than the actual essence of his administrations' press contact. Nevertheless, he was personally on excellent terms with many members of the press, which decreased its watchdog role and, therefore, increased Roosevelt's political leeway.[81] Citing a reporter's surprise at the general enthusiasm Roosevelt aroused among his colleagues, Richard Polenberg argues that "Roosevelt made so favorable an impression on the working press largely because of his informal, colloquial manner."[82] While Roosevelt proclaimed the press to be a strong element in democracy, he did not actually encourage its watchdog capacity.[83] Rather, he wanted to secure space in the news media for White House news from his perspective. He would not personally have said so publicly, but his press secretary acted on that basis. For example, his press secretary organized press conferences twice per week, which obviously created a regular expectation of White House news.

Roosevelt opened his first presidential press conference with "It is very good to see you all and my hope is that these conferences are going to be merely enlarged editions of the kind of very delightful family conferences I have been holding in Albany for the last four years."[84] The suggestion that press conferences should, or even can, be delightful and familial has remained an important notion since. The press conference as an institution—set up by Theodore Roosevelt, who used it very successfully for influencing the news directly—had been languishing throughout the previous three presidencies. Roosevelt, who had already had success with press conferences as governor of New York, revived it. He was the first president to employ a former newspaper man, Stephen Early, as press secretary, and to give him responsibility for the public relations and media policy of the White House, rather than regarding it as a merely administrative job.[85] Roosevelt was active, and often successful, in influencing the press, mostly because he strategically provided them both with large amounts of information, and with good—though noncommittal—quotes, photographs, and other materials. Roosevelt's belief that the press disliked him despite his efforts to be accessible is only partly justified. Many newspapers were indeed critical of the New Deal but also gave a great deal of attention to Roosevelt and the White House news he chose to present to the press.[86]

Stephen Early's role was difficult at times because he both had to ensure that the press had good access to White House and executive news stories while also having to protect the privacy of the First Family and the public image of the president. Early was widely known as particularly fair and respectful to journalists. He was liked as a former colleague, despite the difficulty he had in protecting Roosevelt against the press and, conversely, in defending his colleagues from Roosevelt's conviction that the press disliked him. His attitude was ambivalent, sometimes even hypocritical. It is telling that Roosevelt, who greatly profited from the new photo magazines, was deeply chagrined when Henry Luce, owner of the most important ones—*Time*, *Life*, and *Fortune*—established a foundation to study the freedom of the press, out of worries about government control over the American mass media.[87]

Early himself was less negative about the intentions of the press and attempted to give all news media equal chances at obtaining news stories and photos. Thus, the practice was established that Roosevelt would give press conferences twice a week, once on a Tuesday afternoon and once on a Friday morning, so as to give reporters for morning and evening papers equal chances at news scoops. Early also prepared the conferences, discussing with Roosevelt what might be asked and what Roosevelt might want to say. Few notes were taken during these meetings—Roosevelt generally discouraged note-taking in meetings, in itself a form of obscuring his autofabrication—but Early did make presidential quotes on paper available for the press, which they were allowed to cite.

While they were allowed to ask questions at press conferences without submitting them previously, as had been the habit under previous presidents, they were not free to quote what the president said during those conferences. Most of what Roosevelt said was "off the record" or "as background" and was not supposed to be explicitly attributed to Roosevelt. Moreover, despite Roosevelt's claims to delightfulness and familiarity, Early set up a rather intimidating process for the press of waiting and being checked before they were allowed to enter the Oval Office in which the conferences were held.[88] This created an ideal setting for Roosevelt to be apologetically late and to do what he was good at: "In twenty minutes Mr. Roosevelt's features had expressed amazement, curiosity, mock alarm, genuine interest, worry, rhetorical playing for suspense, sympathy, decision, playfulness, dignity, and surpassing charm. Yet he said almost nothing. Questions were deflected, diverted, diluted. Answers—when they did come—were concise and clear. But I never met anyone who showed greater capacity for avoiding a direct answer while giving the questioner a feeling he had been answered."[89]

Although this elusiveness eventually did harm Roosevelt's popularity with the press, as journalists increasingly understood that the press conferences were not always useful, they did help Roosevelt to develop a public image of amiability and hospitality, and they were an excellent way to launch "trial balloons" to test public opinion through the reactions of correspondents.

Roosevelt's personal, jovial, bantering behavior toward reporters stands in some contrast with the kind of rhetoric he used when he addressed the larger public, as he did in his Fireside Chats. In both cases, his rhetorical skill would lie primarily in the presentation; his words were generally coauthored, or at least discussed beforehand with one or more assistants. But in larger addresses to a less tangible and visible audience, Roosevelt needed to be less tongue-in-cheek and to provide the key message without cynicism. Thus, he became what he had once said he hoped to be, "a preaching president—like my cousin Theodore." The actual preaching was not to the press, as it was in Theodore's case, but rather to the people in his more direct addresses.[90] FDR's preaching was lightened by his jolly image and stood out all the more clearly, because it formed a serious note among many more frivolous ones.

Roosevelt was good at sending messages that inspired trust and confidence, but he was also an excellent listener. He was extremely sensitive to public opinion, both in the sense that he was good at picking up the general sentiment about issues, and in the sense that he found it very important. As his speechwriter Stanley High wrote: "The President seldom goes wrong in his forecast of public reaction. He is sensitive to public opinion as some people are sensitive to weather."[91] However, as Melvin Holli has shown in *The Wizard of Washington: Emil Hurja, Franklin Roosevelt, and the Birth of Public Opinion Polling*, Roosevelt did not only go by his own sentiments and predictions; he was also the first president to use and hold mass opinion polls to estimate the public sentiment on political issues.[92] Previously, public opinion had mainly been gauged during election campaigns by relying on local party members' reports on what was thought and felt in their district, a strategy Roosevelt used as well. Moreover, the *Literary Digest*, phone companies, and some other organizations held polls that were generally nonrepresentative and not random. For instance, they only polled people with phone lines, that is, members of the upper-middle classes, and as a result their predictions were usually skewed. While the *Literary Digest* at times polled millions of people, these were all from among their own readership and, therefore, a biased sample. Emil Hurja, originally a mining engineer, transferred statistical methods he used for sampling raw materials to public opinion polling. On the basis of the essentially flawed data from the *Literary Digest* polls, he created corrected versions, controlling for the *Digest*'s biases, which predicted election outcomes more accurately.[93]

The Democratic National Committee (DNC) in 1928 did not see the value of Hurja's randomized samples, but in the months leading up to the 1932 campaign, Hurja did convince DNC Chairman James Farley. This was partly an effect of another poll, carried out by New York Democrat Jesse Strauss, which predicted that Franklin Roosevelt would win the nomination at the 1932 Chicago convention. Soon after Roosevelt's nomination, many commentators became convinced that this poll had actually influenced the convention's choice for Roosevelt. Thus, the DNC became aware of the possible self-fulfilling effect of polls, in which the poll itself created a bandwagon effect, which, according to Holli, convinced the committee to employ Emil Hurja in the presidential campaign. Hurja's polls helped FDR's campaign in various ways, particularly because they determined very precisely where campaign funds could most fruitfully be spent. Roosevelt regularly spoke with Hurja about which issues he should particularly address in different areas.[94] After Roosevelt's election, Hurja first became patronage dispenser in the administration, but he later returned to public opinion polling for the DNC for the 1934 congressional campaign. For Roosevelt, he measured the public reactions to particular speeches and policies as well as more general approval ratings. Holli argues that "we cannot say for certain that it was Hurja's advice that moderated the president's behavior,

but . . . we can say . . . that Roosevelt was the first president to make system-
atic use of public-opinion polls such as Hurja's to measure reaction to his
policies and speeches."[95]

Roosevelt generally operated on the side of public opinion but simultaneously
tried to steer and inform it. In his "Arsenal of Democracy" speech, for instance,
he campaigned for American military intervention in the war in Europe.
Roosevelt used public opinion reports to navigate his course but did not uncritically go along with their outcomes, unless something seemed to be the only
decision the American electorate would accept. He received more letters from
citizens than any other president, and took these seriously, as a qualitative insight into—and quantitative indicator of—public sentiment. As he said to Louis
Howe, he especially valued personal mail from everyday folks, because it constituted the "most perfect index to the state of mind of the people."[96] He interpreted the number of letters, as he told reporters, as a clear sign of "an increasing and wholesome reawakening of public interest in the affairs of government."[97]
But most importantly, the Fireside Chats and the letters written in response
constituted a form of direct contact between himself and the public.

   This contact seemed synecdochic, involving FDR's actual hand, and metonymic, involving his handwriting and choice of words. It was, in fact,
symbolic—an act performed mostly not by FDR but by staff members substituting for him—yet creating the sense that the president was available for direct
interpersonal contact. FDR's autofabrication as an intimate and strong presence
was created by the efforts of a wide range of staff members and associates. Collectively, they produced FDR's voice, writing the voice in the case of speechwriters and representing it in the case of Eleanor Roosevelt. In doing so, they intermingled his individual voice and manner of speaking, which suggested that
he represented one individual "random" American citizen, with a metonymic
voice that was designed to represent and speak for the entire nation.

CHAPTER THREE

Negotiating FDR Remembrance

FDR dedicated the Franklin D. Roosevelt Presidential Library with these now famous words:

> To bring together the records of the past and to house them in buildings where they will be preserved for the use of men and women in the future, a Nation must believe in three things. It must believe in the past. It must believe in the future. It must, above all, believe in the capacity of its own people so to learn from the past that they can gain in judgment in creating their own future.[1]

In asserting a belief in the capacity of the people "to learn from the past" so that they might "gain in judgment in creating their own future," Roosevelt expressed trust in future generations' ability to learn from his papers and draw lessons from his work. Roosevelt tellingly suggested that it is the nation that "bring[s] together the records of the past," although, in this instance, it was he who personally initiated the creation of the presidential library. FDR presented himself as embodying the nation in a situation that accrued momentum as a national event—the dedication of the first presidential library—but served his personal interest. It has since become standard practice for presidents to create individual presidential libraries, regulated by federal law;[2] these words by Roosevelt are cited time and again in justification.[3]

David Reynolds has suggested that "had Roosevelt survived the war, he would probably [like Churchill] have produced his own account."[4] This seems unlikely to me. Roosevelt, during his life, very actively organized for others to tell his story and to produce accounts of the key events of his presidency. FDR and his staff put a great deal of thinking and strategizing into this, both with regard to FDR's and the administration's communication at the time and for the future. Very many people who had worked closely with FDR in a range of capacities wrote a book about this after his death (many more than I will be able to discuss). One telling example is his son Elliott Roosevelt's 1946 biography *As He Saw It*, which included a foreword by Eleanor Roosevelt and had, as Reynolds has noted, "almost autobiographical force."[5] Almost is not entirely

FDR formally dedicating the Roosevelt Library and opening the museum galleries to the public on June 30, 1941. Courtesy of the Franklin D. Roosevelt Library and Museum, Hyde Park, New York

though, and this difference is important to the understanding of FDR's style of autofabrication for future remembrance.

While FDR did not leave his own account, he did try to control and hand-pick the narrators of his legacy behind the scenes. However, on the record, Roosevelt publicly stressed his belief that he would primarily be judged by future generations on the basis of his political choices and decisions. At the dedication of the library, he explained that he wished to make the papers underlying these decisions available to the future public. This suggests that Roosevelt believed in the justifiability of his political choices but especially in the willingness of future generations to judge him fairly. Unlike Winston Churchill or Eleanor Roosevelt, FDR did not write books to interpret his own presidency; instead, he left his papers to be reordered into new narratives by new generations as they might deem appropriate. Roosevelt was no doubt also aware of another kind of legacy he was creating: the memory of himself as a cultural icon and as a persona associated with much more than politics in the narrow sense.

This chapter argues that remembrance practices are always ideologically charged, reflecting the agency of the people or groups that consciously assume power over whom and what is remembered. This chapter explores the ways that FDR himself crafted his public image with an eye to posterity, trying to shape his own future remembrance, as well as some of the ways that he has been represented and remembered since his death. The chapter first considers FDR's autofabrication for the future—his efforts to influence his own future remembrance—by examining the paper legacy that FDR created through *The Public Papers and Addresses* as well as the FDR Library. Next, the chapter explores the complex nature of FDR's posthumous representation by Eleanor Roosevelt, one of FDR's most important narrators both during his life and after his death. Finally, the chapter delves into the topic of *lieux de mémoire*, spaces in which various memory communities try to implement differing remembrance practices, through a discussion of Four Freedoms Park.

Autofabrication for Posterity's Sake: FDR's Paper Legacy

Most of Roosevelt's autofabrication during his presidency was directed at people living and voting at the time, though he was aware that newspaper articles, radio speeches, and photos would also influence how he would be remembered by future generations. Although he sometimes commented on this, it is difficult to measure the level of conscious impact on particular decisions created by this awareness. Two of Roosevelt's autofabrication projects, however, stand out as being aimed at future generations. Both had to do with preserving the documentary evidence underlying his decisions, and more broadly, the paper trail of his presidency and life. The first of these projects was the compilation of the authoritative *The Public Papers and Addresses of Franklin D. Roosevelt*, a selection of Roosevelt's writings and speeches in thirteen volumes published between 1938 and 1950. The second is an expanded version of that: the Franklin D. Roosevelt Presidential Library and Museum in Hyde Park, New York, where all of Roosevelt's papers are housed.

The Public Papers and Addresses

The Public Papers and Addresses of Franklin D. Roosevelt, 1928–1945 was for decades the most comprehensive and readily available overview of Roosevelt's public media expressions. They contain a selection of the official papers of FDR and of the texts of his speeches, from his governorship through his presidency. What sets this selection apart from other works is that Roosevelt officially sanctioned this publication and wrote—or at least signed—introductions and notes to the first nine volumes, which were published during his life. This official selection, made by chief FDR speechwriter Samuel Rosenman, cannot be thought of as an impartial representation of all Roosevelt said or wrote publicly, but it does reveal what aspects of his public life Roosevelt thought it important to publicize. As such, it is not only a place to read what exactly Roosevelt said and wrote in public, but it is itself an instance of Roosevelt managing his own public image. The volumes' paratext, and their selection of Roosevelt's public expressions, shed at least as much light on his autofabrication as the documents contained in the series.

Rosenman, who edited *The Public Papers* and was a key figure in the creation of the FDR Library, also wrote one of the first Roosevelt biographies. In the introduction to *Working with Roosevelt*, Rosenman stressed the importance of words in Roosevelt's presentation: "One measure of him as a President and as a man is what he said and wrote in his public life. More than any other president—perhaps more than any other political figure in history—Franklin D. Roosevelt used the spoken and written word to exercise leadership and to carry out policies."[6]

This is a stark statement—made by someone who was clearly a partisan figure—but it conveys a sentiment that is expressed more widely, that Roosevelt's rhetorical skill was without equal. It's also clear that Roosevelt found words and text important, not just as a matter of democratic principle, but because he was a nimble user who considered them to be his primary tool for exerting influence over others. Even if Roosevelt did not technically use the spoken and written word "more than any other president," both of the major autofabrication projects discussed in this section iconically represent him through his words rather than through visual images, although the museum has increasingly turned to visual representations as well.

The thirteen volumes of *The Public Papers and Addresses of Franklin D. Roosevelt* appeared in three installments. Volumes 1 to 5, treating the period 1928–1936, came out in 1938; the next four, about the period 1937–1940, were published in 1941; and volumes 10 to 13, covering 1941–1945, became available in 1950. Thus, each subseries was dedicated to one term of Roosevelt's presidency, with the first also including his governorship of New York, and the last also including the early months of his fourth term until his death in April 1945. The titles of the volumes are partisan, even tendentious. If one were to take one's idea of the Roosevelt governorship and presidency from the volume titles alone, the story would read:

1928–1932: The Genesis of the New Deal
1933: The Year of Crisis

1934: The Advance of Recovery and Reform

1935: The Court Disapproves

1936: The People Approve

1937: The Constitution Prevails

1938: The Continuing Struggle for Liberalism

1939: War, and Neutrality

1940: War, and Aid to Democracies

1941: The Call to Battle Stations

1942: Humanity on the Defensive

1943: The Tide Turns

1944–1945: Victory and the Threshold of Peace

These titles obviously indicate strong pro-Rooseveltian interpretations of events that are in some cases still highly debated. Did Roosevelt really develop the New Deal in the years before 1933? The phrase "New Deal" was coined by Rosenman for FDR's 1932 acceptance speech of the Democratic Nomination. While Roosevelt certainly wanted to claim continuity in his social and economic philosophy between his governorship and his presidency, many New Deal programs were based on older progressive ideas, whereas others were improvised briefly before their actual enactment. Similarly, in a global context, it is hard to see 1934—the year the Dust Bowl hit the Great Plains, the year Hitler assumed the title of Führer—primarily as the year in which recovery and reform advanced. From the viewpoint of the Roosevelt administration at the time, these examples would perhaps have seemed far-fetched; it is easy for a historian to point out with hindsight what was important in the past.

Nevertheless, a notable amount of Roosevelt-centered storytelling occurs in these titles. For instance, the titles "The Court Disapproves," "The People Approve," and "The Constitution Prevails" together suggest a sequence of events which puts a positive spin on the Supreme Court Crisis of 1937. Following FDR's attempt to "pack" the Supreme Court, the court (which had rejected most early New Deal measures) changed course in 1937 to allow the federal government to regulate the economy to a larger extent, a revolutionary change. From FDR's perspective, this change was positive, since it expanded the power of the executive significantly. Up until that point, the court—led by a conservative faction of "Four Horsemen"—had adhered consistently to the traditional conviction that the national government could not constitutionally regulate commerce in any situation. After that point—but before the Four Horsemen and two further justices had retired—the court had shifted to a radical new position of upholding all New Deal legislation after 1937, including far-reaching and controversial acts such as the Wagner Act (that ensured workers' right to collective bargaining and includes the first mention in legislation of affirmative action) and the Social Security Act.

Indeed, over the years since 1937, the Supreme Court has hardly restricted the federal or state regulation of commerce at all, even while it has taken on new authority with regard to guaranteeing civil liberties, civil rights, and the democratization of the political system under the constitution.[7] The Roosevelt court backed up many of the basic steps that the New Deal took in order to lay the groundwork for what FDR called "the Second Bill of Rights" (guaranteeing economic security to American citizens) in his January 1944 State of the Union address. The Roosevelt court's decisions in turn helped usher in all kinds of legislation, including future Social Security Acts and the Civil Rights Act of 1964.

The sweeping changes in the Supreme Court's interpretation of the Constitution in 1937 were certainly important and, from a progressive perspective, positive. Nevertheless, FDR's court-packing proposal during the legislative crisis that preceded these changes was badly received at the time and continues to be understood by historians as a desperate attempt at executive overreach for the sake of rescuing the New Deal.[8] Rather than the Constitution "prevailing" or being restored to its former power, as the title for the 1937 volume of Roosevelt's *Public Papers and Addresses* indicates, the Supreme Court changed direction to give more power to the government to regulate commerce and move away from its older laissez-faire interpretation of the Constitution.

"Humanity on the Defensive" (the title of the 1942 volume) is even more striking in terms of Roosevelt's long-term image creation. Roosevelt did not create this title himself; Rosenman did, after FDR's death. Rosenman was one of the first people after FDR's death to follow FDR's pattern of rhetorically universalizing events he was involved in. Rosenman used a kind of all-encompassing rhetoric that Roosevelt himself often employed, also often found in later hagiographic assessments of him. An example of Roosevelt's own tendency to universalize his position is his coinage of the name "United Nations" for the world body to be created after the war, named after the nations united to fight the Axis powers: the United States, Great Britain, the Soviet Union, and China.[9]

Many of the public papers and addresses themselves were obviously drafted by Roosevelt and his staff, often including Rosenman, and all were sanctioned by Roosevelt. The paratext of the series—the introductions to each volume, the

general introduction, the notes to individual documents—largely carry Roosevelt's name and signature, except for the last four volumes published in 1950.
While the exact extent to which these were ghostwritten by Rosenman and
others remains unclear, Roosevelt personally conceived the project as part of
his larger plan to establish the presidential library at Hyde Park and, as such,
took it very seriously.[10] He had already published selections of his gubernato-
rial papers and addresses prior to his election and prior to meeting Rosenman.
Some of these selections appeared again in the first volume of *The Public Papers
and Addresses*, accompanied by extemporaneous remarks, probably ghostwritten by Rosenman during the Hoover–Roosevelt interregnum.[11]

Roosevelt in the general introduction to *The Public Papers* rather offhandedly
explained that he knew "of no one better equipped for this task" than Rosenman.[12] The choice to appoint his main speechwriter—not officially a member
of the White House staff, but a New York Supreme Court judge appointed by
Roosevelt—as editor of *The Public Papers* is important and unique in presidential history. It gave Rosenman great power over the composition and selection
of what would become history. Historian Samuel Hand identifies Rosenman as
the "Thucydides of the New Deal"—the only, and, therefore, forever used and
reused source on Roosevelt's role in the New Deal. "Although Franklin D. Roosevelt deliberately set in motion the machinery which established Rosenman's
position, it is highly improbable that the President ever anticipated the full
impact which Rosenman would assert on New Deal historiography."[13]

It is clear that Roosevelt trusted both Rosenman's talents and his loyalty and
that the two men seem to have agreed on the historical importance of *The Public Papers*. Both draw particular attention, within *The Public Papers* and elsewhere, to the fact that the papers are addressed in the first place to future generations of historians. All modern presidents of course know that their words
will be weighed by future generations, but Roosevelt and Rosenman seem to
have been particularly aware of this and have openly addressed themselves to
future historians as a key audience for *The Public Papers and Addresses*.[14] Rosenman in his editorial foreword to the series excuses possible redundancy in the
eyes of current-day readers:

> The important papers in these volumes are covered by comments and notes
> written by President Roosevelt. This feature is unique in editions of Presiden-
> tial papers. It is hoped that these books in the years to come will be a source of
> historical data about this significant period in history. If some of the notes seem

to deal with subjects well known to readers of today, it should be remembered that they are written not only for the present, but for those who in the future may seek to interpret the policies of President Roosevelt from his public utterances and acts, and from his comments with respect to them.[15]

Rosenman here explicitly combines *The Public Papers'* aim of informing future readers and the fact that Roosevelt contributed his own comments and notes to enhance the future understanding of his presidency. Thus, *The Public Papers* set out to offer FDR's own interpretations of his presidential acts and documents to a future audience. Roosevelt, too, explicitly identified his future audience in his "Word of Thanks": "As these volumes will be principally useful in the future to Government officials and students of history, the contribution of those who have assisted is of great value to permanent accuracy in assaying the period in which we live."[16] More grandly, the series' motto— ostensibly in Roosevelt's voice—is "These volumes are dedicated to the people of the United States with whom I share belief in the principles and processes of democracy." Though both Roosevelt and Rosenman were aware of the emotive effects of such grand claims, neither seem to have been cynical or insincere in making them.

The FDR Library

The FDR Library and Museum was the world's first presidential library. Reactions to the idea of creating such an institution were extremely diverse from the beginning. On the one hand, the idea was well received, presumably in light of the newly strengthened interest in the preservation of heritage. However, the FDR Library was also easily interpreted as a monument created by Roosevelt to celebrate himself. Benjamin Hufbauer has called presidential libraries shaped on the blueprint of the FDR Library "presidential temples" and "American pyramids," arguing that presidential libraries essentially are a kind of memorial.[17] Whether or not that is true, the FDR Library and Museum Roosevelt built at Hyde Park, on the site of his family home, where he was later buried, functions metonymically. Of course, the site of the library has undergone change since his death, yet the FDR Library has over time represented Roosevelt broadly as he wished to be represented. Whereas New Deal buildings, infrastructure, and other cultural artifacts that remain indexically associated with Roosevelt are spatially widespread, the FDR Library functions as a metonymic representation confined to one particular place. It has been a constant reminder of how FDR wanted to be remembered. The physical adjacency of the FDR Library and his lifelong home Springwood strengthens the iconic nature of the library.

The Franklin D. Roosevelt Presidential Library was set up and dedicated by Roosevelt personally, making available his own presidential archives and most of his personal documents. It is one of the key building blocks that have contributed to Roosevelt's continuing renown and popularity, perhaps in place of a memoir or autobiography, such as Churchill's extensive memoirs. The FDR Library as an institution has received relatively little critical scholarly attention—except from Benjamin Hufbauer and Richard Cox, and more recently from Anthony Clark. Otherwise, there are only a number of FDR Library chapters in larger books about presidential libraries and collections, which tend to be neutrally descriptive, and a number of articles written by staff members of and policymakers concerned with the library.[18] The latter are, understandably, mainly celebratory of the project.

Nonetheless, it is the key Roosevelt archive for researchers as well as the key museum for general audiences, tourists, and students; as such, it is an important example of how Roosevelt contributed to the cultural memory of his presidency. Roosevelt envisaged it mainly as a site for ritualized remembrance, in the sense that much of his archive was not actually meant to be accessed by the larger public. Rather, he wished to display particular elements of his relationship with the people: "Of the papers which will come to rest here, I personally attach less importance to the documents of those who have occupied high public or private office than I do to the spontaneous letters which have come to me . . . from men, from women, and from children in every part of the United States telling me of their conditions and problems and giving me their own opinions."[19]

The letters which Roosevelt refers to here are indeed among the easiest documents in the FDR Library to access because a selection of them is exhibited at the entrance of the ground floor museum. The actual archive is primarily meant for academic researchers. Roosevelt himself sketched drawings for the building in Dutch style, to honor the family's Dutch origins, and initiated the library's building and dedication. The design of the library and its floor plan is Roosevelt's: a ground floor that is basically a museum and a second floor that houses the actual archive, accessible to researchers. Tourists visit the museum and the house on one ticket, including a tour of the estate, where Franklin, Eleanor, and Franklin's dog Fala are buried.[20]

The FDR Presidential Library was the first presidential library in America. All following presidents have housed their archives in a personal presidential

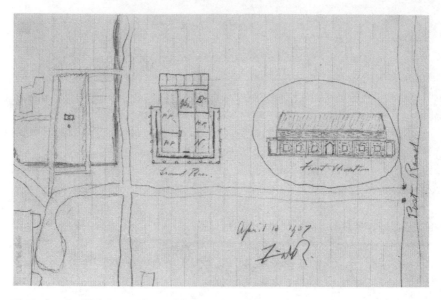

FDR's sketch of his vision for a presidential library at his home in Hyde Park, New York, April 12, 1937. Courtesy of the Franklin D. Roosevelt Library and Museum, Hyde Park, New York

library since, although, unlike Roosevelt, usually after their presidency. Indeed, some preceding presidents' presidential libraries—such as Herbert Hoover's—have also been set up following FDR's example. Before Roosevelt, no law or policy existed to prescribe what should happen with the personal archives of former presidents. The archives of most presidential papers of nineteenth-century presidents have been collected or bought by the National Archives and Records Administration or the Library of Congress in Washington, DC. The archive of George Washington is a painful example of how some of these collections were treated before. Washington himself left his papers to his nephew who lent them to someone else. They ended up in an attic, where they were recovered many years later, damaged heavily by rats and water.[21]

Roosevelt started to make serious plans for his paper legacy in 1937. He had clear ideas about where and how his documents should be kept: "Because these papers relate to so many periods and activities which are not connected with my service in the Federal Government . . . it is my desire that they be kept as a whole and intact in their original condition, available to scholars of the future in one definite locality." He also knew where this should be, writing that he had "carefully considered the choice of locality and for many reasons . . . decided that it would be best that they remain permanently on the grounds of my family home at Hyde Park, Duchess County, New York." He did not give, though, the "many reasons" for choosing the family home specifically. Rather, he stressed the advantage of keeping the entire collection together: "An opportunity exists to set up for the first time in this country what might be called a source material collection relating to a specific period in our history."[22] While these are good arguments to create the library FDR had in mind—and many Roosevelt scholars, including myself, have to be grateful that this collection centering on his person stayed together—it still remains a powerful and conscious feat of autofabrication. It incidentally also alleviated FDR's expenses to manage his own estate, which became federal property (Roosevelt Library Act 1939).

Roosevelt's wish to keep his archives together, concentrated around his person, is not surprising. This is easily read as vanity: he felt that his person, indeed his public persona, should be the central figure in the history of his presidency. Roosevelt was clearly also convinced that it was important that there should be an academic institution for the study of himself and his presidency. Alongside that, he wanted an exhibition space to show a general public his many personal collections—stamps, ship models, books—but also letters and gifts he received as president, including a two-meter-tall, papier-mâché sphinx with Roosevelt's own face. The sphinx and other gifts were exhibited for many years in a special room called "Oddities" in the museum.[23] After a long absence, the 2013 refurbishment brought back the Oddities room, including the sphinx.

That Roosevelt called his archive the Franklin Roosevelt Presidential Library is confusing but significant. To the historians who backed his plan and to the press, he represented it as a plan for an archive, but he also intended to be a museum. As he wrote already in 1937 to his friend, the building's architect Henry Tombs, he expected at least three thousand visitors to the museum per day. This made him suggest that the library's "reading room would not be a reading room at all for students but rather a very carefully designed living room, which would contain portraits, several of my favorite paintings and perhaps a thousand of my books . . . This room, incidentally, I could use myself in the work preparing the collections during hours when the public was not admitted."[24] So, the new institute was to be a museum for the majority of the visitors, an archive for later historians, and a library in the secondary sense of a gentleman's "reading room." Although Roosevelt did not himself want to name the library after himself, he did insist on "library" as part of the new institute's name; more accessible than "archive" and more serious than just "museum."

Despite that well-considered name, which invokes the aura of academic rigor and objectivity, the museum did and still does function in part as an FDR monument. It celebrates the life and memory of Roosevelt, but before, as after the renovation of 2013, the museum has, certainly compared to other presidential libraries, been evenhanded in assessing Roosevelt's decisions. It offers many opportunities for "confronting the issue," as the permanent exhibition has it, of problematic acts and episodes in FDR's presidency, such as the Japanese internment, the fact Roosevelt did not allow more Jews to enter the United States in the late 1930s and early 1940s, and his unfitness at the Yalta peace conference. At the same time, the exposition of letters and gifts from fans gives a strong impression of how popular he was. The museum now, in accordance with modern theories about experiential learning, also offers an interactive and immersive experience, making visitors—most of whom are presumably sympathetic already—come away with a positive and nostalgic sense of FDR, his era, and legacy.

Roosevelt attached great importance to ensuring that his plans for the library would have the support of historians, partly to give form and lend weight to the academic character of the pursuit, but presumably also to avoid accusations that it was a display of self-congratulation.[25] The latter succeeded in part. The December 11, 1938, *New York Times* headline, "Roosevelt Estate to House Archives, Go to Public Later," had as subheading, "Historians Back Idea."

Both *The Public Papers and Addresses* and the FDR Library are iconic representations of Franklin D. Roosevelt. I mean iconic here in the Peircean sense. Charles Sanders Peirce, an American philosopher who theorized the link between representation and represented object, saw three categories: indexical, symbolic, and iconic representations. *Indexical* representations point to the object (for instance, an arrow sign "bathroom" that points to the bathroom). *Symbolic* representations do not resemble or point to the object but still represent it (for instance, specific words). *Iconic* representations resemble the object, as with a photograph; texts, unlike individual words, can also be iconic representations in the sense that they can draw up a likeness through words. Both *The Public Papers and Addresses* and the FDR Library represent FDR textually, that is, in an iconic fashion. The museum portion of the library is also rife with photos of FDR and objects he owned, including his car, his leg braces, his shoes, and letters and gifts people sent him. Such objects outline his silhouette by charting the physical and social fabric he fitted into and, thus, are iconic. At the time that Roosevelt created the FDR Library, the museum profiled him indexically by showing collections he had brought together.

FDR Library, research room, upstairs. Courtesy of the Franklin D. Roosevelt Library and Museum, Hyde Park, New York

FDR's study with wheelchair and portrait of Sara Delano Roosevelt, downstairs. Photograph by Adam Jones from Kelowna, BC, Canada

Eleanor Roosevelt as Narrator of FDR's *Nomos*

Franklin Roosevelt has been portrayed and represented by a host of agents with varying agendas, both during his presidency and after his death. Eleanor Roosevelt was a key representative who—in addition to doing her own political work—worked on behalf of her husband's autofabrication, carrying it beyond his lifetime. She also engaged in autofabrication on her own behalf and sometimes used her role as her husband's narrator to advance her own autofabrication. It seems that ER sometimes represented her late husband for his own sake and other times appropriated her representation of him to suit her own interests in the present. While it is impossible to determine ER's intentions with any certainty, it seems fair to say that ER's remembrance of FDR—like anybody's—was ideologically charged. Other actors who played a role in FDR's autofabrication, whether during his life or by shaping his remembrance after his death, no doubt also appropriated their representations of FDR to suit their own interests. We can see this general pattern, for instance, in the many books that FDR's staff and cabinet members, including secretary Grace Tully and Secretary of Labor Frances Perkins, wrote about working with him. Many people who worked closely with FDR wrote about their experiences, presumably in part because their stories contained important information, but definitely also because doing so was a way to market one's experience and have one's voice heard.

Eleanor Roosevelt in particular functioned as a narrator of FDR's *nomos*, which Robert Cover defines as a "normative universe" that turns on the constant creation and maintenance of "a world of right and wrong, of lawful and unlawful, of valid and void."[26] As head of the executive branch of federal government, FDR was profoundly involved in the creation and maintenance of that "world of right and wrong" on a political and legal level. From very early on until her own death, seventeen years after his, ER narrated his person and presidency. Her "My Day" columns for instance, before as well as after FDR's death, were filled with references to "the President" and "my husband," often explaining what FDR thought, said, believed, or would have said. She comes to function as a kind of megaphone in the public debate of FDR's opinions, even if she also often said she did not agree with them. After his death, she retained this function as FDR's narrator. On April 4, 1955—ten years after FDR's death—ER weighed into the Cold War debate about the meaning of the Allied conferences at the end of World War II, writing: "I am . . . sure that my husband said nothing to Stalin that he had not previously said to Mr. Churchill."[27]

The most important way in which Eleanor Roosevelt filled a gap left by her husband was through writing. Franklin Roosevelt spoke and acted, suitably for an executive and a dramatic actor. He left voice recordings as well as a library filled with documentary material of his presidency, but he wrote very little, and often prohibited note-taking in meetings with cabinet members or advisers. His signature was primarily performative, an act to transform a formulaic text into law, not a narrative kind of writing. ER, in contrast, signed off her writings with her name to stress their personal nature. Unlike Churchill, who, as the subtitle of David Reynolds's book *In Command of History: Fighting and Writing the Second World War* has it, was both a major actor in and narrator of World War II, FDR did not "write" the war or any event during his presidency.[28]

Reynolds's idea that FDR would have done the same if he could have over-simplified the matter: Churchill, a former journalist, was much more of a his-torian and a writer than FDR. I would instead argue that FDR's creation of his library, as he said explicitly in dedicating it, attests to his comfort with hav-ing others write his story, based on the cues he left. This is, as the previous chapter has shown, in line with his approach to his autofabrication as a col-lective effort that he managed, and also with the fact that he left the project of publishing his *Public Papers and Addresses* entirely to Samuel Rosenman.

FDR was more of an orator than a writer. It is possible that the fact that Franklin Roosevelt did not leave much writing or any memoir is coinciden-tal, but it seems more likely that this reflects his preference for modern media—radio, photography, newsreels—that would accrue even more importance in the future. Also, writing would perhaps to FDR, who regularly forbade aides and cabinet members to take notes during meetings, have seemed too much of a commitment to one particular version of events. His style—as Warren Kimball discussed at length in *The Juggler*—was to keep things open to allow for a variety of interpretations.

Eleanor Roosevelt, on the other hand—in addition to being a great orator in her own right—was a writer as well. She wrote a daily newspaper column, prac-tically without missing a day, from December 31, 1935, to September 26, 1962, and hosted radio, and later television, shows.[29] She also wrote articles (often monthly) in numerous magazines as well as a total of four autobiographies: *This Is My Story*, *This I Remember*, *On My Own*, and *The Autobiography of Eleanor Roosevelt*. ER's writing contributed proverbially to FDR's immortality, further-ing the issues and ideals of his nomos through narrative.

In telling stories about Franklin Roosevelt's public and private life and her own days as First Lady in her "My Day" columns, Eleanor Roosevelt engendered cultural narratives and memories of both. In many of her columns, she also addressed her audience, recommending and endorsing various cultural artifacts representing FDR's presidency and their lives. On March 18, 1949, her column was dedicated to a pictorial narrative book to appear soon titled *Franklin Roosevelt at Hyde Park*. She commended it as "the story of a whole era that has passed," stressing the book's narrative force, and, by implication, FDR's synecdochic quality as a representative of that era and a normative universe: "It is not just a pictorial history of my husband. It is the story of a whole era that has passed. Few people in the future will live the kind of life depicted in this book but the record will be there, and I think it is well for us to remember that out of this kind of living came great democratic leaders."

Eleanor Roosevelt claimed that "a pictorial history of my husband" had the potential to represent an era, and indeed a bygone world. She asserted the importance of remembering it as an example because "this kind of living" produced "great democratic leaders." ER suggested that the book indeed represented a normative universe, a seemingly apolitical paradise that brought forth great leaders.

By writing, moreover, that "I know my husband would have enjoyed [it] tremendously," she endorsed the book by proxy, as if it were authorized by Franklin Roosevelt himself. In so doing, she produced and amplified FDR's narrative in his absence, while casting it as officially endorsed. In this manner, Eleanor Roosevelt gave the book a place in FDR's autofabrication by suggesting it carried his personal approval, while absolving him of any accusations of scheming to put himself in the picture posthumously.

In another column, Eleanor Roosevelt reviewed the opening performance of Dore Schary's play *Sunrise at Campobello*, a dramatic rendering of FDR's illness with polio and initial rehabilitation (see chapter 5).[30] She, on the one hand, emphasized the play's fictionality but, on the other, gave estimates of the distance between individual characters in the play and in real life. Louis Howe, for instance, looked differently but "could easily have said any of the things that were put into his mouth" and actor Ralph Bellamy "suggested my husband very successfully." About the dramatic rendering of herself, she wrote: "Miss Mary Fickett did an excellent job of being a very sweet character, which she is in the play. I am afraid I was never really like Mr. Schary's picture of myself, so I could even look upon the portrayal of myself in a fictional light!" Especially the latter comments, about FDR and herself, were carefully phrased to both affirm the narrative portrayal as legitimate and at the same time to mark the distance between the dramatized version and the real experience in the Roosevelts' private life in the 1920s. Her comment on Mary Fickett's portrayal of herself as "very sweet" shows that she refused to regard herself as such. While endorsing the idea that sweetness is a positive trait, she herself was impervious to that compliment within the negotiation of power.

Her presence at the opening night and her positive review of the play, however, in themselves already lent weight as well as a suggestion of veracity to the play. *Sunrise at Campobello* was turned into a successful film in 1960, nominated for four Academy Awards and winning a Best Actress Golden Globe Award for Greer Garson's role of Eleanor Roosevelt. Thus, within the cinematic universe of *Sunrise at Campobello*, the ER character is crucial to the narrative's success. Outside of it, the real Eleanor Roosevelt enabled the film's making—she mentioned in a June 1960 column that the filming was "in full swing" at the main house and her private cottage at Hyde Park. She also advertised and officiously authorized the film.

Eleanor Roosevelt's role as the agent of FDR's legacy, and particularly as a key narrator of his story, has itself become part of a tradition of remembering FDR. In the 1976 television movie *Eleanor and Franklin* (Daniel Petrie, based on the book by Joseph Lash)—until the 2014 broadcast of Ken Burns's *The Roosevelts* series, the most authoritative television biopic of FDR—the ER character is the focalizer of the narrative. Her narrativization naturally stresses their youths, their relationships with each other and with the rest of their family, friends, and Franklin's colleagues. This personal and intimate perspective profoundly influences the portrayal of FDR. Indeed, nowhere in the current or previous chapters have I been tempted to write "Franklin," except in the previous sentence: the film presents him, through Eleanor's eyes, as a Franklin, someone addressed intimately by his first name. I have discussed examples of FDR's attempts in speeches to cast himself as an open and amicable person, for instance, through his repeated use of the word "frank" and "frankly" in his first inaugural address. If this strategy was successful at the time, it has not carried on into a tradition of calling him "Franklin" without "Roosevelt," except in combination with "Eleanor" or through her character's focalization. Thus, despite his seeming informality, FDR has remained at a distance, except through ER, who became a conduit to his private life.

In *Eleanor and Franklin*, a young FDR reflects on this issue in a conversation with ER, saying: "I've always felt I was an actor—I consciously have to charm people. Some people think I'm insincere."[31] This use of the word "actor" is important, primarily because this cinematic FDR interprets the historical FDR as having to "consciously charm people." The film thus suggests that

FDR was consciously fabricating his own public image, and that his construction of his own sincerity was not always believed when he was a young man. This scene foregrounds autofabrication as a matter of being able to produce a convincing construction, because the person playing FDR (who says "I've always felt I was an actor") is obviously an actual actor (Ted Eccles). What may seem insincere about being an actor in the case of the young FDR character is transparent and congruous in the person playing him. That genuineness will emerge for the FDR character as well, when he is no longer just an actor in the nomos but also a character, played by an actor, in later narratives. As president, FDR's political and legal power allowed him to enact and embody a normative universe bigger than himself. This was a dynamic in which he needed to consciously charm people, at times unsuccessfully or at the cost of being thought "insincere." Eleanor Roosevelt, however, could cast FDR's power in his nomos in a favorable light, and, at times, keep that power out of the limelight, by turning him into an actor or character in her narrative.

Eleanor Roosevelt wrote in a 1942 "My Day" column about an inscription that a friend had sent her from a statue of the Pioneer Woman. ER noted that the line in the inscription that she liked best was as follows: "And with all she lived with casual unawareness of her value to civilization." ER reflected in her column on the unsung heroism of the women of her day who were "'casually unaware' of [their own] great accomplishments." She suggested that while these women were "unsung in the present"—because culturally, their heroism included their renunciation of any claim to recognition in the present—they would be "recognized by history." ER both drew attention to women's uncashed checks and praised their generosity for not demanding recompense. ER's own strategy was similarly modest, although she was by no means unaware of her value to the dominant forces around her.

Using this awareness, Eleanor Roosevelt did not only serve her husband's autofabrication but also her own, by attributing her own political priorities and ideals to him during his presidency, and in his name during and afterward. She did so literally after his death, by signing off "Mrs. Franklin D. Roosevelt," where she had previously usually used her own name "Eleanor Roosevelt." Perhaps when FDR was still alive there was more of a need to demarcate the distinction—precisely to allow ER her freedom to speak for herself—but using his name as a widow, she clearly projected herself as his proxy. At the same time, ER had to remain "casually unaware" of her contribution, publicly devoting herself to narrating FDR with the honesty and the openness which indeed has remained essential to her image. When she did act on her own behalf, or better, in the interest of others whose causes she applauded, she had to do so implicitly. ER's political agency, however, remained subliminally present after FDR's death. This was in part through her public roles, mainly as US delegate to the general assembly of the United Nations and chair of the UN Commission on Human Rights, but also in a vaguer cultural sense. In a December 1945 *Gallup* poll, respondents were asked to name potential candidates who "might make a good president," and Eleanor Roosevelt came fourth.[32]

Eleanor Roosevelt's political clout hinged, as said, on her invisibility in the political sphere. Much as she continues to be remembered as a First Lady politically astute enough to be a potential president, her overt absence equally survives in cultural remembrance. This means that she is often overlooked as a political agent or at least granted less attention in mainstream remembrance than the groups she promoted—women, ethnic and racial minorities—consider to be her due. This is an effect of the same casual unawareness that was essential in negotiating her position of power. Thus, few visitors to the Roosevelt Historic Home and FDR Presidential Library make it to ER's cottage Val-Kill. ER is only implicitly present at the Four Freedoms Park in New York, and she has only thirty-five minutes out of fourteen hours dedicated to her in Ken Burns's *The Roosevelts: An Intimate History.*

After Franklin Roosevelt's death in April 1945, Eleanor Roosevelt continued to be politically active, though not in elected office. She was, most famously and importantly, the United States' first delegate to the United Nations General Assembly and chairperson of the UN Committee on Human Rights Within that capacity, she helped to draft the Universal Declaration of Human Rights. Within the United States, ER became a public intellectual, who wrote and published many opinion pieces and books, appeared on a wide range of radio and television shows, and chaired various boards and committees. She was also involved, as her husband had been in the first decade of the twentieth century, in battling the enormous power of the Democratic Party machine of Tammany Hall. However, on the whole, her position as a public intellectual, educating the American public, was the role that suited her best in the years between 1945 and her own death on November 7, 1962.[33]

Although Eleanor Roosevelt remained very influential in her post-war career, her lowered visibility was an explicit choice. She was often invited to run for political office but continued to present herself rather as FDR's "aura," even if her projects in reality were more her own than extrapolations of FDR's. As she wrote about this in an article in *Look Magazine* in 1946, following her refusal to run for vice-president with Harry Truman: "At first I was surprised that anyone should think that I would want to run for office, or that I was fitted to hold office. Then I realized that some people felt that I must have learned something from my husband in all the years that he was in public life! The simple truth is that I have had my fill of public life of the more or less stereotyped kind."[34]

This representation of her plans in 1946, suggesting a retirement from public life, was a far cry from what Eleanor Roosevelt actually did after her husband's death. In fact, she became more politically active and more visible in the public eye than ever. Clearly, she continued to autofabricate herself as FDR's wife, suggesting that any fitness for political office that people might assume would have been learned from him. She continued to exert great influence, never missing an opportunity to make her voice heard, and she continued to pose as someone who did so only reluctantly—despite herself and to her own surprise. In discussing the period after FDR's death, Binker and O'Farrell, in a *Historical News Network* article about ER in *The Roosevelts*, note indignantly that "this period is a complete mystery to most Americans who usually associate ER with Franklin and assume that her role in American life ended with his death in 1945 or that her postwar life merely echoed his New Deal. Neither of these statements is true."[35] While they are right about this, it was ER's own conscious autofabrication that produced for "most Americans" this perception of "mystery" and strong association with "Franklin" as well as the impression that ER's independent and autonomous later politics always remained a continuation of the New Deal.

Remembering the Four Freedoms

As outlined in the introduction, I interpret cultural memory as the archive of culturally acceptable narratives. This interpretation is close to, yet different from, Jan Assmann's celebrated definition; Assmann understands cultural memory as concerning culturally inherited events that are no longer part of "lived" memory in society.[36] Assmann sees these events as becoming congealed legends or myths that function as cultural touchstones. He sees cultural memory as distinct from communicative memory, which comes into existence in everyday interaction between people.

In between cultural and communicative memory there is, to borrow Jan Vansina's expression, a "floating gap."[37] What occurs in this gap is a negotiation that can be considered in both temporal and spatial terms. Whereas Assmann may be said to favor the temporal approach, another foundational memory theorist, Pierre Nora, approaches this negotiation as primarily a spatial process. Both approaches may be productive, but what interests me specifically—and what they seem to gloss over—are the processes that take place in the "floating gap."

Rather than thinking of cultural memory as a congealed and set outcome of communicative memory processes that temporally follows the demise of lived memory, I see cultural memory as the collection of narratives that have not yet been but stand a reasonable chance of becoming solidified. This process is crucially driven by agents in the present and occurs at what Pierre Nora has called *lieux de mémoire* (sites of memory). Pierre Nora supposes a clean-cut opposition between *lieux de mémoire* and *milieux de mémoire* (environments of memory). He is nostalgic about *milieux de mémoire* but does not quite place them; rather, he suggests that up until the nineteenth century, people were in their day-to-day invested in remembering the past in such a way that it "stayed alive." So *milieux de mémoire* were public spaces (churches, village squares, town halls, bars) in which the past continued to live on among common people. *Lieux de mémoire*, according to Nora, are the modern re-placements of the more diffuse and omnipresent *milieux de mémoire*: designated geographical locations where memory "lives," although, according to him, in a kind of frozen state.

Both Pierre Nora and Jan Assmann thus attend particularly to the "last" and most explicitly congealed form of memory, which disregards precisely the crucial negotiation carried out in the "floating gap."[38] However, this negotiation does actually occur at *lieux de mémoire*, despite Nora's pessimism about such sites' deadness. It is important to recognize this, because, as within autofabrication, disguising the fact that there is a negotiation artificially increases the authority of the remembrance practices that emerge as dominant.

This negotiation occurs normally between interested parties, who each want a different narrative to become the dominant, set narrative, often, but not necessarily, for ideological reasons. To stress the agency involved, I follow Jay Winter's suggestion to use "remembrance" to denote acts that reconfigure elements of memory.[39] In acts of remembrance, agents draw narrative elements from the broader archive of cultural memories, configuring them in specific ways in order to have others invest in particular versions of particular stories. Remembrance is not only driven by recognizable agents; it also usually involves a practice, often including rituals.

The archive as a metaphor for memory is well-known, as is the realization that archives, like memories, are sites and products of an ongoing negotiation about how to interpret the past.[40] Various issues are at stake: which past gets most attention, what meaning that past is attributed in the present, how the relevant past is to be selected, how historically correct it is, and to what extent remembered agents can themselves influence later cultural memory. It is difficult to pinpoint precisely where this negotiation takes place. Although Nora set out specifically to expose the power dynamics in such negotiations, both his own term *lieux de mémoire* and Henk Wesseling's Dutch equivalent *Plaatsen van herinnering* tend to confirm the canonicity of the dominant narrative rather than engage with cultural debates about how to remember particular sites.[41]

Ann Rigney defines "sites of memory" as "actual locations or symbolic points of reference that serve as dense repositories of historical meaning . . . and hence as communal orientation points in negotiations about collective self-definitions." She conceives of *lieux de mémoire* as places that are variously used and interpreted by a multitude of "memory communities," or social groups, each with their own ideas of what is important and thus worth remembering.[42] My own conception of *lieux de mémoire* is similar to Rigney's; I see *lieux de mémoire* as denoting places, concrete or abstract, where cultural memory continues to be in flux. Such places—where the public, institutions, scholars, educators, and other stakeholders continue to negotiate cultural memory and remembrance—are active sites of identity politics.

The Four Freedoms have been and continue to be echoed endlessly in various political and cultural contexts. They were part of the Atlantic Charter drawn up by Roosevelt and Churchill and from there found their way into the charter of the United Nations. They were also the basis for a renowned series of war propaganda posters by Norman Rockwell, discussed in the next chapter. The central words are also repeated in many FDR memorials, most centrally in the Four Freedoms Park on Roosevelt Island in New York City.[43] Also, the Roosevelt Institute annually awards four "Four Freedoms Medals," one for each freedom.[44] In those and other forms, the Four Freedoms Speech has continued to resonate and to be rekindled time and again in new contexts.

Within the academic debate about FDR and his role in US and world history, too, the Four Freedoms continue to provide a "site of memory" and locus for debate. Cases in point are Harvey Kaye's monograph *The Fight for the Four Freedoms: What Made FDR and the Greatest Generation Truly Great*[45] and Jeffrey Engel's edited collection *The Four Freedoms: Franklin D. Roosevelt and the Evolution of an American Idea*.[46] Kaye's book in particular can be viewed as doing the work of remembrance: it employs the history of the Four Freedoms and the "Greatest Generation" in an unapologetically progressive narrative about what can be learned from the past. Engel's edited volume, like the present book, is less of a direct voice in the negotiations around the place Roosevelt and the Four Freedoms should occupy in American culture. Instead, the authors of the collection present the Four Freedoms as they are understood in the twenty-first century, as the ultimate result of a long process of universalization of American values, to which FDR contributed in a major way. Nevertheless, both books—much like Emily Rosenberg's *A Date Which Will Live: Pearl Harbor in American Memory*—engage in the question of how an individual idea or event, and FDR's words about it, contributed to the creation of cultural icons with broad appeal.

While I see FDR's formulation of the Four Freedoms as being itself an abstract *lieu de mémoire*, I focus in this section on a physical *lieu de mémoire*: the Franklin D. Roosevelt Four Freedoms Park. Located at the southernmost tip of Roosevelt Island, New York, Four Freedoms Park is Louis Kahn's last design, built posthumously and opened in 2012.[47] The memorial is a project driven mainly by the Roosevelt Institute, the previously mentioned foundation, and especially by Ambassador William vanden Heuvel.[48] The Roosevelt Institute is linked to the Roosevelt family: both the board of directors and the board of governors are chaired by Roosevelt grandchildren. The Roosevelt Institute is committed to "carrying forward the legacy and values of Franklin and Eleanor Roosevelt."[49] The Franklin D. Roosevelt Four Freedoms Park has a highly abstract and stylized design, basically triangular, with a walkway on each side leading through a highly schematically constructed park to a square outdoor "room" at the very tip of the island. The room provides space to sit and a box that contains a bust of Franklin Roosevelt facing away from the room. The outside of the box that can be seen when sitting in the outdoor room is engraved with a section of the Four Freedoms speech. The pointed triangular shape of the memorial indexes the United Nations Headquarters—Roosevelt's distant vision, which he did not live to see fulfilled—like a compass needle. The memorial clearly is the project of an ideological institution, built with private funds from likeminded philanthropists remembering FDR as a champion of freedom and visited by a presumably sympathetic public.

The FDR Four Freedoms Park Conservancy, the board that built and now manages the memorial, is linked to the Roosevelt Institute. The Conservancy is active in proposing remembrance practices at the site, such as an annual wreath-laying ceremony to remember FDR's death, and educational programming, such as the FDR Four Freedoms digital resource—a smartphone application offering spoken and visual explanation and interpretation of FDR and the memorial. At the same time, the memorial is Louis Kahn's last design,

Four Freedoms Park, Roosevelt Island, New York City, 2014. Photograph by Albert Vecerka, Esto.com

inviting an audience interested in memorial architecture rather than in Roosevelt, an element that is not so much part of the agenda of the Conservancy. Kahn is discussed briefly on the website and on the park billboards, but primarily in the context of his reverence for FDR, and the fact that Kahn was helped early in his career by Roosevelt's New Deal.[50] Despite the Conservancy's stress on FDR, it is also clearly a site for remembering Kahn. Although posthumous building of an architect's design is no doubt always slightly unfaithful to his original intentions, Gina Pollara, the executive director of the building project, cited faithfulness to Kahn's design and a commitment to his architectural intentions as her primary motivation in accepting her commission.[51]

The remembrance of FDR and of Kahn do not conflict at the site. Some individuals and institutions are more interested in the one, others in the other, but both groups are essentially contributing to and recalling different areas of cultural memory through the lens of this site. A more territorial contest has to do with the space the site occupies. Roosevelt Island was previously called Blackwell's Island, after its colonial owner since the late seventeenth century. Located off Manhattan, it was a logical place to isolate people. It housed prisons, various hospitals (most famously, the smallpox hospital at the entrance to the memorial), and a lunatic asylum (in a peculiarly literal illustration of Foucault's phenomenology of the othering of aberrance in *Madness and Civilization*). For this reason, the island was renamed Welfare Island in 1921. It was then renamed Roosevelt Island in 1971, in memory of FDR's commitment to the poor, old, and incapacitated.[52]

It is perhaps no surprise, then, that the Roosevelt Island Disabled Association vehemently opposed the fact that the Four Freedoms Memorial contains no explicit reference to Roosevelt's own disability. To stick to Kahn's design means to focus on FDR's ideals of freedom and worldwide internationalism, rather than to give undue attention to a handicap that clearly did not obstruct him in carrying his ideals to fruition. On the other hand, not to show the disability can be construed as portraying FDR as merely charitable to disabled people, glossing over the fact that he was one of them. An acknowledgment of the disability would emancipate the site from a place of exclusion to a place of redress. The outraged response of the Roosevelt Island Disabled Association is connected directly to the irritation that some disabled people, like Hugh Gallagher, have expressed with FDR's passing as nondisabled, in part through performing a kind of magnanimous attitude toward people with disabilities that denied his own identification as one of them. In not referring to his disability—even decades later, when FDR had become more identified with

A look into the future of the FDR Hope Memorial.

Rendering of the future FDR Hope Memorial, sculpture by Meredith Bergmann. Roosevelt Island Operating Corporation

his disability than ever before—the site continues FDR's own style of autofabricating his disability as an absence.

The practical outcome was that the Roosevelt Island Disabled Association embarked on building the FDR Hope Memorial, in front of—but not as part of—the FDR Four Freedoms Park, with an initial donation from the Roosevelt Institute. The FDR Hope Memorial will portray FDR in his wheelchair, reaching out to a girl on crutches, in order to "educate future generations about FDR and about Roosevelt Island, a vital community of "enabled" residents."[53] Thus, the Four Freedoms Memorial functions as a *lieu de mémoire*, used by various groups to implement particular remembrance practices, shoring up particular narratives of the site, and of Roosevelt's meaning to it and to the world. It remains a site—not just a *lieu*, a placeholder, but a geographically and socially located *milieu*—alive with debate and memory-making as long as various interpretative remembrance practices continue to vie for the same ground, literally and figuratively, in cultural memory.

This chapter has focused on ways in which FDR's autofabrication extended into the future after his death, orchestrated in large part by himself and his most trusted agents. Of these, the Franklin D. Roosevelt Presidential Library was most clearly his own idea, designed and executed by himself according to his own plan, even against the wishes of his mother (who still lived on the estate at the time of the library's dedication in 1941). But although creating this library was perhaps a pet project, it has had great influence on the broader culture of presidential remembrance practices and on the role of the National Park Service in preserving cultural legacies next to natural heritage.

The Public Papers and Addresses of Franklin D. Roosevelt were primarily Samuel Rosenman's project. They were commissioned by FDR to bring together and publish his main speeches, press conferences, and other documents as a reference work for researchers. The papers and addresses simultaneously offered insight into the primary sources to allow readers to draw their own conclusions, and on the other hand included a specific selection and spin toward what Roosevelt and Rosenman themselves considered important elements of future cultural memory and potential remembrance practices.

Finally, a key agent in the shift from FDR's autofabrication in the political and cultural context of his presidency to autofabrication for the sake of posterity was Eleanor Roosevelt. In many ways, she narrated Roosevelt's presidency, both as an avid columnist and contributor to all kinds of mass media publications and broadcasts, and as a "voiceover" in later representations of

FDR's presidency. The documentary *Eleanor and Franklin*, for example, drew on her journals for their narration and used the ER character's voice to explain and frame the events shown. In this chapter, I have wanted to show how ER simultaneously worked hard to establish and cement her husband's cultural and political legacy after his death, while at the same time furthering her own political causes according to her own beliefs. FDR might well have disagreed with these, but ER nonetheless retained a great deal of authority based on the premise that she knew best what he would have wanted and increasingly—as Allida Black has put it—"cast her own shadow" in politics and culture. The United Nations' Declaration of Human Rights, for instance, both continues the work that FDR started with the New Deal and his statement of the Four Freedoms, while also executing ER's own more eagerly radical stance on global human rights.[54] It is typical of ER's silent yet crucial role in progressing FDR's vision beyond his death that she is not represented explicitly at the Four Freedoms Park on Roosevelt Island. The memorial points across the East River toward the United Nations Headquarters in Manhattan: without being visible, ER has played a key role in bridging that interval.

This also brings my larger narrative to a point of transition. Whereas so far, I have focused on FDR's autofabrication (carried out both by himself and by trusted advisers), this chapter has also emphasized sites of memory that have become places of negotiation in the decades since FDR's presidency. While I have stressed the continuing agency of FDR's autofabrication thus far, these processes are also driven by agents and interests at the time of negotiation. The following chapters will increasingly focus on processes of memory-making by examining how remembrance practices are produced. The ghost of FDR's autofabrication will remain present and will remain an object of scrutiny.

CHAPTER FOUR

The New Deal Depoliticized in Cultural Memory

At the start of Roosevelt's presidency in March 1933, the American economy was at an all-time low. Millions of Americans had lost their savings, become unemployed, or seen their mortgages foreclosed.[1] During his 1932 campaign, Roosevelt promised "a new deal" for all Americans, especially those "forgotten men at the bottom of the economic pyramid."[2] He was elected by a landslide in November 1932. He then kept extremely quiet in the months between his election and inauguration, to the point that Hoover later accused him of doing nothing on purpose so as to let the economy sink lower and make his entry to the presidency more dramatic.[3] Whether Roosevelt was actually that calculating remains hard to prove or disprove, but Hoover was unprecedentedly unpopular by that time, while expectations of Roosevelt were soaring. His first inaugural address has remained an iconic moment, setting the tone for a period of major new legislation and reforms. Roosevelt called Congress into special session to pass emergency laws. While he did not actually bypass Congress at all, his first inaugural demanded "broad executive power" from Congress, such as the president is usually only granted as commander in chief during war.[4] However, debate and activism in Congress, rather than the executive, was eventually decisive for much of the New Deal's policies, as Ira Katznelson has argued.[5]

The Great Depression and the New Deal together remain a crucial episode in American twentieth-century cultural memory. The 1930s and particularly the New Deal have been essential to how FDR has been remembered in America since his presidency. As the first enormous challenge Roosevelt faced as president, the Depression—to which the New Deal was his response—has always been strongly associated with FDR in cultural memory. "Dr. New Deal," his own coinage, remains one of FDR's most popular nicknames.[6] However, the remembrance of Roosevelt's New Deal does not accurately reflect the political measures that comprised the program, as historian Anthony Badger notes.[7] This chapter sets out to understand why remembrance of the New Deal tends to engage so little with the actual political program, even while the New Deal remains central to the Roosevelt icon. FDR is still widely perceived as the epitome of a universally beloved people's president. When looking at cultural representations of FDR, it seems clear that the New Deal is one of the standard ingredients contributing to that image, together with World War II, Eleanor Roosevelt, and the fact that he was disabled.

The New Deal has left a wide range of cultural legacies that continue to provide indexical links to FDR. Most of these legacies are no longer controversial political issues or at least no longer blamed on FDR. Political opponents of federal involvement with healthcare and welfare issues, for instance, would now sooner blame the heritage of Johnson or Clinton than Roosevelt. To some extent, the New Deal has acquired a place in cultural memory as Jan Assmann uses the term: the small handful of congealed narratives a nation shares. Because of those well-known narratives, and a few often-seen stock varieties of New Deal architecture, it is easy to think of the New Deal as having been primarily a cultural (rather than a political) phenomenon—a fact that, in itself, constitutes a depoliticization. The political changes spawned by the New Deal have now become so detached from it that the association is all but lost.

The changes in the physical and cultural American landscape have been preserved as cultural and material capital, rather than as government efforts to intervene in the capitalist market economy, although the New Deal has clearly also done that. This particular remembrance of the New Deal as a progressive and (with hindsight) inevitable landscape and electrification effort that remains architecturally visible, rather than a crucial expansion of federal executive and legislative power (which it also was), constitutes a depoliticization in cultural memory enabled by the tangible nature of the objects involved. At the same time, and paradoxically, one of the most politicizing legacies of the New Deal is that the narratives of American heritage came to be produced by federal agencies. As such, the publicly presented interpretations of American history are inevitably products of negotiated consensus between different stakeholders and synchronic with mainstream cultural memory. This is because as preservation became a duty of federal agencies like the National Park Service (NPS), instead of being privately owned and managed, it became necessary for them to be neutral and nonpartisan.

In this chapter, I will show how the New Deal, which was highly controversial throughout the 1930s, was depoliticized in cultural memory in various ways, turning into a friendly but ideologically vacuous attribute to Roosevelt. This process of depoliticizing the New Deal in cultural memory, I will argue, followed two routes: personalization, in which the New Deal came to be conflated with FDR's person, and mediatization, in which a "First Hundred Days" media practice developed that was dissociated from the politics of FDR's First Hundred Days. Both routes made use of and expanded the ideological plasticity that Roosevelt himself already embodied. However, in this process of cultural memory, depoliticization can never quite escape being politically charged.

In fact, depoliticization is a deeply political process in which FDR was profoundly engaged, in a manner that could be described as manipulative, even devious. I think of depoliticization in two contexts. Michael Kammen's theory that depoliticization results from myth building—a theory that is exemplified by the musical film *Annie*—provides the first context.[8] In the second context, I treat depoliticization as a partisan political project, in which FDR employed presidential rhetoric to gloss over the partisan and radical nature of the New Deal. These two contexts are not separate. Indeed, I will explain— with the help of political theorist Chantal Mouffe—that the cunning manner of depoliticization FDR employed was characterized by the (often convincing) claim that unifying the nation and rallying around his specific progressive politics were the same thing. That strategy of bland, hard-to-disagree-with rhetoric that "masked" politically controversial and perhaps even radical ideas is one of the main things that irked FDR's opponents, even decades after his presidency.

The chapter's first two sections explore FDR's own efforts both to autofabricate himself through the New Deal—though without using it for obvious self-aggrandizement—and, conversely, to protect the politically controversial New Deal by identifying it with himself personally. The first section takes up FDR's ideological plasticity, while the second looks at the way in which FDR employed the New Deal's success and widespread reputation to silently forge a popular consensus about his administration. The third and fourth sections of the chapter show how such strategies took root, so that the New Deal began to appear in cultural representations in a depoliticized manner. The third section focuses on New Deal nostalgia, such as portrayed in the musical film *Annie* (1982). The fourth discusses the development of the "First Hundred Days" as a presidential media tradition that started with FDR but that has gradually lost its New Deal connotation.

It is important, however, to realize that the New Deal itself, both during FDR's presidency and in the decades afterward, functioned as an iconic program. This is true in the general sense that many New Deal projects that remain visible in the American landscape are perceived as constituting authentic proxies of the era and context that produced them. This is also true in the Peircean sense: these projects, with their sweeping impact and pretensions, *resemble* the culture and aesthetic that they represent. In the context of American politics, certainly in the years during and after World War II, the New Deal was arguably even more iconic than FDR; the New Deal characterized FDR more than vice versa. Probably in part for this reason, FDR himself was keen to think of his plans for the future of international relations as a global New Deal. A 1944 article in the magazine *The Nation* also called for a "New Deal for the world," suggesting that this manner of considering FDR's domestic rescue program would be scalable to global proportions.[9] In doing so, the magazine employed the New Deal, rather than FDR, as an icon and blueprint of Americanism.

This iconic nature and marketability of the New Deal did not only bleed into American international relations but also temporally into following administrations. The idea of a formula whose core tenets consist of a renewed role of the state in the economy, as well as on the expansion of the federal government vis-à-vis the states, and on the construction of an American socio-democratic experiment, have remained politically viable over time. As William Leuchtenburg points out in *In the Shadow of FDR*, a host of later federal-level social and economic programs had to deal with the iconic nature of the New Deal and explicitly or implicitly are named after it. For instance, Truman's Fair Deal and Johnson's Great Society take not just the gist of their progressive policies but also their branding from the New Deal less than from Roosevelt. An interesting exception to this is Kennedy's *Brain Trust*, which actually refers to another typical FDR brand, his "brain trust" consisting of a team of policy advisers (discussed in chapter 2).

Of course, the New Deal has simultaneously also remained politically controversial and not only in right-wing circles. Katznelson, for instance, has shown in detail how white supremacist factions in the southern states politically enabled the New Deal in exchange for permission to continue their ingrained and habitual racial cruelty; they then excluded African Americans from the New Deal's benefits.[10] Similarly, Jewish leaders had to more or less choose between supporting the New Deal (which did benefit many American Jews) and calling out FDR's initial inertia in response to the rise of violent anti-Semitism in Germany.[11]

FDR's Ideological Plasticity

Roosevelt's resistance to ideological profiling has often been regarded as a political advantage. As, for instance, Patrick Renshaw has said in *Franklin D. Roosevelt*: "Where Hoover's greatest handicap in dealing with the depression had been his philosophy, FDR's greatest asset was his lack of one. 'Philosophy?' he once quizzically told a questioner. 'Philosophy? I'm a Christian and a democrat—that's all.'"[12]

Renshaw surely was only referring to Hoover's "handicap" in metaphorical terms, and not to FDR's disability. However, it remains striking that he noted FDR's "lack of" a philosophy as his "greatest asset." In the same way that FDR passed as nondisabled, he also managed to project an unusual nimbleness in seeming apolitical.

I use the term "depoliticization" to denote either a rhetorical shift away from the political and into the cultural realm, or a universalization (such as when FDR termed himself "a Christian and a [lower-case d] democrat" while carrying out an agenda that was then and would always be considered radical in the US political tradition). FDR associated himself only with labels that the overwhelming majority of Americans at the time would identify with as well, however much they might have opposed Roosevelt's actual politics. Roosevelt was successful in presenting a kind of emptiness or enigma: he used words that appeared to commit him to a particular stance, which he then denied. Roosevelt used this strategy to seem less partisan and thus depoliticize himself, albeit to his political advantage.

The formulation of the Four Freedoms, which remain important in projections of Roosevelt as a public icon, similarly precludes a great deal of opposition. Wherever one is on the political spectrum, at least two of the Four Freedoms are likely to be compelling. The two "freedom *of*" tenets, speech and religion, point to individual liberties, while the two "freedom *from*" tenets, fear and want, promote collective freedoms that require an active role from government. The Four Freedoms balance left-wing and right-wing priorities as well as individual and collective needs, offering a set of principles that contain something for almost everyone.

One of the most persistent representations of the Four Freedoms, and thus indexically of FDR, is a set of Four Freedoms posters created by Norman Rockwell in 1943 and used by the Office of War Information to sell war bonds. Each poster represents one of the Four Freedoms. Each also represents a

Four Freedoms posters by Norman Rockwell. Collection National Archives at College Park

Christian, white, middle-class nostalgic view of America, interpreting the Four Freedoms as concretely referring to American family life, Thanksgiving, workmanship, and Protestantism. The controversial aspects of freedom from want—the ideological foundation for what was for many Americans a highly suspect New Deal—is stifled by the huge Thanksgiving turkey Rockwell uses to represent white, middle-class American family life.

Roosevelt commissioned and later praised Rockwell's representations of the Four Freedoms, writing to him: "I think you have done a superb job in bringing home to the plain, everyday citizen the plain, everyday truths behind the Four Freedoms . . . I congratulate you not alone on the execution but also for the spirit which impelled you to make this contribution to the common cause of a freer, happier world." To *The Post*, in which they were first published, he wrote: "This is the first pictorial representation I have seen of the staunchly American values contained in the rights of free speech and free worship and our goals of freedom from fear and want."[13] Thus, FDR sanctioned this representation of the Four Freedoms as representing "staunchly American values," allowing Rockwell to gloss over FDR's activist social and economic agenda, as well as the presence in America of people who were non-white, poor, or not Christian, while avoiding doing so himself. As such, through this obviously problematic yet popular representation, FDR's Four Freedoms became ingrained in American memory in a new way: in a new medium as well as with a concrete narrative content that the original formulation does not have. FDR was especially successful in his autofabrication and at surviving in cultural memory through remembrance because he understood this. He autofabricated himself as being on some level an empty container and then allowed artists like Rockwell—independent to some extent but paid by his administration—to fill in his abstract words with visual narratives that resonated in new ways.

Roosevelt also used history to depoliticize himself in the then-present. Roosevelt was sensitive to the potentially unifying and consensus-building effect of historical analogies; he surrounded himself with formal and informal advisers in such matters. During campaigns, FDR stressed his connection with heroic statesmen such as Lincoln and Jefferson, partly in order to associate himself with the entire electorate rather than with Democratic voters only.[14] In 1936, for instance, he acted on the advice of his assistant secretary of state, R. Walton Moore, who argued that "while the campaign is under way, a stop at Jefferson's home might be highly productive in terms of public relations."[15]

Also in 1936, Roosevelt unveiled the head of Thomas Jefferson at Mount Rushmore, saying in his dedication speech:

> We can perhaps meditate a little on those Americans ten thousand years from now when the weathering on the face of Washington and Jefferson and Lincoln shall have proceeded to perhaps a depth of a tenth of an inch—meditate and wonder what our descendants, and I think they will still be here, will think about us. Let us hope that at least they will give us the benefit of the doubt—that they will believe we have honestly striven every day and generation to preserve for our descendants a decent land to live in and a decent form of government to operate under.[16]

Here, FDR explicitly raises the question of future remembrance. By shifting the perspective so far into the future, to "Americans ten thousand years from now," he directly aligns himself with "Washington and Jefferson and Lincoln," who are portrayed at Mount Rushmore. The effect of this far horizon is that he can easily suggest he is in a league with those illustrious presidents because he shares their broad ambition for "a decent land to live in and a decent form of government to operate under." While this ambition seems so vague and bland that it is an empty claim to make, FDR does implicitly include "to preserve" as one of the government's duties. Preservation of American landscape and Americana was much more his specific agenda than that of Washington, Jefferson, or Lincoln, but this speech suggests that, like honoring the Founding Fathers, preservation through the public sector is one of the sacred duties of American patriotism. Thus, he affiliates himself with Washington, Jefferson, and Lincoln through a rhetorical figure that seems to make irrelevant their ideological differences, while at the same time suggesting they shared his political agenda. Thus, Roosevelt both acted as an agent in idealizing a supposed consensual American history and activated that history to his own electoral advantage.

Historian Michael Kammen argued that using cultural memory to depoliticize the past is a crucial American strategy for dealing with American history; he saw Franklin Roosevelt as an exemplary proponent of that tendency. The above example illustrates what I think he meant, both because it is an instance of how looking back into the past can provide a sense of collectivity in the present that sidesteps partisan differences, and in the sense that it shows how FDR could make this effect operative for his own political and partisan ends. However, Kammen uses the term depoliticization without making clear what precisely he means by it. When he says, "Americans have been inclined to depoliticize their past," he suggests that American memory tends to become apolitical, that is, to lose its political charge. But the fact that Roosevelt could depoliticize himself by forging a link with national historical figures to his electoral advantage implies that this was, after all, a political phenomenon. Indeed, in FDR's case, it seems to have been a political strategy, though perhaps driven more by practical opportunism than by ideological conviction.

Political theorist Chantal Mouffe argues that modern democracy is characterized by an irreconcilable combination of liberalism, focused primarily on individualism and human rights, and democracy, focused primarily on equality and popular sovereignty. This uncomfortable combination inevitably leads to conflicts of interest between the majority vote on the one hand and the pluralism of individuals on the other. Mouffe sees consensus as impossible and argues that modern democracies need spaces in which opposing voices can clash. In *The Democratic Paradox*, she argues against late-twentieth-century political movements like Tony Blair's "third way," which was intended to transcend the left-right opposition in politics, and the "Clintonization" of politics in America.[17] She considers such movements purely "aggregative," reducing democratic politics to "the negotiation of interests" without transforming antagonism in plural societies to a productive political agonism.[18] One might argue that Roosevelt is a kind of archetype for consensus-driven politicians like Blair, Bill Clinton and Gerhard Schröder. Mouffe sees consensus-driven politics as a risk for the health of society's pluralism, and particularly for those groups in society that need to seek emancipation. Arguably, for example, FDR's noncommittal friendliness to African Americans may actually have worked to delay the growth of the Civil Rights Movement until well into the 1950s.

For Kammen, "political" seems to mean the same as "partisan." "Depoliticization of history" then refers to the fact that historical narratives in an American context tend to become more collective because they lose their partisan colors to a blander, generically patriotic American mode of cultural memory. However, as we have seen in Roosevelt's case, the movement from controversial partisan issues in the present to a projected memory of an affable national consensus is itself a shift of framework with a highly political impact of a kind that Mouffe deplores. In Mouffe's view, FDR's and other politicians' tendency to suggest that a bland general consensus has evolved about the interpretation of events in cultural memory—however fabricated it may be—robs the democratic process of a positive site for confrontation between opposing interests. Roosevelt's projection of himself as an ideologically empty body politic was incongruous with Mouffe's ideal that the political should be agonistic.

How FDR Silently Defined a Mainstream

Through the New Deal—and inspired by the progressivism that he shared with Theodore Roosevelt—FDR contributed to a cultural context in which preservation of American cultural heritage was perceived as a government function. Because this preservation was a national effort, it was logical to de-politicize the cultural legacy concerned, divorcing it from its partisan con-text and casting it as a broader collective legacy. However, this shift in itself was politically charged. The suggestion that it was nonpartisan and "belonged to everyone" actually antagonized people who really mistrusted it and is, in part, the reason Roosevelt continues to be hated so viscerally in some circles that oppose the idea that preservation is a government task in the first place.

At Roosevelt's instigation, Congress enacted a massive number of new laws, including dramatic ones like the ending of Prohibition and the release of the Gold Standard. Roosevelt made enormous appropriations, among others for the Civilian Conservation Corps, through which millions of young, un-employed urban men were put to work in national parks and forestry projects. The scale of the New Deal meant that hundreds of agencies were set up to carry out the plans and new legislation.[19] This led to what was soon called the "alphabet soup" of New Deal agencies. Most were involved in providing relief for the poor and unemployed, stimulating economic recovery and reforming the financial system. The scope of the New Deal and speed with which new legislation was drafted and enacted meant that Roosevelt had to give the lead-ers of the individual programs a free hand. Much of the New Deal was, even more than normally, carried out without Roosevelt's direct involvement.[20]

Roosevelt's administration commissioned public works on a massive scale. There is little evidence that Roosevelt ever thought of the products of New Deal programs in terms of autofabrication, but some have so tangibly shaped the physical and cultural landscape of the United States that they cannot be disregarded as an ingredient of Roosevelt's public image. Among the best con-served and most visible today are the many parks, roads, and public buildings that were built as part of the New Deal. Iconic landmarks such as the Tennessee Valley Authority and the Golden Gate Bridge are associated with the New Deal and thus with Roosevelt.[21] Moreover, there were New Deal programs to provide jobs for white collar workers, intellectuals, and artists without work—historians, writers, photographers, visual artists, film makers, actors—most notably, the Federal Writers Project.[22] Some of their most famous products included the American Guide Series, in which historical guidebooks were written for every state and many smaller regions, and the so-called "Negro Culture in America" project, which collected oral histories of surviving formerly enslaved persons.[23] Extremely famous, also, are the post office mural paintings and photographs of the Dust Bowl sand storms by Dorothea Lange and others.

These cultural artifacts can be seen as indexical references to Roosevelt, not because they resemble him, but because they are connected to him, both historically and in cultural memory. Such indexical references recall FDR's enormous influence on the American cultural, intellectual, and physical landscape. In that respect, objects and cultural artifacts produced in the New Deal also symbolically represent FDR.[24]

As Kammen has argued, the New Deal not only changed the physical and cultural landscape but also the American mindset with regard to its cultural heritage: "There is a very real sense in which Americans broke with an ingrained habit of mind (let the private sector do it) in order to rescue and restore to prominence a range of particular traditions. Needless to say, impoverished yet creative people were also salvaged in the process. That was the principal objective, in fact. The circumstances were such that assisting Americans helped to save Americana."[25]

Although the shift in "habit of mind" sparked by these programs—designed with "the principal objective" of helping "impoverished yet creative people"— was not an explicitly expressed aim of the New Deal, FDR welcomed it abundantly. One key legacy of the New Deal was the move toward a paradigm in which people considered Americana worth saving with public money. This shift from private to public sector in perceived responsibility for "rescu[ing] and restor[ing] to prominence a range of particular traditions" has important political implications, which FDR applauded. This intensifies the indexical connection between FDR and the artistic products created and artifacts preserved through the New Deal. FDR did not, however, use the agency he had as New Deal president to promote himself in iconic terms.

Kammen, in *Mystic Chords of Memory*, argues that the principal objective of the New Deal was not to let the talent of "impoverished yet creative people" go to waste; he cites "help[ing] to save Americana" as a resultant effect.[26] Others, like artist Edward Laning, have argued that the Roosevelts' personal loyalty to their artist friends played a role in the Roosevelt administration's patronage of the arts; he alleges that the Roosevelts, further than being humanitarians with artist friends, had no particular interest in art.[27] However, like any political leader, Roosevelt was—humanitarianism and loyalty to art-loving friends aside—also well aware that acting as a patron for artists could boost his public image. This practice among political leaders is obviously much older than Roosevelt, and he must have been aware of its potential. However, what distinguishes him from others is that he did not use New Deal buildings and other artistic products directly to blow his own trumpet, but rather to forge a climate of public responsibility for American heritage in which his own initiatives could thrive.

However little Roosevelt may personally have been interested in art in a highbrow aesthetic sense, he strongly felt that the American federal government should be more involved in the preservation and management of American cultural heritage. This conviction was part of a larger trend in American society. The 1920s saw a great rise in the collective interest in objects that are specifically American cultural artifacts, such as American books, antiques, and objects of American folk culture, as well as in less tangible objects of patriotic Americanism, such as frontier narratives. The latter is evidenced for instance by the foundation and immediate success of a monthly called *The Americana Collector*.[28] Such Americana were mostly collected by individual collectors but were also—in the belief that the laboring masses must be educated and entertained—often displayed for the public in (often privately owned) museums.[29] Before the stock market crash of 1929, many private collectors also simply invested in Americana. After that, the New Deal essentially took over the project of "saving Americana" and making patriotic folk history accessible to the masses. It created a cultural practice of historical awareness in the federal government and a new sense of responsibility for the public sector to take care of, and assume power over, cultural heritage and remembrance.

Buildings, infrastructure, national parks, and lasting cultural artifacts—such as the many artworks, murals, American state guidebooks, oral histories, and photographs that were produced as part of New Deal programs—are classical objects for statesmen to want to leave behind. The link with the world's great mausoleums, monuments, and examples of royal patronage is easily made, as Roosevelt must have been aware, and he may have consciously stayed away from such arguably dictatorial gestures. Given that he later suggested that he did not want a personal memorial after his death to visually portray him, it seems likely that he did not wish artists and others paid by his unprecedented, and by no means universally accepted, public spending to heroically and iconically portray and idolize him all too explicitly. Yet, even if the legacy of the New Deal in the American landscape does not refer to Roosevelt in an iconic sense, the New Deal's distinctive style remains recognizable and indexically connected with FDR.

Rhetorically, the New Deal relied heavily on the sense that restoring the American economy was a matter of modernizing concepts of civilization and patriotism. In his first State of the Union address as president, on January 3, 1934, Roosevelt said:

> Civilization cannot go back; civilization must not stand still. We have undertaken new methods. It is our task to perfect, to improve, to alter when necessary, but in all cases to go forward. To consolidate what we are doing, to make our economic and social structure capable of dealing with modern life, is the joint task of the legislative, the judicial, and the executive branches of the National Government. Without regard to party, the overwhelming majority of our people seek a greater opportunity for humanity to prosper and find happiness.

Although he does not mention the New Deal explicitly, Roosevelt here practically equates his social and economic program with civilization and inevitable progress. He states explicitly that such programs are the task of National Government and a need of "the overwhelming majority of our people . . . without regard to party." Of course, his paraphrase of what that majority of people seek is so broad—"greater opportunity for humanity to prosper and find happiness"— that it would be hard to oppose, wherever one stands with "regard to party." Such attempts to unite the nation by stressing the national importance of federal political choices are in part the president's function. To argue that policies or programs serve the entire nation's interests is politically strategic, and the New Deal was intended to help everybody. However, what makes the New Deal exceptional as a broad social and economic program is that its aims included nation-building, preservation of cultural and natural heritage, memory-making, and stimulating what has since come to be called the heritage industry. Thus, FDR's key political program came to occupy a wide range of historical sites and cultural arenas through a neutralizing national framework. The language of this framework distanced it from the New Deal's political ideals.

The New Deal needed to create nationally constructive, uncontroversial, and useful projects. This need may have suggested the idea to organize projects that would develop, research and glorify American heritage, which then became an end in itself. History and Americana were good topics for New Deal art projects exactly because, at a time when native and African American points of view were largely ignored, they tended to be regarded as uncontroversial. They also could be argued to be useful to "the entire nation," even if that did not include most minorities. Karal Ann Marling has argued that the reason most of the twenty-five thousand post office murals presented historical tableaux is that

Industry in Rockdale by Maxwell B. Starr in the post office in Rockdale, Texas. Painted circa 1940. Larry D. Moore CC BY-SA 4.0

they supplied the "most popular mode and theme in federal and other public facilities because the past was comparatively non-controversial."[30] Marling seems to mean that historical themes were uncontroversial compared to themes from the present. She argues throughout that, while both history and future were acceptable since "yesterday ensured all of America's happy tomorrows," a certain taboo rested on representing the Depression and the present of the 1930s.[31]

A seeming consensus about historical themes was also perhaps still comparatively achievable at that particular time. This possibility has since been overturned by a range of cultural agents as well as emancipatory movements, memory wars, and other broad cultural developments. These agents and developments have in various ways reassessed which people, events, structures, and perspectives deserve priority in historiography and rethought the meaning of historians' authority in a fundamentally fragmented world. Many post office murals with historical themes that perhaps seemed comparatively uncontroversial at first became controversial in the 1960s and 1970s. To give an example, murals like the one above, by Maxwell Starr in the Rockdale, Texas Post Office—which depicts black and white laborers working together on mining and harvesting cotton—may have looked harmless in the 1930s. However, the Civil Rights Movement unmasked such bland depictions of suggested racial harmony as painful misrepresentations of past and present.

Another example of a historical scene in a post office mural is the painting in the post office in Mart, Texas, done in 1939 by José Aceves. It is a classic frontier scene, showing an American family going west to carve out a better life and tame the wilderness. The men stand and hold guns; the women sit in the wagon, which forms the family's temporary domestic sphere. The baby in the left woman's lap suggests the fertile future this family is moving toward. This mural depicts a cliché of American history, in which a supposedly empty continent was discovered, developed, and civilized by white agrarian frontier families like this one—simple but courageous and honest people who domesticated the wilderness. Variations on this American grand narrative have become suspect: the American continent was hardly empty or in need of salvation, and this formation narrative does not apply to most Americans. However, in 1939, it still worked as a historical and, therefore, not immediately controversial, illustration of "the" American past.

McLennan Looking for a Home by José Aceves in the post office in Mart, Texas. Painted circa 1939. Jimmy Emerson DVM

In the 1930s, history was not only a convenient source for artwork; the sense that historical sites and national heritage must be created and managed was also fashionable. Alfred Kazin has called the American Guide Series symbolic of the "reawakened American sense of its own history."[32] In incorporating the American Guide Series into the New Deal, Roosevelt was nimbly jumping onto an existing bandwagon.[33] Kammen argues that "part of FDR's success in projecting an appealing image lay in his distinctive capacity to connect innovation with tradition."[34] FDR's early conviction that the federal government should preserve, manage, and make accessible American cultural heritage was also distinctive. In particular, he politically valorized the strategic benefits in taking charge of portraying the past through the New Deal. FDR did not dictate that portrayal, but the mere fact that it was a federal effort depoliticized it.

FDR believed the federal government should be involved in preserving American heritage. Another important innovation that FDR was personally involved with was the creation of the National Historic Sites Act of 1935, which commissioned the NPS to preserve and manage publicly accessible national historic sites, along with managing the national parks.[35] This would, he argued, enhance patriotism: "The preservation of historic sites for the public benefit, together with their proper interpretation," he declared to Congress in 1935, "tends to enhance the respect and love of the citizen for the institutions of his country, as well as strengthen his resolution to defend unselfishly the hallowed traditions and high ideals of America."[36]

The choice for the NPS to carry out the management and presentation of historic sites is interesting, because the NPS had traditionally only taken care of protecting and making accessible the United States' natural heritage. To let the NPS manage the American historical legacy as well carries a rather deterministic and self-congratulating suggestion that American history, too, must be seen as a kind of natural wealth and resource. Because the decisions about which sites are "of national significance for the inspiration and benefit of the people of the United States," as the National Historic Sites Act has it, is a federal one, only sites whose historical importance is consensually agreed upon can achieve that status. Kammen might argue that this process depoliticizes the past. At the same time, the consensus is a political compromise that only takes place between some agents, usually not the more radical ones.

It is, in that context, a significant act of autofabrication on Roosevelt's part— in two related ways—that he bequeathed his Springwood estate, including the Roosevelt home and his own grave, to the NPS. In the Peircean sense of the words, his life-long home indexes him (that is, it references him by pointing in his direction). On a secondary level, it represents him iconically (that is, it resembles him) both because the place molded FDR's character, and because the home outlines him by providing a kind of photo-negative perspective conjuring up an FDR-shaped space. This perspective is reflected in the FDR Library Museum, too, through the exhibition of shoes, clothing, leg braces, and wheelchairs that he filled, and which continue to carry a visible impression of his body. Moreover, turning the Springwood Estate into an NPS historic site posits Roosevelt's home and, therefore, Roosevelt himself as an iconic figure in the more general sense, as somehow akin to a kind of natural national heritage. As such, FDR's Hyde Park home presents him as a part of a quintessential American heritage to be managed federally. Roosevelt seems to claim a future position for himself as an occupant of the empty space at the heart of political power.

Through the New Deal and its contiguous tendency to make heritage preservation a federal issue, Roosevelt shaped a context in which the past could be depoliticized. This choice was political in the present at that time. The selection of representable history itself had political implications, not so much in partisan terms, but rather in the sense that it silently defined a mainstream—a selection that was supposedly inclusive but in effect left very little room for political agonism.

Even critical voices such as Dorothea Lange's and Arthur Rothstein's iconic photographs of the Dust Bowl, or John Steinbeck's novels, which effectively showed the impotence of the Roosevelt administration to protect American citizens, were also directly associated with or employed by New Deal programs, neutralizing their criticism by incorporating it. Moreover, many of their images, in part through their wide dissemination, soon acquired a nostalgic quality. Lange's most canonical photo of a woman who has fled the Dust Bowl to California with her children is a case in point. Despite the fact that it portrays real despair, it is also an aesthetically beautiful, pieta-like portrayal of sorrowful motherhood. Because Lange's and others' implicit and explicit criticism of the administration was itself part of the New Deal, it was both expressed and immediately also domesticated. This control through inclusion was only rarely, and much later, replaced by actual censorship, for instance in Lange's case, once she started to take photographs in Japanese relocation centers that exposed their atrocities. Many of those photos were impounded by the army and only resurfaced in 2006.

Destitute Pea Pickers in California. Mother of Seven Children. Age Thirty-Two. Nipomo, California, 1936. Dorothea Lange; Farm Security Administration—Office of War Information Photograph Collection (Library of Congress)

A Nostalgic Treatment of the New Deal: The 1982 *Annie*

FDR successfully set the stage for many others to take up—not necessarily consciously—the various depoliticization strategies that he and his staff used, including the strategy of personalization (shifting focus from political issues to FDR's personal characteristics or personal life). In this section, I examine a scene from a popular representation of the New Deal that focuses on FDR's personal qualities: the 1982 musical film—and Christmas television classic—*Annie*. For many Americans born after 1970, this film would have been the first cinematic representation of Franklin Roosevelt they had seen, possibly even their first exposure to his iconic character. Orphan Annie and her benefactor Oliver Warbucks make a trip to the White House in order to keep from Annie's view the hundreds of couples who claim to be her parents after Warbucks has offered a large reward. They are received by Franklin and Eleanor Roosevelt and have tea with them. The story is presumably set in 1933.[37]

White House lawn—Franklin and Eleanor Roosevelt (FDR and ER) await the landing of Oliver Warbucks' (OW) helicopter.

FDR: Aren't Republicans ostentatious?

ER: Franklin behave! It's astonishing that he's here at all.

FDR: Hahaha!
        (to Warbucks) What do you call this thing, Oliver?

OW: An autocopter. Don't need an airport, just a backyard. They say it can land on a dime, whatever that may be.

FDR: Hahaha! I appreciate your coming down, it means a great deal.

OW: It means nothing. It means only that Annie wanted to meet you.

Annie: It's nice to meet you, Mr. President Roosevelt.

FDR: My pleasure, Annie. And thank you for bringing the old goat. We'll make a New Dealer of him yet.

OW: Inconceivable.

ER: Don't mind him, Oliver.

FDR: Come along, Annie! My uncle Theodore, Teddy Roosevelt, used to teach his children to walk on stilts. Now I can't teach you to walk on stilts, but I can teach you to roll in a chair with wheels, my own private rollercoaster.

Inside the White House.

OW: The New Deal, in my opinion, is badly planned, badly organized and badly administered. You don't think your programs through,

	Franklin. You don't think what they're going to do to the economy in the long run.
FDR:	People don't eat in the long run.
ER:	People can't feed their children.
FDR:	The lucky ones end up in orphanages.
ER:	The older ones are abandoned to steal, to starve.
OW:	The business of this country is business. You have to organize . . .
FDR:	Take them off the dole and put them to work! That is precisely what I intend to do.
ER:	In the national parks, building camps, clearing trails, fighting fires, planting trees . . .
OW:	Hold it, hold it!
FDR:	I want to feed them, and house them, and pay them, not much but enough so they can send home to their parents, so they can hold up their heads again and be proud to be Americans.
Annie:	That's a swell idea!
OW:	It isn't a swell idea, Annie, it's mistaken foolishness! Big-hearted and empty-headed. Which parks? Which children? What will it cost? Who's going to organize it? Who's going to run it?
FDR:	I, er, was hoping you would.
OW:	Me?
FDR:	And Annie.
Annie:	Leaping lizards!
OW:	Out of the question!
Annie:	How could I help?
OW:	Wait a minute!
FDR:	You could help us recruit the young people.
OW:	Now hold everything!
FDR:	Many of them have given up hope, Annie, they think their government doesn't care whether they live or die. With your help, we can convince them that with a little extra effort on their part . . .
OW:	I want to say something!
Annie:	There's a song I used to sing in the orphanage, when I'd get sad, it always cheered me up.
OW:	Eleanor . . .
Annie:	Just thinking about tomorrow / Clears away the cobwebs and the sorrow / Till there's none

When I'm stuck with a day that's grey and lonely / I just stick out
my chin and grin and say:
The sun will come out tomorrow / so you gotta hang on till
tomorrow / Come what may . . .
Tomorrow, tomorrow, I love you tomorrow / You're only a day away

ER: Oh Frank . . .

FDR: You'll help us too, won't you Oliver?

OW: Er . . .

ER: Think of the children! Think of Annie!

Annie: The sun will come out tomorrow . . .

FDR: Sing Oliver, that's an order from your Commander in Chief!
           You too, Eleanor!

ER: I can't sing!

FDR: Sing!

All sing.

All the iconic and long-standing FDR attributes are present: Eleanor Roosevelt, the compassionate yet shrewd wife; the armless wheelchair made of a
common dining room chair; the White House; and FDR's cigarette holder,
hat, pince-nez glasses, and buoyant manner. Letting a president appear in a
children's musical film in itself depoliticizes him, or otherwise, can be seen as a
mark of how depoliticized he had, by this time, already become. However, the
content of this scene is surprisingly political. FDR pounces on the occasion to
enlist Oliver Warbucks's astronomic funds and organizing capacities for the
execution of New Deal employment programs, which Warbucks, as a staunch
and self-made Republican, obviously opposes. (The name "Oliver Warbucks"
is an obvious pun on "all of our war bucks" that is not further developed in the
movie.) Welcoming as they sound, Roosevelt's first words to Annie clearly express the fact that he is mainly interested in her as a conduit for approaching
her benefactor: "My pleasure, Annie. And thank you for bringing the old goat.
We'll make a New Dealer of him yet." He is in fact addressing Warbucks, and
ER—"Don't mind him, Oliver"—accordingly responds directly to Warbucks.

The entire scene works in a similar fashion. Annie's presence is primarily
important because she enables the exchange in the first place, and because she
presents a kind of live specimen case of the people whom the New Deal purportedly aims to help. This lends a sentimental dimension to FDR's plea, which
has its effect on Warbucks as on the viewer. Warbucks raises the quintessen-

tial rational argument against the New Deal—"The New Deal, in my opinion, is badly planned, badly organized and badly administered"—one that, in hindsight, was to some extent justified. Roosevelt immediately steers the discussion, with his wife's help, in the highly emotive direction of poor, underfed orphans. He does not actually engage with Warbucks's argument, although it appears that he does because he repeats the phrase "in the long run." Only later, when Warbucks repeats his case—"Which parks? Which children? What will it cost? Who's going to organize it? Who's going to run it?"—does Roosevelt address the issue by taking a set of more or less rhetorical questions literally and making Warbucks himself responsible for the program. This response not only defuses Oliver Warbucks's reasoning against the New Deal as "mistaken foolishness, big-hearted and empty-headed" but also the viewer's possible hesitation. This effect is enhanced by the fact that the movie's heroine immediately decides that the New Deal is "a swell idea."

When FDR says, "the lucky ones end up in orphanages," Warbucks and the viewer obviously already know how bad Annie's experiences in Miss Hannigan's Dickensian orphanage have been, and how much luck a healthy and self-reliant American child needs to survive there. The same maudlin line of argument is continued by Eleanor Roosevelt, who introduces the aspect of the potential moral decay of the poor children: "The older ones are abandoned to steal." She sums up what the poor would do, as part of the New Deal, to earn money to feed their children, work "in the national parks, building camps, clearing trails, fighting fires, planting trees." This elaborates on the emotionally patriotic line of argument that FDR has taken up earlier when he said he wanted people to "be proud [again] to be Americans." This direct link between New Deal laborers' patriotism and preserving and embellishing the American landscape was indeed very Rooseveltian. This link has the same depoliticizing effect here as in the 1930s historical context, because it shifts a central point of partisan disagreement to the realm of national American pride.

The weakness of this cinematic Roosevelt's argument comes at the only time when he does have to really address Annie. He suggests that she "could help us recruit the young people," but after all, how many "young people" does Annie know? And are these children supposed to support the New Deal by contributing to the workforce? Recruitment for the relief programs was an administrative matter, not one of convincing the poor to accept the offered work. On an extradiegetic level, that is, beyond the film's universe, however, Roosevelt and Annie's joint effort to sell the New Deal to "the young people" does work. The fact that Annie is convinced works both to counter Warbucks's cynicism and to signal to the movie's presumably young audience that the New Deal is indeed a swell idea. This movement depoliticizes the New Deal in a way that is a blueprint for the personalization strategy: the persuasive power comes from Annie's charming and charismatic personality.

Within the universe of the film, too, Annie's reaction, in accordance with her protagonist role in the narrative, does eventually resolve the situation: the song unites all present and effectively Americanizes the New Deal, even for Republicans. The early New Deal did, besides immediately and concretely help people, function to restore confidence in a vague and generalized way, like "Tomorrow." However, the song lyrics "When I'm stuck with a day that's grey and lonely / I just stick out my chin and grin and say: / The sun will come out tomorrow" are actually much more obviously Republican-style self-sufficient and independent than the plan Roosevelt is presenting, which is aimed at people who can emphatically not wait until the sun will come out again to save them from poverty.

Ideals of self-reliance, rags-to-riches social mobility, and strong family values—even for those who, like Annie and Oliver Warbucks, have no family to begin with—are visually born out in the above still from the same scene. It casts Franklin and Eleanor Roosevelt, together with the portrait of George

Still (1:25:00) from *Annie* (1982) with Annie, Oliver Warbucks, the Roosevelts, and George Washington

Washington, as parental figures framing the orphan Annie and her wealthy patron Oliver Warbucks. The presidential couple and their illustrious predecessor in the White House foster the American Dream of common people that purportedly typifies the American experience. Annie is the striking presence and the focus of the picture. The others are arranged around her as exemplary historical, feminine, financial, and political antecedents, offering all the ingredients Annie needs to attain her own dazzling success. Annie and Oliver Warbucks as a combination represent both ends of the classic, supposedly unassisted progression from rags to riches, although the film's plot shows that this progression may not actually be feasible without help from the president. Annie and Oliver Warbucks also encompass both extremes of other spectrums: poor to rich, starting to arrived, female to male, recipient to benefactor. Together, they span (in a sense) the entire American populace, proudly surrounded and shielded by Franklin and Eleanor Roosevelt, as parents of the nation. The portrait of George Washington in the background nationalizes the situation still more, by lending it the validation of national history and unity. However, Mouffe and others would be quick to point out that nonwhite people, queer people, and other minorities are silently marginalized as nonexistent within this supposedly inclusive representation of American citizenship.

This crudely sentimental scene obviously did not actually take place. This cinematic Franklin and Eleanor externally look dissimilar to the historical figures they represent. And there are no known cases of FDR bursting into song, using his power as commander in chief to get political opponents to join in, or demanding that he himself be allowed to sing a solo. Roosevelt's Secretary of Commerce and New Dealer Harry Hopkins actually did once respond to an attack on the New Deal by saying, "People don't eat in the long run,"[38] as FDR does here. But although the phrase is associated with the New Deal as an argument and a catchphrase, it is not Roosevelt's.

However, many elements of this Roosevelt representation are strikingly faithful in one way or another to Roosevelt's autofabricated public image. He famously claimed the role of commander in chief in peacetime, a role previously reserved for presidents during wartime only. This role brought him increased executive power during the Depression, although he did not in practice bypass Congress in making key decisions.[39] FDR's rhetoric casting the New Deal as a war against want, beginning in his first inaugural, has remained extremely influential. Later adaptations of this rhetoric have stressed the New Deal's victory in restoring American morale, even if it was not overly success-

ful economically. Roosevelt soon took the opportunity to link the New Deal
to the threat of war and the survival of American democracy, saying on June 27,
1936: "Here in America we are waging a great and successful war. It is not alone
a war against want and destitution and economic demoralization. It is more
than that; it is a war for the survival of democracy."

Such reasoning has taken attention off the memory of the New Deal's economic problems and focused it on remembering its moral success, and following that, the success of the democratic United States in World War II. As
Jonathan Alter has formulated it in his national bestseller, *The Defining Moment: FDR's Hundred Days and the Triumph of Hope*: "The first time he saved
democracy, in 1933, he accomplished it more on his own, by convincing the
American people that they should not give up on their system of government.
Before he confronted fascism abroad, he blunted the potential of both fascism and communism at home."[40] Examples such as this one show how the
New Deal has become depoliticized in mainstream American memory: attention moved away from controversial economic measures, toward much vaguer
democratic and patriotic ideals that were harder to disagree with.

"Tomorrow," in all its vagueness about what exactly it is that will bring relief, equally exemplifies that shift of attention from the economic details of
the New Deal to its triumph in saving American morale. The song offers restored confidence more than material relief, mirroring both the Republican
stance at the time and the main remembered outcome of the New Deal. However, there was a difference between the Hooverian confidence in Emersonian rugged individualism and the New Deal's social activism, as Alter notes:
"The result was a new notion of social obligation, especially in a crisis. In his
second Inaugural, in 1937, FDR took stock of what had changed: 'We refused
to leave the problems of our common welfare to be solved by the winds of
chance and the hurricanes of disaster.'"[41]

There is an obvious political dispute here about the role of government in
a crisis but also an intriguing agreement between Roosevelt's rhetoric and that
of "Tomorrow." When referring to "the winds of chance and the hurricanes of
disaster," Roosevelt couches chance and disaster in terms of unsettling weather
circumstances, a simile which was peculiarly appropriate during the Dust
Bowl years. Although, unlike FDR, the song essentially advertises waiting for
better weather—"The sun will come out tomorrow"—both invoke meteoro-
logical metaphors. These metaphors are depoliticizing because weather is a
quintessentially uncontroversial and apolitical conversation topic. Moreover,

they invoke a much older national frontier discourse of both enduring, but also fighting and subjugating, weather circumstances.

Despite what was for a children's musical film relatively unapologetic political content, the 1982 *Annie* had come a long way in depoliticizing the New Deal when compared to its forebears. The film both loosens and ritualizes ties with the actual political New Deal; the film invokes the New Deal like a sort of incantation, without considering or explaining what the historical New Deal actually entailed. The film was based on a 1977 Broadway musical written by Thomas Meehan (book) and Martin Charnin (lyrics). The Broadway musical included songs like the scathing "We'd Like to Thank You, Herbert Hoover" and "A New Deal for Christmas" and featured, alongside Franklin Roosevelt, a number of his New Deal staff.[42] In "We'd Like to Thank You, Herbert Hoover," a chorus of impoverished Americans sarcastically comment on Hoover's broken election promises:

Prosperity was 'round the corner
The cozy cottage built for two
In this blue heaven
That you gave us—Yes!
We're turning blue!

They offered us Al Smith and Hoover
We paid attention and we chose
Not only did we pay attention
We paid through the nose.

In ev'ry pot he said "a chicken"
But Herbert Hoover he forgot
Not only don't we have the chicken
We ain't got the pot![43]

Such personal Hoover-bashing, written more than forty years after Hoover had left office, suggesting that Hoover cheated his people in the elections and had not got the least idea of the extent of their poverty, echoed the Roosevelt campaign of 1932. "Prosperity is just around the corner" is a legendary Hoover quotation repeated endlessly by the Democratic campaign, even though Hoover never actually said it.[44] The scene is set in a "Hooverville"—a popular name for the shanty towns of the unemployed and homeless erected during the Depression—a coinage from one of FDR's ghostwriters, Charles Michelson.[45]

That Roosevelt was personally involved in the hate campaign against Hoover is clear from the following memo, which he dictated to Howe:

> Here's a subject for a campaign cartoon:
> Caption: Are you carrying the Hoover banner?
> Below this: Picture of a man holding his trouser pockets turned inside out
> Underneath: The words "nuff said."[46]

The 1932 FDR campaign expressions "Hoover flag" for empty pocket and "Hooverville" both survive in American idiom. While Hoover did not make social security for all American citizens a federal responsibility, his administration did more to battle the Depression than Roosevelt's campaign suggested, and Roosevelt largely continued Hoover's domestic policies to fight the Depression.[47] Nonetheless, renderings of New Deal cultural memory like the *Annie* Broadway musical show that the memory of a dramatic break—from total stagnation and indifference to the despair of the multitudes (under Hoover) to a new sense of confidence and support (under Roosevelt)—has survived in mainstream popular culture. Anecdotes indicating the emotionally radical nature of the shift from Hoover to Roosevelt evolved at a very early stage. Jonathan Alter cites the famous story of Eleanor Roosevelt's visit to the "Bonus Army," a group of impoverished First World War veterans who marched on Washington early in 1933 to demand advance payments on their war pensions, and whom the Hoover administration had sent the army to disperse. As one marcher approvingly said: "Hoover sent the army and Roosevelt sent his wife."[48] Even though FDR did not advance the veterans' money any more than Hoover did, this sums up the sentiment underlying most surviving narratives and anecdotes from the early New Deal and Roosevelt's assumption of office.

Harold Gray's comic strip *Little Orphan Annie* (1924–1964), on which the musical was loosely based, did not endorse FDR's domestic politics at all. This makes it all the more striking that the most famous musical and film performances of *Annie* are so adamant in their positive assessment of Roosevelt and the New Deal. Gray was highly conservative and used the comic strip to vent his frustration about the New Deal, which to his mind went against the most fundamental principles of American liberty. As he wrote in 1952: "I . . . have despised Roosevelt and his socialist, or creeping communist, policies since 1932, and said so in my stuff, so far as I was allowed to do so. I hate professional do-gooders with other people's money."[49] The comic, according to Jeet Heer, was not specifically conservative in the 1920s but became so after the start of Roosevelt's New Deal, which sparked increasingly virulent reactions from the political right. Over the course of the 1930s, *Little Orphan Annie* became so explicitly conservative that some newspapers stopped running the comic, despite its enormous popularity.[50]

Annie moved from a politically controversial comic strip during the 1930s to a blander but still fairly explicitly partisan musical (albeit partisan in the opposite direction than the comic), to a milder film, which nonetheless remains clearly nostalgic in its treatment of FDR and the New Deal. This trend is continued in a yet more recent *Annie* film: the 1999 television movie directed by Rob Marshall. This latest cinematic rendering of *Annie* confirms the depoliticizing development seen in earlier versions. Roosevelt makes a historically unlikely but iconic grand entrance in his wheelchair. Some other New Dealers—for instance, left-wing Supreme Court Justice Louis Brandeis—appear in the movie as well, but only in direct relation to Annie's narrative and without even the mention of broader political issues. The shift from criticism of the New Deal in the 1930s to nostalgia in later versions of *Annie* as well as the increasing depoliticization of Roosevelt throughout *Annie*'s development represent wider trends in the reception of Roosevelt as a cultural icon.

"The First Hundred Days" Dissociated from the New Deal

The diachronic development of various versions of *Little Orphan Annie*—comic strip, musical, and film   forms an exemplary case study of how the New Deal was depoliticized in cultural memory through personalization. Later versions of *Annie* portray the New Deal as character attribute of Franklin Roosevelt. The next section focuses on a separate route by which the New Deal was depoliticized: the media practice of highlighting the First Hundred Days of a new president. The First Hundred Days of Roosevelt's presidency were marked primarily by the unprecedented bulk of political measures, bills signed, appropriations made, and agencies founded. Because the amount of new legislation and appropriations was so enormous, beating FDR's First Hundred Days in terms of legislative and executive impact became a practically unreachable goal for presidents to aspire to.

Over time, the phrase "the First Hundred Days" has come to merely signify "the end of a president's honeymoon," a moment that is marked by catchy phrases and the potential for easily marketable news. The First Hundred Days are associated with Roosevelt's astuteness in public relations but have become detached entirely from the New Deal as a political program. The practice of marking a new presidency's First Hundred Days, which Roosevelt started, has turned the end of the First Hundred Days of any new presidency into a moment for measuring the new executive against Roosevelt and conversely created an unofficial but important recurring opportunity for ritually remembering FDR's legislative success at the inception of the New Deal. As a result, the New Deal has in cultural memory lost much of its political poignancy to a blander and more general sense of nostalgia. The First Hundred Days custom is now mainly a media ritual practically divorced from the New Deal; it remains only tentatively indexically linked to Roosevelt, and even more loosely to the New Deal. This process was instrumental in the depoliticization of the New Deal for the sake of cultural remembrance.

Leuchtenburg's *In the Shadow of FDR: From Harry Truman to George W. Bush* comments on how later presidents had to deal with Roosevelt's legacy to the office and with the political and sometimes the cultural or media practices that he left. For instance, since FDR, the president was expected to hold many informal press conferences in which journalists could ask questions without submitting them beforehand—if they did not do so, the press would complain.[51] Leuchtenburg convincingly argues that the effect of such customs is that later presidents have had to live up to standards set by Roosevelt. The First Hundred Days of any new administration have become such a central initial yardstick and media moment for new presidents that no presidential First Hundred Days can escape comparison with Roosevelt's legendary First Hundred Days. To organizations committed to nurturing the remembrance of FDR in American culture, those occasions also provide a logical moment in the American public arena to bring back to public consciousness the First Hundred Days of the New Deal.

As a political program, the New Deal is—of the themes discussed in this book—perhaps the one that is still most seriously criticized, partly because left–right polarization in American politics remains relevant. However, as a feat of mass communication to restore national confidence in the economy and government, it remains widely admired. The many historical analogies with the New Deal that have appeared since the onset of the 2008 credit crisis and Obama's election attest to this duality.[52] On the one hand, they discuss, with varying conclusions, the question of how economically successful the New Deal was, and, on the other, they present FDR's rhetorical success in quickly restoring confidence as exemplary. Many such analogies appeared briefly after Obama's election and reelection, and during his presidency's First Hundred Days.

A honeymoon period at the start of a new presidency—or political leadership in general—has probably always existed in one form or another, but the specific reference to a president's First Hundred Days in office has been in vogue since FDR used it on July 24, 1933.[53] Roosevelt did so to refer to the length of the special session of the seventy-third Congress—which he had called immediately after his inauguration and which had produced a record amount of new legislation. However, it came to be used first by FDR confidant and brain truster Raymond Moley as an expression to refer to Roosevelt's First Hundred Days in office.[54] Ever since, a new executive's First Hundred Days have formed an inescapable litmus test. The comparison of the First Hundred Days between presidents obviously gives FDR an unfair advantage. In his case, the phrase was invented precisely because he had achieved so much, even just in terms of new legislation, in one hundred days, whereas for any following president the length of the period is arbitrary. Nonetheless, using and marketing the First Hundred Days of a presidency as an indicator of the new president's executive power and ability to make a mark has become a tradition with considerable weight, not only within America but worldwide. This ritual of reviewing this first period is extremely popular with the press. Politicians, too, seem to favor the public assessment of their performance after hundred days, since on the one hand they will usually already have achieved things they are proud of, and on the other, will not yet be accused of ineffectiveness or failure to keep campaign promises, since after hundred days it is obviously premature to write off a new leadership as ineffective.

As Leuchtenburg has shown, the only president after Roosevelt who did not have to deal with the First Hundred Days custom was Harry Truman, who became president when FDR died. In the grave circumstances of world politics in the spring of 1945, it would have been inappropriate to celebrate the First Hundred Days. Even on his reelection in 1948, the phrase came up less than Truman's domestic reform agenda, the Fair Deal—obviously named after the New Deal, in part because it aimed to continue the New Deal legacy.[55] For Eisenhower, it was different; journalists focused on his First Hundred Days, even if he himself as a Republican did nothing to compare his honeymoon months to FDR's. In a broader sense, Eisenhower did feel he had to continue New Deal programs, perhaps to his chagrin. As he said in 1956, "Should any political party attempt to abolish social security and eliminate labor laws and farm programs, you would not hear of that party again in our political history."[56] So by comparison, the First Hundred Days custom was for Eisenhower possibly a relatively welcome FDR tradition, because it did not actually interfere with politics. John Kennedy, as a Democrat with an old and well-known family friendship with the Roosevelts, intended to make much of celebrating his own First Hundred Days as president. Indeed, the speech he was to give on the occasion was written, but the event was canceled. As Leuchtenburg says, "It was painfully clear that April 28, 1961, bore no resemblance to the hundredth day of FDR's first administration."[57] Johnson was less modest, believing soon that he overshadowed Roosevelt ("This Congress is a lot more impressive than the Hundred Days Congress"): an attitude that backfired.[58]

By Richard Nixon's presidency, the Roosevelt inheritance was hardly directly political anymore; it was limited to the expression "first 100 days" and the custom that had survived of paying special attention to that period. This was a media practice that later presidents expanded—notably Bill Clinton, but Ronald Reagan, in fact, much more successfully.[59] Thus, the First Hundred Days became more of a cultural media practice than a political touchstone, practically devoid of actual New Deal remembrance, let alone remembrance of the New Deal as a controversial political program. On the other hand, it remained a moment to look back to FDR's early days in a highly formulaic, ritualized manner.

Obama, who had in his campaign primarily positioned himself as the cultural and political inheritor and executor of Abraham Lincoln's emancipation agenda, at the start of his presidency nonetheless had to actively deal with this Rooseveltian legacy. In his speech held at the May 2009 White House Correspondents' Association Dinner, in which the president traditionally "roasts" himself, his administration and White House journalists, Obama said about this:

> All in all, we're proud of the change we've brought to Washington in these first hundred days, but we've got a lot of work left to do, as all of you know, so I'd like to talk a little bit about what my administration plans to achieve in the next hundred days.
>
> During the second hundred days, we will design, build, and open a library dedicated to my first hundred days. It's going to be big, folks. . . .
>
> In the next hundred days, we will housetrain our dog Bo . . . In the next hundred days, I will strongly consider losing my cool.
>
> Finally, I believe that my next hundred days will be so successful I will be able to complete them in 72 days.[60]

Obama wisely embraced a tradition he could not get away from anyway in a spirit of self-mockery: no president's First Hundred Days have truly measured up against Roosevelt's own massive achievements in the spring of 1933. However, Obama's anaphoric repetition of the phrase "In my next hundred days . . ." is not only self-mocking: it simultaneously draws attention to the rather arbitrary journalistic stress on "Hundred Days" as a particularly conclusive period of time. Thus, Obama's joke is not only directed at himself, but also at the media practice. Similarly, the references to opening a library, and to "our dog Bo" are part of—and make fun of—Rooseveltian customs that dedicated presidential libraries and included the presidential family dog in speeches (see chapter 1).

Thus, the First Hundred Days have since Roosevelt become a cultural phenomenon that new presidents cannot avoid dealing with. However, the reverse is also true: with every new administration, the First Hundred Days media practice provides an opportunity for various organizations and other agents interested in stimulating Roosevelt's cultural remembrance to give attention to the New Deal and FDR. A comment of Obama's that he had read a book about FDR's First Hundred Days massively increased the sales of all three books mentioned above that fit the description: Jonathan Alter's *The Defining Moment: FDR's Hundred Days and the Triumph of Hope*, Anthony Badger's *FDR, The First Hundred Days*, Adam Cohen's *Nothing to Fear: FDR's Inner Circle and the Hundred Days that Shaped Modern America*, even though none of these probably was the book that Obama did read.[61]

Obama's election in 2008 also provided the ideal context for the Franklin D. Roosevelt Library Museum at Hyde Park to organize a temporary exhibition, "Action and Action Now—FDR's First 100 Days." The title is a Roosevelt quotation but can also be read as "Action [then] and Action Now." As such, it implicitly sets audiences up for a comparison between the economic and financial crises of 1933 and 2008. The exhibition guidebook actually cites the seventy-fifth anniversary of FDR's First Inauguration as its inspiration, but the fact that 2008 was an election year and 2009 saw the First Hundred Days of another new Democratic president promising change and restored confidence probably gave the exhibition its relevance more than the seventy-fifth anniversary. The exhibition's title is taken from Roosevelt's inaugural address: "This Nation asks for action and action now" (March 4, 1933). The exhibition invoked and repeated a plethora of famous FDR maxims, including "the forgotten man at the bottom of the economic pyramid," "I pledge you, I pledge myself to a New Deal for the American people," "This is a call to arms," and "the only thing we have to fear is fear itself." The exhibition more or less chronologically took visitors through the year 1933, on March 4, of which the First

Hundred Days started, showing photos taken in 1933, newspaper articles, cartoons, letters to FDR and recreating the presumed atmosphere of the 1930s in terms of entourage. Thus, one could sit in a reconstructed 1930s living room to listen to a recording of FDR's inaugural address "over the radio," to create a sense of identification with American citizens in 1933.

The narrative started in a room titled "America, 1933" and represented the situation of the country in the depths of the Depression. The room was a black box, indicating the darkness of the situation, and showed the iconic picture of unemployed men queuing outside a Depression soup kitchen (actually taken in 1931). The exhibit then highlighted the immediacy of the crisis and explained the main things Roosevelt and the New Deal did. Special attention was given to "FDR's Conversation with America," which displayed many letters FDR received after his inaugural address and first Fireside Chat. Like other original documents, these came from the archive part of the FDR Library. On the whole, the exhibition was, as might be expected given the exhibition's location, organizers, and fundraisers—the Roosevelt Institute— positive and celebratory of Roosevelt and the New Deal. The focus on the First Hundred Days was conducive to that effect: results could not yet be measured at that point. One thing the exhibition did well was to recreate the honeymoon feeling of a new presidency, which also existed in the 2008–2009 present.

The "Action and Action Now" exhibition did eventually ask "Did it Work?" and was nuanced in its analysis. The conclusion, taken from the exhibition guide booklet, is: "The coming years would be difficult. There would be many setbacks. But a confident new president had set a course, boldly committing the government to battle the Depression. In the process, he restored most important element needed for recovery—hope."

This summarizes exactly those difficulties that the rest of the exhibition— given its focus on the First Hundred Days—does not have to show. It mentions the increasing resistance from businesses everywhere, the New Deal programs that turned out to be unsuccessful and ill-organized, the Supreme Court cases about the constitutionality of many New Deal programs. This conclusion acknowledges those problems, without attributing blame to FDR. Indeed, the first two sentences are passive and suggest difficult circumstances rather than flaws in the president's own policies. At the same time, it ritually repeats what is by now a cliché in cultural memory: if the New Deal did nothing else, it at least restored hope.

Impotent Opposition

Michael Kammen in *Mystic Chords of Memory* argues that cultural memory in America, especially in the twentieth century, functions as a nationally shared sense of history, creating an atmosphere of consensus that can be used to overcome partisan or other political divides. This seems by now a rather naive reading, especially in the light of the "memory wars" of the last decades, in which various memory communities have clashed over what should be the "official" national memory of a particular event.[62] Especially since the 1960s, such confrontations have actually more closely resembled Mouffe's ideal of radical opposition in the locus of power than Roosevelt's implicit model of friendly but noncommittal consensus.

Kammen, however, rightly shows that both Theodore Roosevelt at the beginning of the century and Franklin Roosevelt to an even larger extent became experts at using cultural memory to stress the unity of America rather than the fragmentation. As an example, Kammen explains how Roosevelt depoliticized American party history by associating himself with Abraham Lincoln. Whereas Lincoln was a Republican president and Roosevelt a Democrat, Kammen notes that many Americans "simply assumed that Roosevelt and Lincoln surely shared a party affiliation and represented a prominent line of continuity in American leadership."[63] FDR's uses of the past were eventually "shrewd and self-serving":[64] he used the impression of national consensus for his partisan and controversial political aims. The same American tendency to depoliticize the past that FDR used to present himself as Lincoln's political descendant also occurred when Roosevelt himself became a historical icon.

However, this trend of using the past as a depoliticizing and consensus-building force is not specific to FDR. The first half of the twentieth century also saw a strong tendency toward the creation of shared cultural memory without any involvement of FDR, such as the creation of many "American Studies" programs at American universities in the late 1930s.[65] It seems as though Roosevelt was correctly sensing and riding a wave that was already there and that had, in fact, started to gain momentum in the late nineteenth century.[66] The growing accessibility of memory sites, and thus the increased presence of ritualized remembrance practices as a force in society, can and does also work the other way. The fact that a much wider range of memories were mediated and far more rememberers could find channels to make themselves heard also created divergence in the general gist of cultural memory and a clearer difference between various memory communities with different agendas. Both effects are visible in the cultural memory of the New Deal, but the consensus-focused, depoliticized, ritualized, and generally positive assessment of the New Deal remains the dominant force in mainstream cultural memory. Both the case of *Annie* and that of the First Hundred Days practice exemplify this trend.

However, such celebratory exhibitions as that in the Franklin D. Roosevelt Library museum in Hyde Park, New York, inevitably only reached those who were already open to a positive interpretation of FDR's political program. The opposite pattern exists as well. To this day, highly polarized responses to the New Deal keep appearing. Such histories are agonistically political in the way Mouffe proposes, although she seems to have expected such reactions in general more from the political left than from the conservative right that produces them in the case of FDR and the New Deal.

One example is Jim Powell's popular *FDR's Folly: How Roosevelt and His New Deal Prolonged the Great Depression*. The chapter titles are all along the following lines: "Why Did FDR Seize Everybody's Gold?"; "Why Did New Dealers Make Everything Cost More in the Depression?"; and "Why Did the New Dealers Destroy All That Food When People Were Hungry?"[67] What is striking about those titles, other than their belligerence, is that they are not solely focused on FDR. Other, more depoliticized "New Deal" memory practices tend to have lost sight of the actual New Deal; and they have instead adopted a strong focus on the person of FDR (in the case of *Annie*) or on ritualized and repetitive invocations of particular phrases and media customs. *FDR's Folly*, however, directly confronts the politics and ideology underlying the New Deal. Although most of the book's claims are highly tendentious, there is a core of righteous indignation with which Mouffe would agree. The cultural memory of the New Deal is, as Powell repeatedly stresses, too much concerned with "Franklin D. Roosevelt's charismatic personality, his brilliance as a strategist and communicator, the dramatic One Hundred Days, the First New Deal, Second New Deal, the 'court-packing' plan, and other political aspects of the story."[68] It is striking that Powell considers these issues "political," because they are also exactly the topics that have been central to depoliticizing the New Deal.

The political aspect for Powell lies in the fact that the catchphrases he sums up function to create a kind of empty consensus about the New Deal as a nostalgically remembered past, when it should be treated as a phase in which liberal democracy was seriously endangered. Powell quotes law professor Richard Epstein saying: "A fine despot may do wonders for a while: public roads may be constructed, the trains may run on time, and the Dow may reach three thousand. But a bad despot, or a good despot turned bad, has quite the opposite effect. Our concerns go beyond potholes, train delays, and the bear market. We worry about tyranny, terror, confiscation, segregation, imprisonment, and death."[69]

Here, and elsewhere, Powell comes closer than most would dare to comparing FDR's strategy of depoliticizing the political in order to claim power to similar strategies used by Hitler and Stalin at the same time in Europe. While I do not think his negative analysis of the New Deal is correct, his point that FDR's approach to the New Deal entailed a risk to liberal democracy has some truth to it. Roosevelt remains a kind of despot in cultural memory exactly because his autofabrication and remembrance are so consensus-focused that, in their relative emptiness, they all but eliminate the space for substantial disagreement, the locus of power which should function as a site for conflict. The fact that arguments such as Powell's have so little effect on mainstream representations of the New Deal indicates, however, how successfully the New Deal was depoliticized into the future. Such arguments are essentially confined to a relatively small circle of right-wing Republicans, who cannot revive the political debate beyond their own radical margin. This may in part be because they are so radical, but primarily, it is because almost all other cultural representations of the New Deal have become so consensually depoliticized.

CHAPTER FIVE

FDR's Disability in Cultural Memory

When journalism professor Ray Begovich discovered an eight-second film clip of President Roosevelt in his wheelchair in early July 2013, the clip became instant world news. No such footage had been found previously. The film did not reveal new information; ever since the news of Roosevelt's illness spread in 1921, it was widely known that he had had adult-onset poliomyelitis.[1] The emergence of the clip was major news simply because—with the exception of a single well-known photograph of FDR in his wheelchair taken in 1941 by Margaret Suckley—no photographic images of Roosevelt in his wheelchair had ever been widely disseminated.

This scarcity of photographs or films showing FDR's wheelchair was a result of his successful negotiation with the press. FDR had a well-honored "gentlemen's agreement" with press photographers and journalists that they would not photograph or describe his wheelchair; in exchange, they received relatively easy access to the president and informal presidential press conferences. If photographs of the wheelchair were taken, they were not published, and film footage like that which Begovich discovered remained unknown. The widespread cooperation of the press demonstrates why the concept of "passing" (introduced in chapter 1) is more appropriate than words such as "deception" or "hiding" that have been commonly used to describe FDR's mode of dealing with his disability in public. FDR was not the only person working to downplay his disability. Rather, there was a shared collective negotiation in which the disability was deemphasized to the (perceived) advantage of all involved.

Minimizing public awareness of his disability was a major part of FDR's autofabrication. One crucial element in Roosevelt's choice not to show the extent of his disability may have been the long cultural tradition of seeing the body of the Head of State as representative of the state. As Ernst Kantorowicz has theorized in *The King's Two Bodies* (1957), medieval kings formally (and later heads of state officiously, in cultural perception) embodied the state and thus could be said to have two bodies: a *body politic* and a *body natural*, united in one. This duality is exemplified in the maxim, "The King is dead, long live

FDR in his wheelchair, with Fala and Ruthie Bie, 1941. Photograph by Margaret Suckley, FDR Presidential Library and Museum

the King." Although this maxim denotes the fact that the body politic is not dependent on the body natural, of course FDR and other political leaders have logically intuited that a visibly disabled (or dead) body natural could suggest to the population a weak embodiment of the nation. As these final two chapters explore, this body metaphor from medieval Europe can help us to understand FDR's iconification as an embodiment of America in the twentieth century.

In the case of FDR's disability, cultural memory has diverged sharply from his autofabrication: his disability is now a key attribute of FDR as a cultural icon. This chapter traces the shifts in public perception, delineating two distinct phases in the decades after FDR's death. The chapter also examines the phenomenon of changing cultural needs that have led to "prosthetic memories" of FDR's disability (and wheelchair) as having been highly visible during his presidency, when this was not the reality. These prosthetic memories reflect a shift in men's dominant social strategies for dealing with disability, from passing (prevalent during FDR's lifetime) to a performance of masculinity focused on the disability and the prosthetics that were employed. This latter strategy became the more commonly employed mode in FDR remembrance.

Roosevelt's wheelchair, which during his life was invisible to the public, was rolled into the cultural memory of his presidency by various stakeholders—in particular, by disability rights activists, documentary and filmmakers, and memorial and exhibition designers. For various reasons, these groups of representers shifted from a role in which they aided FDR's passing as nondisabled to a role in which they showed FDR's disability abundantly. In doing so, they focused on concrete and metaphorical prosthetic devices, often staging FDR as a kind of hypermasculine superhero. They furthered the visibility of disability in society, in a sense that was superficially positive, but included a wide range of presumptions about the impact of disability on a disabled person. This positive and visible presentation of disability and prosthetics often happened without engaging the perspective of disabled people, and could thus have a socially disabling effect, in exactly the same way as projecting negative prejudices about disability could have. In this vein, the chapter argues, finally, that FDR's disability and wheelchair came to function as a "narrative prosthesis" for the nation, a metaphor for the nation's ability to "conquer" adversity.

FDR's Strategy of Downplaying His Disability

Franklin Roosevelt became ill in February 1921 when vacationing at Campobello Island (New Brunswick, Canada), probably having been infected on a visit to a boy scout camp.[2] He was diagnosed with "infantile paralysis," as polio was then commonly called. When it became clear that he would probably remain disabled, his mother Sara Delano wished for him to withdraw from political and professional life and retire with his wife and children to the family estate in Hyde Park.[3] At the time, many believed polio affected the mental as well as the physical capabilities of people who had survived the disease. In the late nineteenth and early twentieth century, as Kim Nielsen has noted, "physical 'defects', both scientists and the casual observer increasingly assumed, went hand in hand with mental and moral 'defects.'"[4] Most people who were physically disabled through polio ended up institutionalized in Spartan polio hospitals that increased their dependence on the help of professional caregivers. As an elite survivor, FDR would in that paradigm be expected to become a wealthy "invalid" (in the terminology of the time), withdrawn from public life and taken care of by family servants. Eleanor Roosevelt and FDR's personal adviser Louis Howe, however, supported FDR in reentering the public arena and resuming his political career, despite a disability that was both met with social stigma and with a wide range of practical accessibility issues.[5]

FDR himself strongly and against all odds believed in the possibility of a future in which he would no longer experience the aftereffects of polio, and was committed to doing all in his power to walk again, to the point of seeming to be in denial. He pursued a large number of classical, new, and alternative therapies to strengthen and get control of his leg muscles. Many of these involved walking in water, which allowed him to feel able to walk (and to say things like: "I walk around in water 4 feet deep without braces or crutches almost as well as if I had nothing the matter with my legs").[6] Considering FDR's situation through the lens of passing, one might argue that FDR tried for years to pass as nondisabled in his own eyes.

Roosevelt returned to politics as leader of Al Smith's 1924 presidential campaign. This culminated in his historic "Happy Warrior" address nominating Smith as Democratic candidate, a speech that put him squarely back into political focus.[7] This occasion was also the first time Roosevelt "walked" to the rostrum to deliver the speech, aided by a stick on one side and his son James's arm on the other. He was paralyzed from the waist down and could only stand due to the steel braces on his legs, the fact that the rostrum was screwed to the floor, and his well-developed arm muscles.[8]

When Roosevelt became governor of New York in 1928, his physical health became a topic of public interest, initially because the Republican campaign tried to prove Roosevelt's unfitness for the office. Smith reacted famously to such suggestions during a press inquiry: "But the answer to that is that a governor does not have to be an acrobat. We do not elect him for his ability to do a double back-flip or a handspring."[9] Christopher Clausen indeed asserts that "Republicans soon stopped talking about Roosevelt's physical condition for fear of creating a sympathy vote for him."[10] During his first presidential election campaign the issue returned; this time, Roosevelt invited Republican journalist and sympathizer Earle Looker to have him examined physically. Looker's article in *Liberty Magazine* (July 1931) "Is Franklin D. Roosevelt Physically Fit to Be President?" in its opening paragraph says: "It is an amazing possibility that the next President of the United States may be a cripple. Franklin D. Roosevelt, Governor of the State of New York, was crippled by infantile paralysis in the epidemic of 1921 and still walks with the help of a crutch and a walking stick."[11]

Although Looker cast himself as a Republican, he worked closely with Roosevelt's adviser Louis Howe, who bought fifty thousand reprints of this issue of *Liberty Magazine* for the Roosevelt campaign.[12] The article was typical in its framing of Roosevelt's disability in the 1930s: while it clearly said that Roosevelt was "a cripple," it made no mention of a wheelchair. The mention of "a crutch and a walking stick" is helpfully ambiguous. Readers might assume that Roosevelt possessed both and used either the one or the other, but he needed two supports to walk even the shortest distance. The statement that FDR "still walks with help" suggested both that he continued to walk and that he may have soon stopped needing help. It also guided attention away from the fact that it was debatable whether Roosevelt's way of moving himself while upright constituted walking at all. Although the word "amazing" in "an amazing possibility" primarily denoted surprise, it also carried a positive connotation. The assertion that FDR was "Governor of the State of New York" implied that he was already fit for high office, while the reference to "the epidemic of 1921" framed him as one of many innocent victims of a malevolent virus. Looker, in short, portrayed FDR as essentially nondisabled and free of any of the negative consequences that contemporaries might associate with disability.

Clearly, both before and during Roosevelt's presidency, Americans knew that the president had had polio and was "a bit lame" as a result.[13] Roosevelt did not so much hide as play down his disability in public; it was not widely known that he was unable to walk or stand unaided. He was publicly active in setting up charitable institutions: he famously founded the March of Dimes, still one of the United States' largest charities, which supported polio survivors and financed research toward a vaccine. This drew attention to his own polio history but also framed it as *history*. The implicit suggestion was that while FDR had had polio, he was now no longer affected by it and was now able to put his powers to helping others reach the same state. Polio survivors likely felt regular pressure, often from rehabilitation doctors and nurses, to emulate FDR's example in passing as nondisabled.[14]

The March of Dimes charity is discussed at some length in Paul Longmore's book *Telethons*.[15] Longmore argues that the exposure of disability in the inter-

est of fundraising, as was done in telethons (television fundraising mara-
thons, as set up by, among others the March of Dimes) sets up the disabled as
an object of pity, and the donors as the able-bodied norm who, out of *noblesse
oblige* help them.[16] FDR's role as a philanthropist for polio research can easily
been seen in that context as signaling that he had "overcome" the disease to a
point where he could operate on the other, able-bodied side of it, employing,
as Longmore put it, his patronage "to renew [his] humanity," which Longmore
sees as the key selling point of disability charities.[17]

In his public functions, Roosevelt was careful not to be seen, photographed
or filmed in his wheelchair or while being lifted, for instance from his car. This
strategy was successful at the time—press photographers did not shoot, much
less publish, pictures or film footage that showed Roosevelt in such vulnerable conditions.[18] Such norms have changed dramatically: Roosevelt representations now deal very explicitly with the fact that he could not walk. Roosevelt presented himself mainly to the public through radio speeches, which
obviously do not include a visual representation. He was generally silent about
his disability, accommodating it without drawing attention to doing so. The
famous photos from Yalta, showing Churchill, Roosevelt, and Stalin—all
seated—exemplify this. One exception occurred weeks before his death. In one
of his last public speeches, he explicitly apologized for addressing Congress
from his chair: "I hope that you will pardon me for this unusual posture of sitting down during the presentation of what I want to say, but I know that you
will realize that it makes it a lot easier for me not to have to carry about ten
pounds of steel around on the bottom of my legs; and also because of the fact
that I have just completed a fourteen-thousand-mile trip."[19]

While this apology was a departure from his previous silence on the issue
of his own bodily condition—especially during the 1944 campaign, when he
was visibly unwell and made intense efforts to appear as energetic as ever—this
opening was not entirely inconsistent with his previous treatment of his disability. Although he did not stand at this particular moment, he talked about
standing and about the physical energy he usually brought to public speaking,
alluding (through his mention of just having traveled fourteen thousand miles)
to the energy he had even then.

Roosevelt died of a cerebral hemorrhage on April 12, 1945, at the Little
White House in Warm Springs, Georgia, his cottage at the site of "his" polio
treatment center. Here, he had worked for years on trying to minimize the aftereffects of polio and their visibility and had made important contacts with
fellow polio survivors. The occasion of his death drew a great deal of attention

to his physical body. This was perhaps in part because of the surprising location and the unexpected moment. It was surely also in part because Roosevelt's body, previously invested with political power and thought of primarily as representing the nation, suddenly became provokingly natural. In the wake of the news of how and where he died, obituaries gave far more attention to his general health and physical condition than had been typical for news reporting during his presidency, and White House journalists started to become more open about having witnessed Roosevelt's physical appearance.[20]

In a probing study of "Reactions to the Death of President Roosevelt," Harold Orlansky in 1947 established that "Republican Party propagandists had publicized reports of Roosevelt's poor health during the November 1944 election campaign," but that "after Roosevelt's reelection, the press was silent on the subject, although ill-health of the President is a major news story." Orlansky mused that "apparently the myth of a vigorous, energetic leader is not restricted to dictatorships. The cult of physical strength reaches deep into the body politic."[21] While Orlansky refers only to Roosevelt's ill health on the campaign trail in 1944, by mentioning "the myth of a vigorous, energetic leader," he suggests that FDR's physical disability contributed to the news value of his sickness in 1944. Orlansky further hints that the press's silence about Roosevelt's health after his reelection may have been a cautious response in the context of World War II, in order not to suggest any kind of "weakness" to enemies.

In the 1930s and 1940s this was a very sensitive topic; many would consider it inappropriate to discuss the president's physical body. However, it was also highly relevant. During the 1944 campaign, some Republicans wondered aloud whether one should, in the middle of a world war, elect a leader who was clearly physically unwell (conveniently conflating FDR's disability and ill health). However, after FDR was reelected, they stopped bringing the issue up, just as they had stopped mentioning FDR's disability when FDR was elected the first time. After the war and FDR's death, it became possible to discuss these questions in a more abstract context.

Narratives of Conquest: The First Phase of Increased Public Awareness of FDR's Disability (1945–1985)

Around the time that they moved into the White House, Franklin and Eleanor Roosevelt themselves started to frame FDR's disability—if they did refer to it at all—as a victory. ER said in an interview with the *Ladies Home Journal*: "I think that probably the thing that took most courage in his life was his

Churchill, Roosevelt, and Stalin at Yalta, February 1945 (US Government Photographer). The National Archives, Kew, Richmond, Surrey, United Kingdom

meeting of polio and I never heard him complain . . . And with each victory, as everyone knows, you are stronger than you were before."[22] The language of FDR's own speeches, too, however sporadically and obliquely, suggested that his disability might be a source of strength for the nation.

For instance, the first inaugural address, which warned the country against "paralyzing terror," suggested that FDR—because of having privileged knowledge about illness from his own experience—would be able to help heal the nation. However, representations of FDR after his death increasingly (and explicitly) presented FDR's disability as having been a source of strength for him personally. In the fifteen years or so following Roosevelt's death, it became increasingly widespread knowledge that the effects of polio had disabled FDR to a larger extent than was visible during his presidency. The stigma surrounding polio had decreased, and the public increasingly regarded FDR's disability as a "misfortune" that nevertheless "conferred extraordinary prowess on other senses"—strengthening other parts of his body and mind instead of weakening them, as many had previously believed.[23] FDR was one of the key actors driving this shift in popular belief.

In the late 1940s and early 1950s, the most common reading of Roosevelt's disability was that it had been—as Eleanor Roosevelt had once said in an interview—"perhaps a blessing in disguise."[24] If the episode had affected Roosevelt's character development, the perception at this point was that it was only to make him stronger, more resilient, and more capable of empathy with those in trouble. FDR's daughter Anna Roosevelt elaborated on the same idea, writing a piece in 1949 for the magazine *The Woman* titled "How Polio Helped Father."[25] Of course, the belief that FDR's disability in various ways conferred strength constituted an overdetermination and generalization of the effect of disability, just as the earlier belief that physically disabled people were mentally unfit did (albeit in a different direction).

From his presidency until the 1970s, practically all narratives of Roosevelt's illness and disability on the one hand understated the extent to which it affected him and on the other suggested that it was something that had been successfully "conquered." This framing of disability as something to be "conquered," "healed," or "overcome" fits within the medical model of disability. It is not perhaps strange to see it in that context, certainly in this case, given that the disability was an effect of an illness. Instead of fighting that notion, and the stigma it implied to all who dealt with the effects of a disability, FDR employed it by passing as no longer disabled and suggesting he had "overcome" polio (and was thus especially gifted at "overcoming"). The effects of illness in FDR's case were interpreted as primarily positive on the level of character development, strengthening his determination and teaching him empathy. This interpretation was a clear departure from former attitudes toward disability and polio, away from earlier practices of ostracizing people with the disabilities. Roosevelt contributed to that change through his example: after a disabled president had been so successful in the nation's highest office for so long, it was impossible to argue that disabled people were unable to participate in public life.

Roosevelt also contributed to changing the outlook for polio survivors by creating, funding and developing the polio treatment center in Warm Springs, which he had "discovered" in his own rehabilitation process. His charity, the March of Dimes, was highly visible and popular, and Roosevelt held annual birthday balls to find sponsors for these efforts. What is important here is that he never cast himself as a someone who was himself disabled as an effect of polio, but as a philanthropist who picked this cause because polio had affected him *in the past*. The announcement to the world of the discovery of Jonas Salk's polio vaccine on April 12, 1955—on the tenth anniversary of FDR's death—completed a triumphant narrative. In this triumphalist framing, which still adhered to the medical model of disability, the challenges and sacrifices of the fabled radio president led, through the March of Dimes, to a victory over an epidemic disease for the entire world.

An important moment in the coloring in of the narrative of FDR as a character strengthened through polio was when, in 1960, the biographical film *Sunrise at Campobello* (dir. Vincent Donehue) came out, based on a 1958 play by Dore Schary. The run of the play was important in "breaking the silence" about FDR's experience as a polio survivor, and the narrative was disseminated nationally with the film. Beginning in the summer of 1921 at the family's vacation home on Campobello Island, New Brunswick, on the border between Maine and Canada, *Sunrise at Campobello* depicts FDR in early scenes as vigorously athletic. He enjoys games with his children and sailing his boat until suddenly he becomes ill with fever and then paralysis. Subsequent scenes focus on the conflict in the weeks that follow between the bedridden FDR, Eleanor Roosevelt, his mother and Louis Howe over FDR's political future. A later scene portrays FDR literally dragging himself up the stairs as he painfully strives to deny his physical limitations. In the final triumphant scene, FDR is shown reentering public life as he walks to the speaker's rostrum at the 1924 Democratic National Convention, aided by heavy leg braces and the arm of his eldest son, a "Happy Warrior" as much as Al Smith (whom FDR nominates in his address with that title).

Also in 1960, one of the first books about Roosevelt's manner of handling his disability appeared: Jean Gould's *A Good Fight: The Story of F.D.R.'s Conquest of Polio*. As the title suggests, the book stresses a victory narrative in which Roosevelt had "won the battle" against polio as a prelude to taking on the nation's major crises of the twentieth century. Both of these narratives follow a pattern that David Mitchell and Sharon Snyder outline in their influential book *Narrative Prosthesis*: the disability is the reason for telling the story in the first place, and narrative closure is provided by the suggestion that the disability is "conquered." Mitchell and Snyder introduce the term *narrative prosthesis* to describe the use of disability in literary works as a "stock means of characterization" or as an "opportunistic metaphorical device."[26] A disabled character, they argue, can easily become a kind of "crutch" for the narrative itself. Disability is often a starting point and justification for storytelling, and disabled people are commonly objectified by being cast in this role. Through their disability, they can easily become prosthetic devices employed, in a metaphorical sense, to bear up a narrative. Certainly, we can view victorious narratives that draw comparisons between FDR "overcoming" his disability and the United States "overcoming" national crises as an example of narrative prosthesis. But whereas Mitchell and Snyder stress the injustice that being projected as a narrative prosthesis does to disabled people, FDR often positioned himself as such and profited from being understood as a prosthetic figure. This certainly has been the case in cultural memory.

Prosthetics in FDR's Autofabrication

FDR's self-positioning as a prosthetic figure points to a key aspect of his autofabrication: the use of prosthetics, as well as "the adornment of various technologies that serve as disability markers."[27] Before discussing the second phase of increased public awareness of FDR's disability, I must detour to discuss the term "prosthetics" and to explain the role of both physical and metaphorical prosthetics in my book. At the crossroads of disability pride and passing are a range of such "technologies that serve as disability markers," the category broadly referred to as "prosthetics." This term has often been employed outside of the field of disability studies—for instance, by Alison Landsberg and Robert Burgoyne, whose work I will discuss later—often acquiring metaphorical meanings. While it is indeed attractive for scholars of, say, posthumanism or science fiction to theorize as "prosthetics" all kinds of technologies that are worn on the body, complementing it or giving it extra powers, this does not attend to the material facts of actual prostheses as worn by disabled people in their day-to-day. Disability studies can, by centering a disabled perspective and experience, show how prosthetics are both more and less than they are sometimes claimed to be by scholars who do not take into account actual users of actual prosthetics when employing the term.

As Katherine Ott writes in the introduction to *Artificial Parts, Practical Lives*, the authors want to correct the "the vogue for prosthetics as found in psychoanalytic theory and contemporary cultural studies." Many scholars use the term "prosthesis" regularly, and often reductively, as a synonym for common forms of body–machine interface. From such a point of view, it is easy to regard any machine or technology—cars, telephones, sexual devices—as prosthetics. Ott, however, stresses that actual historical prosthesis users "are not cyborgs or bionic beings. Nor are they merely metaphors for empire, nationhood, or modernist anomie. Prostheses can certainly fill all those roles. In scholarly literature, prostheses usually perform cultural work unrelated to the practicalities of everyday life. One does not need real people to do a deep metaphorical analysis of symbolic forms; in many cases, putting real people into these scenarios would subvert or nullify the analysis."[28]

When applied to the study of Franklin Roosevelt, both perspectives on prosthetics are relevant. I discuss the prosthetics he used, and the ways in which he did so, in some practical detail. However, I will also show that FDR, as a real person in a historically unique scenario, did become a metaphor and an icon for a range of things, especially through his disability and his use of prosthetics. For instance, Roosevelt's car was a highly important attribute for him in shaping his public image. He was often photographed sitting in it, both because the car facilitated his passing as able and because he eagerly associated himself with modern technology. The FDR Library and Museum now explicitly exhibits the car in order to show how it is hand-controlled; thus, the metaphorical implications of a "prosthetic" car and its practical details were inextricably linked during FDR's life, and even more so in his afterlife, when the disability and its impact was made abundantly visible, and when FDR's role as a national icon was expanded. The disconnect between the cultural work of metaphorical prosthetics and the practicalities of their use seems apparent in most cases but is not in FDR's.

The Ubiquitous Wheelchair: The Second Phase in Increased Public Awareness of FDR's Disability (1985–2016)

Roosevelt's wheelchair could not have been remembered from his actual presidency, because it simply was not visible to the public. The wheelchair entered cultural memory through films such as *Sunrise at Campobello* (1960) and *Annie* (1982), films that utilized the wheelchair to emphasize the fact that FDR lived with the effects of polio (presented in the film as a nearly insurmountable setback). In *Annie*, the protagonist is received by Roosevelt in a wheelchair; he offers in passing to teach her to ride one too, an image that recalls the—by 1982 very famous but also anomalous—1941 photo of FDR in his wheelchair with Ruthie Bie. The public image of FDR in a wheelchair that has evolved since the late 1980s differs both from the simplistically triumphalist early portrayal of FDR's disability in such films and from the implicit and indirect public awareness of his disability during Roosevelt's presidency. Later representations tend to pay attention to the idea that his using a wheelchair shaped FDR's identity. While many knew about Roosevelt's disability during his presidency, his wheelchair has come to occupy center stage in public consciousness only relatively recently. In representations of Roosevelt from around 1990 and onward—memorial, cinematic, or documentary—his wheelchair has practically become FDR's most defining and recognizable feature. In movies about World War II made since then, whenever viewers see a man in a wheelchair enter the scene, they understand immediately that this must be FDR.

Part of the reason for the increasing omnipresence of wheelchair imagery whenever Roosevelt is represented is no doubt that Roosevelt representations have increasingly become visual, necessitating the inclusion of the wheelchair. During his presidency, Roosevelt reached the public mainly through the radio, so he himself could easily choose not to refer to or represent the wheelchair. In newspapers there was, beyond the initial interest in FDR's physical fitness for office, little focus on the matter, perhaps because of the common desire on the part of audiences to treat disability as invisible, as FDR himself did most of the time.

A further explanation for the rise to fame of Roosevelt's wheelchair is that, in the wake of the success of the Civil Rights Movement and other emancipation movements, disabled Americans also started to demand more equal opportunities, culminating in 1990 in the Americans with Disabilities Act.[29] As part of that process, Roosevelt was roped into a rigorous campaign of identity politics, but, in a broader sense too, interest in the "human-angle" perspective on his disability increased throughout US society. A scholarly classic from the early era of disability activism was Theodore Lippman's book *The Squire of Warm Springs*, which cast FDR as an early disability rights activist and a visionary therapy designer who hailed the radical belief that for polio survivors, physical treatment allowed for contact with peers, and was necessitated by social expectations, rather for medical reasons.[30] This reading of FDR's role in early disability rights activism seems to attribute to FDR a more modern attitude to disability than is warranted, however savvy FDR was in dealing with his disability in the primarily social context of his autofabrication. Nonetheless, Hugh Gallagher did explain his experience in Warm Springs in 1953 (where he briefly met Eleanor Roosevelt and acquired his lifelong fascination with FDR) was a key moment in his process of personally and socially accepting his disability.[31]

But the real turning point in terms of remembering Roosevelt's disability came with Hugh Gallagher's paradigmatic *FDR's Splendid Deception: The Moving Story of Roosevelt's Massive Disability—And the Intense Efforts to Conceal It from the Public* (1985). This book created and reinforced popular narratives about FDR's experience of polio and the resultant disability. Hugh Gallagher, himself disabled as a result of polio, suggests that Roosevelt actively, indeed obsessively, tried to hide his disability. Gallagher argues that the polio episode and FDR's failure to recover fully were traumatic and had a formative effect on his character. According to Gallagher, Roosevelt went through periods of intense depression as a result.[32] Various authors have argued that Gallagher may have been projecting his own post-polio depression on FDR.[33] This, of course, is itself speculation about the reason why Gallagher would have commented on FDR's unexpressed feelings.

Nonetheless, Gallagher's book—which foregrounds FDR's disability and his presumed physical, emotional, and social suffering—has helped shape the cultural memory of FDR's disability. Although Roosevelt himself had downplayed his disability, keeping it vague in cultural perception during his presidency, Gallagher's book helped to cement in cultural memory the notion that FDR's disability had in fact shaped his identity. FDR himself would have rejected that notion, against the background of the then-contemporary tendency to equate people with their disability. When FDR became ill in 1921, overwhelming and itself disabling stigma around disability was the norm. FDR responded through a combination of passing as nondisabled and presenting his disability as a positive attribute whenever possible or necessary, even as an occasion for performing explicit masculinity. Later, Gallagher's model—in which disability can be constitutive of identity—included the idea that FDR's autofabrication, which relied on denial about the disability, made it harder for others to embrace their identity.

The question of why 1985—the year that *FDR's Splendid Deception* was first published—was such as watershed moment, and more broadly, why polio survivors were relatively late in advocating for disability rights and visibility, is important. Within the wider spectrum of disability, polio is somewhat unusual. Polio is a disease, and survivors experience its aftermath. Nonetheless, survivors (including disability scholars Hugh Gallagher and Marc Shell) often self-identify as "polios," suggesting that the social effects of the disease become part of their identity. Since polio is a contagious disease, social stigma specifically connected to contagion is among its long-term effects (as if polio survivors remained contagious for life). Polio went around more or less regularly in the summer in the first half of the twentieth century, killing and disabling mostly children.[34]

In the early phases of disability rights activism, as Marc Shell explains, polio survivors usually did not participate; they could often pass as nondisabled and thus did not consider themselves to be disabled. However, when they did start to become engaged in advocacy, they were often very effective. (This was true of Hugh Gallagher's advocacy in the 1970s and 1980s, which culminated in *FDR's Splendid Deception* as well as activism for inclusion of the wheelchair in the FDR Memorial in Washington, DC.) Shell attributes this effectiveness in part to the relatively high level of education within the community of polio survivors. This may be an effect of an intersection between disability and class: "with acute cases of polio, survival often depended on family wealth," as Shell notes.[35] As a result, it may be that polio survivors were among the groups within the disabled community best equipped both to pass as nondisabled and to effectively demand rights.

Hugh Gallagher perhaps recognized himself in FDR, and FDR's case was indeed often held up to polio survivors in the 1940s and 1950s as a model to emulate. Philip Roth makes a similar comparison between FDR and one of his characters in *The Plot Against America*. The novel features young Philip's cousin Alvin, who goes to war in Europe in 1940—fighting with the Canadian army—and loses a leg. Through Alvin, Roth shows the situation disabled veterans found themselves in, with heavy uncomfortable braces and ill-fitting prostheses. Alvin's ensuing depression and passivity are partly an effect of practical matters such as an uncomfortable prosthesis, but primarily result from the shame and social stigma that he experiences. Roth contrasts the state that many young veterans were reduced to—less by disability itself than by the social stigma attached to it—with FDR's opportunity to continue to be publicly active, due to his wealth and supportive environment. Roth's 2010 novel *Nemesis* does something similar. Its protagonist Bucky Cantor is a vigorous young games teacher who contracts polio and is severely disabled by it. Rather than trying to live with its effects, Bucky withdraws from his community, breaks off his engagement, and leads an isolated and depressed life.

Alvin and Bucky can be seen as foils for Roosevelt, the polio survivor who, in contrast to others, managed—as a result of his privilege and successful autofabrication—to evade the social stigma and ostracism connected with disability. Like *The Plot Against America*, *Nemesis* suggests that Roosevelt was an individual outlier, not because of his disability, but because he could continue his career in spite of his disability, in part by embracing the notion that it had made him stronger and more engaged. Through such foils as Alvin and Bucky, Roth effectively shows how in cultural memory, Roosevelt's disabled body was turned into a materialized metaphor of American grit in the face of adversity. It is no surprise then, that for many disability activists since, FDR has been an ambivalent figure. On the one hand, he was undeniable proof that disability need not check one's political career. On the other hand, FDR himself and most later FDR representations handled his disability in a manner that was problematic and could indeed form an obstacle for others in their process toward integrating disability in their identity.

Documentary films like *Warm Springs*[36] and *FDR: A Presidency Revealed*[37] as well as experiential guided tours like that of the Roosevelt Home in Hyde Park, New York, have echoed the interpretation of Roosevelt as unusually resilient, often even suggesting that being buoyant and irrepressible is profoundly American. Such representations are also potentially problematic, because they can frame FDR's particular manner of coping with disability as patriotic, and possible other responses—for instance, from disillusioned veterans—as somehow un-American. (This happens to Captain Dan in *Forrest Gump*, which I discuss in chapter 6.)

Warm Springs essentially starts where *Sunrise at Campobello* leaves off. It focuses on Roosevelt's discovery of the hot baths at Warm Springs and his development of the pools into a polio treatment center. The film stresses how Roosevelt successfully turned the effects of his individual disease into something positive and constructive for polio survivors throughout the nation, suggesting simultaneously that he single-handedly pulled the extremely poor, backward, and segregated village of Warm Springs from a state of dilapidation into the twentieth century. This narrative functions as a bridge in cultural memory between Roosevelt's personal "conquest" over his disability, and the village as a pilot project for the New Deal.

In modern representations, Roosevelt's disability is practically always portrayed as a nearly insurmountable personal trauma that he nonetheless dealt with successfully, adding to his massive accomplishment, ability to empathize, and charm. This aspect is now overemphasized, initially also by the American disabled lobby, to the point of suggesting that it was Roosevelt's most important characteristic. This is far removed from Roosevelt's own attitude toward his disability. FDR and his team autofabricated the disability, and especially the wheelchair, out of view; the memory of it has appeared after his death, based on later representations. Indeed, Roosevelt's disability and the presumed trauma surrounding it in his private life have become a central aspect of the FDR icon, because they can easily function allegorically for other American traumas in cultural memory. If Roosevelt could survive disaster and trauma in his life then so could the nation. The historic FDR's silence surrounding his disability is an important enabling factor in this metaphor. So although FDR restrained the presence of his disability in his public image, its intensive use is now usually part of directly celebratory remembrance practices.

FDR's Virility in Cultural Memory

Using prosthetics socially often requires a performance of hypermasculinity, as Ott, Serlin, and Mihm have observed.[38] While during his life FDR was consistently focused on passing as nondisabled, this alternative strategy for dealing with disability that has become dominant in FDR representations after his death. Crucial to Roosevelt's role as a celebrated cultural icon in an ableist and patriarchal culture has been the perception that his disability didn't affect his virility, in spite of his paralysis "from the waist down," as it is commonly described. This played an important role during World War II, when there was a strong belief that being nondisabled was a condition of masculinity.[39] This idea had to be renegotiated after veterans came back from the war with disabilities and trauma. The issue of Roosevelt's disability vis-à-vis his masculinity resurfaced in the 1990s, when people wondered openly how paralysis "from the waist down" affected his sexual ability. This was also a decade in which presidential virility was at the forefront of popular attention, because of the sex scandal around and impeachment of President Bill Clinton. In searching for historical examples, many found FDR, whose extramarital affairs were known, although they had not previously attracted a great deal of attention.[40]

One obvious way of culturally asserting FDR's masculinity is via his sexual potency—a route taken, for instance, by teen movie *FDR American Badass!* (2012), in which the FDR character asks, "Does my cock still work?" moments after finding out his legs are paralyzed. Through its very triviality, the film betrays an important aspect of FDR as a public icon in cultural memory: if his legs no longer worked, it is all the more important to know that the commander in chief at least functioned well sexually. Anecdotes of his marriage with Eleanor Roosevelt cannot provide this reassurance because their sexual relationship ended, at least in cultural memory, after a marital crisis in 1918 that was prompted by ER's discovery of FDR's affair with Lucy Mercer. Treatments in popular culture of FDR's mistresses and alleged affairs, such as the film *Hyde Park on Hudson* (2012), have usually functioned at least on one level as proof of FDR's continued virility. Such treatments have introduced narratives about FDR's private life into a broader public sphere, addressing the politically and ideologically charged issue of the president's capacity to function as a sexually potent and thus "able" man.

Ellen Feldman's novel *Lucy* (2003) is an intriguing case because it combines the movement from public to private with a movement from official to unofficial and more speculative history. It is well researched and sticks closely to historical details insofar as they are known in telling the story of FDR's relationship with Lucy Mercer Rutherfurd from her perspective. The fact that the Lucy character is the story's narrator makes her a kind of illicit derivative of Eleanor Roosevelt's role as narrator. Lucy Mercer Rutherfurd did not actually tell her side of the story, but in projecting her as narrator of the affair, Feldman is careful to position the love story within the context of FDR's political work and against the background of the United States' involvement in World Wars I and II. Throughout the novel, the narrative is mainly historical—both in the sense of supported by detailed historical evidence, and in the sense that it reads like a favorable biography of FDR, addressing his political career more than his private life. *Lucy* recounts the narrative of FDR's presidency, while filling up the gaps from a vantage point that is just outside the realm of the political, the public, and the official. Lucy, both protagonist and reminiscing narrator, has a particular position only available to a fictionalized mistress from which to complete the narrative and assert FDR to be sexually able, a private issue that is politically and culturally important to his remembrance.

Other female Eleanor Roosevelt foils showcase FDR's masculinity in cultural memory: not just Lucy, but also FDR's secretary Marguerite LeHand ("Missy"), his distant cousin Margaret Suckley ("Daisy"), and to a lesser extent his private secretary Grace Tully. These women figure importantly in many biographies (e.g., Geoffrey Ward's *Closest Companion,* about Daisy). Grace Tully wrote a biography of FDR herself—*F.D.R. My Boss* (1949)—narrating his story, and thereby occupying yet another element of what might be considered ER's position, reinforcing FDR's masculinity and natural dominance in the process as evident in the title "My Boss."

FDR's Disability Memorialized

According to Roosevelt's personal friend Chief Justice Felix Frankfurter, Roosevelt wanted only a small and simple monument. Frankfurter recalls Roosevelt's wishes: "[It should be] placed in the center of that green plot [in front of the National Archives in Washington DC, and should be] a block about the size of this (putting his hand on his desk). I don't care what it is made of, whether limestone or granite or what not, but I want it to be plain, without any ornamentation, with the simple carving 'In memory of . . .'"[41]

It was typical for Roosevelt to have expressed such a modest wish, while at the same time doing something clearly self-aggrandizing: building the first presidential library for the public on the grounds of his private estate. As a museum and archive dedicated to the study of and education about Franklin D. Roosevelt, the library has often been read as a massive memorial in its own right. However, the one time he explicitly expressed himself on the question of a monument that would serve solely as a memorial, Roosevelt was clear. He did not want to be remembered through a statue of his body natural, but he made a point of being memorialized in connection with the body of his work, near the National Archives, where most of his executive impact is laid down on paper, as the FDR Presidential Library does too. FDR's personal records are in the FDR Library in Hyde Park, but a large part of the archival records of his administrations are in the National Archives in Washington, DC. The memorial that he described to Frankfurter was indeed built in 1965, right where he indicated. Thus, both the FDR Library and the memorial outside the National Archives are personal memorials, built or commissioned by FDR, that do not represent his body in a figurative way, but through an archive that speaks to his executive work.

Nonetheless, there are some statues of Roosevelt in the United States. While other nations have built iconic Roosevelt statues without much trouble, American memorial art signals how sensitive the issue of figuratively sculpturing FDR became in the United States.[42] The eventual national Franklin Delano Roosevelt Memorial on Washington's Cherry Walk was dedicated on May 2, 1997. Art historian Sally Stein writes about the first official memorial representation of Roosevelt, the Roosevelt dime, struck in 1946: "The numismatic portrait exceptionalizes Roosevelt by withholding any indications of a body below the head. Coins admittedly offer cramped spaces for portraiture, the small size of the dime being most restrictive. Even so, the physiognomy on the Roosevelt dime stops unnecessarily short with the chin, especially compared with the way necks and sometimes shoulders figure as prominent supports in the case of the Lincoln penny, the Jefferson nickel, and the Washington quarter."[43]

Stein's argument that Roosevelt is unnecessarily disembodied is true for most early American Roosevelt monument designs. The FDR Presidential Library now features some busts, which obviously circumvent the difficulty of portraying his disability, as well as a statue in the library's Kerr Memorial Garden. The statue is of Eleanor and Franklin Roosevelt and does portray them in full, but this was only made in 2003.[44]

Eleanor and Franklin Roosevelt, sculpture by StudioEIS, Senator Robert S. Kerr Memorial Garden, Hyde Park

The original, privately funded memorial in Washington, which followed FDR's wish to the letter, was dedicated exactly twenty years after Roosevelt's death on April 12, 1965. Preparations for a larger national memorial started in August 1955 with a joint resolution of Congress, Public Law 84-572, establishing the Franklin Delano Roosevelt Memorial Commission to select a design, acquire funding, and oversee the construction of a public FDR memorial in Washington, DC.[45] The initial design by William Pedersen and Bradford Tilney was chosen by the memorial commission in 1962, selected by an expert jury from 574 entries in a national competition. The design consisted of eight giant "steles"—the highest of which was to be 167 feet, higher than the Jefferson Memorial—each inscribed with parts of Roosevelt's speeches. The presence of the texts as the only supplement to abstract form underscored the absence of Roosevelt's body from the monument. As a favorable critic noted, the design "quite literally made FDR's words his monument."[46] While this is essentially what Roosevelt himself did too, through his attempts to associate his memory primarily with his library and radio speeches, the design was criticized for being impersonal and remote from FDR's character and personality. Clearly, although this memorial embraced FDR's strategy of passing as nondisabled, it no longer felt relevant enough in 1962 to function as a site of memory for FDR.[47]

The second major attempt at an appropriate design for a large Roosevelt Memorial was even more abstract and eerily disembodied. After Pedersen and Tilney had resigned their commission in 1965, the Franklin D. Roosevelt Memorial Commission selected Marcel Breuer in 1966 to propose a new design. This consisted of a pinwheel of seven long triangular darts, centered around a granite cube showing Roosevelt's face in an incised halftone photojournalistic portrait. Breuer's reason for choosing the cubic centerpiece is strangely telling: "I chose the cube because it is the very center, the very base of form—practically perfect . . . The globe is comparable, but it isn't static; it moves too much. I preferred the great stability, the 'standing power,' of the cube. FDR had 'standing power' too."[48]

The critique that a globe would "move too much" is striking, since FDR's success often hinged on his flexibility and ability to move quickly politically. Breuer's impulse to fix him in one place is telling. Although FDR's twelve-year presidency did provide stability in a tumultuous era, "standing power" is of course exactly what FDR did not have—the correct expression is *staying power*—but the slip suggests how present the memory of a standing FDR still was in 1967. The cube is an attempt at making the memorial "static," although Roosevelt, despite his disability, was emphatically not, nor is the FDR icon. To make the proposed memorial more of a Roosevelt Memorial—but inadvertently also one that would contribute to his passing as nondisabled—audio recordings of Roosevelt's speeches were to be played continuously as part of the memorial. The new design was thus as abstract as its predecessor. The first design did not include a visual image of FDR, citing in the accompanying statement that this was unnecessary given the abundance of available photos. The second design did contain a visual image of Roosevelt, but halfheartedly, portraying him only vaguely. Both designs used Roosevelt's speeches, and in both cases, this worked to draw attention to the absence of his body.[49]

In 1972, Congress decided to add the assistant director of development from the National Park Service, Raymond L. Freeman, to the Memorial Committee.[50] Educated by the previous failures, Freeman articulated the requirements for the design more precisely than before: it was to be "a 'landscape solution' that would harmonize with the beauty of the existing park-like setting; that water be a significant element of the memorial environment; that no major structure dominate the site; that an image or images of Roosevelt were appropriate; and the recreational area be retained."[51] Landscape architect Lawrence

Halprin made the first version of his eventually successful design in 1974. It consisted of a series of four "outdoor rooms," each one dedicated to one of Roosevelt's four terms as president, as well as to the Four Freedoms. Halprin was torn about the position in which he wanted to show Roosevelt: "In his notes from 12 March 1974 [Halprin] indicated that he would like something 'bigger than life, standing with cape and cane and braces—because that's how most of us remember [FDR].' Four days later, Halprin changed his mind . . . [and] also admitted to himself, 'The statue issue is a tough one in terms of scale. Also should [FDR] be seated as he normally was when we saw him or standing . . . I think sitting is better—but how?'"[52]

It is striking that Halprin remembers Roosevelt in the first instance in a standing position, echoing Breuer's Freudian reference to "standing power." Insofar as Halprin had seen Roosevelt standing at all, only the upper half of his body would have been visible and the cane and braces would have been out of sight. The difference in formulation between "[standing], as most of us remember" and "seated as he normally was when we saw him" suggests that Halprin became aware of the fact that memory, even a presumably collective memory, as the use of the plural pronoun suggests, may have differed from the actual position Roosevelt was usually seen in. However, even Halprin still remembered FDR as able to stand and clearly did not, in the first place, envisage a wheelchair.

While the Roosevelt figure that Halprin eventually chose for the monument was still "bigger than life," it did not have the huge proportions he initially envisaged.[53] Moreover, Halprin eventually chose to include a number of statues by various sculptors in the memorial not only of Roosevelt himself but also depicting scenes, such as men in a breadline, and a man listening to a radio. Such scenes are both vividly visual and invite the visitor to participate. The walls of the memorial have inscriptions of passages from famous speeches and Fireside Chats, but that is practically the only element of the former designs that remained. In contrast to the earlier abstract designs, Halprin's is relatively accessible, functioning almost more like an interactive outdoor museum than a memorial. However, in terms of disability access, it also engages in a degree of "accessibility theater," a display of accessibility put on to satisfy a nondisabled audience without actually being effective in guaranteeing access to disabled visitors (e.g., tactile elements placed higher than a blind person could reach them).

The memorial shows Roosevelt seated and clad in a giant cape, which obscures the object he is sitting in or on, leaving open whether it is a wheelchair.

Statue of Franklin Delano Roosevelt (in his wheelchair), cutout from "Statue . . . and his dog Fala at the Franklin Delano Roosevelt Memorial." Carol M. Highsmith, via Wikimedia Commons

In the version that was officially dedicated in 1997, the memorial remains ambiguous: Roosevelt's disability is not denied, but neither is it openly visible. In that sense, the memorial is strikingly similar to Roosevelt's own manner of dealing with his disability. Halprin thus kept to Roosevelt's strategy of not lying about the disability, but obscuring it fairly actively—a strategy of which some (but not all) members of the Roosevelt family approved. However, this

Sculpture of a breadline at the FDR Memorial, Washington, DC. Carol M. High-smith, via Wikimedia Commons

strategy was under debate in the 1990s, in part as a result of Hugh Gallagher's analysis of FDR's experience of disability.

As Barbara Floyd has shown impressively in an article aptly titled "Hugh Gallagher's Splendid Reception," *FDR's Splendid Deception* had an enormous impact on the long process surrounding the development of the FDR Memorial in Washington, DC. His book was a bestseller and was cited intensely both in arguments against and in favor of including a wheelchair. Gallagher himself saw including it as a form of emancipation that FDR had not been able to achieve during his life and therefore favored it.[54]

Lobby groups such as the National Organization on Disability, headed by Alan Reich, strongly opposed the way in which the memorial, until its first dedication in 1997, persisted in what they perceived as treating Roosevelt's disability as something that still needed hiding. Michael Deland, a board member of the National Organization on Disability, argued that FDR "lived in a wheelchair and history should record it,"[55] thereby raising the question of who should decide what "history" must record. Architecture scholar Reuben Rainey argued, contra Frankfurter's statement about remembering Roosevelt through the memorial that FDR himself favored, that "it is clearly the prerogative and the responsibility of those who benefit from the deeds of an individual to decide how that individual will be appropriately commemorated."[56] By that logic, it makes sense that Michael Deland considered the disabled community as having been

The "wheelchair" part of the sculpture of Franklin Roosevelt at the National Memorial, Washington, DC. Photograph by Sara Polak

particularly impacted by Roosevelt's deeds and image as a disabled president. However, the idea that disabled Americans should take particular responsibility for the Roosevelt memorial, since they benefited from his presidency more than others, is by no means obvious. It rather seems that movements like the National Organization on Disability wanted Roosevelt to represent them retrospectively more than he actually did—claiming the icon thereby as a prosthetic figure, supporting and making visible their claim to emancipation. Hoping to defuse the threatening escalation, Halprin added tiny wheels to the legs of the chair in which Roosevelt is seated in the Roosevelt Memorial's main sculpture.

Protesters against the plans to portray Roosevelt in the memorial without visible signs of his disability, using the slogan "Don't hide FDR's source of strength," threatened to disturb the dedication ceremony of the memorial, until President Clinton asked Congress to mandate an addition to the planned monument showing FDR in his wheelchair. So, the first dedication on May 2, 1997, went on undisturbed, after the appendage to the memorial—itself a prosthesis to sustain an already encumbered monument—had been ordered. At this dedication Clinton said: "It was that faith in his own extraordinary potential that enabled him to guide his country from a wheelchair. And from that wheelchair, and a few halting steps, leaning on his son's arms or those of trusted aides, he lifted a great people back to their feet and set America to march again toward its destiny."[57]

With the juxtaposition of the wheelchair and the march of America toward its destiny, Clinton suggests that the wheelchair was instrumental in lifting the great people. Portraying America as having fallen on the march toward its destiny and needing to be lifted works particularly well because the wheelchair of the man doing the lifting is all too real, if invisible in the memorial at that moment. The suggestion is that America metaphorically went through what Roosevelt had experienced in the body and that the election of a disabled man as its savior was a natural part of America's destiny on the stage of world politics.

After the dedication, Halprin went back to work with the added assignment and asked sculptor Robert Graham, who had already made some of the other sculptures for the monument, to design one of Roosevelt in his wheelchair. In 2001, a "Prologue" was added to the memorial—an anteroom to the four other outdoor rooms, empty except for a sculpture of Roosevelt in his wheelchair—and wearing his glasses—in the middle. The sculpture was life-size, but looked smaller in the large space and was out of style with the rest of the memorial. Artistically, its addition was certainly no improvement, but it did show how political Roosevelt's disability still was. The controversy was resolved to some extent, but the compromise was visibly awkward. In a speech at the dedication of the Prologue to the memorial on January 10, 2001, Clinton remarked: "By showing President Roosevelt as he was, we show the world that we have faith that in America you are measured for what you are and what you have achieved, not for what you have lost."[58]

Clinton did not explicitly mention the wheelchair, but he gave his speech standing beside a sculpture of Roosevelt in a wheelchair that had specifically been added to "show him as he was." The suggestion is that the wheelchair was part of his identity. Clinton specifically staged the wheelchair as proof that in America a disability is no social or practical impediment to success. In doing so, he offered a version of the grand narrative of American exceptionalism: the fact that Roosevelt could be the hero he was shows that America sees people's personally acquired merits and does not judge them by "what they have lost." Clinton here completes the argument he began in 1997, suggesting that the heroism that was first Roosevelt's own great strength was transferred to the nation. Disability activists had managed to realize a specific antechamber dedicated to the wheelchair. At the same time, Clinton's rhetoric here could be understood as ableist, suggesting that it is able Americans' unusual tolerance that allows for disabled people to achieve great things. This fraught resolution to a long and painful process of creating a national Franklin D. Roosevelt Memorial ropes FDR into a long tradition of disabled figures in literature and memory as narrative prostheses.

FDR in his wheelchair, *Prologue to the National Memorial,* Washington, DC.
Kevincartı, CC BY-SA 4.0

Prosthetic Memories of FDR's Disability

As polio historian Marc Shell has argued: "most autobiographies written by
polios and many biographies written about polios depend on triumphant survival as an organizational structure."[59] This both refers to the triumphalist
framing of polio discussed above and also invokes another key mechanism of

disability representation: more than just a theme, disability becomes the basis of many narratives' organizational structure. This pattern occurred in many of the representations discussed in this chapter. However, perhaps it is possible to profit from the structural support that disability can offer to narrative representations without attributing undue meaning to disability as something to be conquered (punished, exorcized, embraced). Developments in public history over the last decades suggest so.

In the 1950s, journalist Freeman Tilden was employed by the National Park Service to research and write about America's National Parks and National Historic Sites. Tilden created guidelines for NPS guides to interpret the sites in order to educate visitors about their national heritage.[60] Tilden's first principle expresses what I regard as a central tenet of American historical tourism: historical sites must offer a sensuous experience to the visitor, presenting history as experiential. Tilden's paradigmatic claim is that national heritage can only take on meaning for the individual visitor when the interpretation offered somehow connects it to his or her own experience. Interpretation is an act of translation from the enigmatic heritage site or object to the personally relatable experience of the visitor. An example he gives comes from the Franklin D. Roosevelt Home at Hyde Park:

> It is the room where the President was born. You could put up a label and say, "President Roosevelt was born in this room." That is accurate information. Or in personal contact with his group the interpreter would be at liberty to state the fact in any elaborated way he might please. But someone had an inspiration here. What you see is a reproduction of the telegram sent by the happy father, James Roosevelt, to a friend announcing the arrival in Hyde Park "of a bouncing boy, weight 9.5 pounds, this morning." It is just what you or I would have done, and you instantly feel kinship not merely with the Roosevelts, but with the whole mansion and area.[61]

The personal and relatable telegram inspires, Tilden suggests, a feeling of kinship in the visitor. The Roosevelts and the whole mansion and area become familiar; one is invited to identify both with the proud father himself, and with the addressee—a close family friend. Interpreting for Tilden means offering a pedagogical bridge from the individual to the larger narrative, through the personal or the experiential, so that the visitor can relate to it on a sensuous and emotional level. Such interpretation must involve "the whole man" and aim to "provoke." Likewise, the wheelchair in the FDR Home and other accommodations became objects that allowed visitors to experience who FDR "really" was, creating a sense of him that American citizens who experienced his presidency could not have had.

The FDR Home is still managed by the NPS, and the guides interpreting the site in group tours still work essentially with Tilden's principles. This includes moments of disability drag that have been criticized heavily within disability studies, because as Alison Kafer notes, "Wearing a blindfold to 'experience blindness' is going to do little to teach someone about ableism," yet suggests that it does, without ever engaging the perspective of disabled people.[62] Most tours include an invitation to "imagine what it was like to be FDR" by imagining what it was like to be in a wheelchair. There is a wheelchair exhibited in the home. On most tours, guides draw attention to the hand-pulled lift by which FDR could move himself upstairs. They mention the fact that he did not want the lift to be electrified, because he was afraid that in case of fire, he would be unable to leave the house. Through such emotive and vividly imaginable fears, visitors are encouraged to sympathize with FDR, almost literally being put in his seat. The goal is to create the impression, mostly through the concrete use of the actual site, that visitors can experience history from the front row. The assurance that "this is where it happened" allows for the employment of disability markers like FDR's wheelchair, turning them into public attributes that they had not been during FDR's presidency. Tobin Siebers theorizes this type of interpretation as a narrative structure that masquerade disability for the benefit of the able-bodied body only.[63]

More recent thinking among public historians about historic house museums often focuses on broader forms of inclusiveness as well as interactivity between the museum, its visitors, and its local community. Franklin D. Vagnone and Deborah E. Ryan in the *Anarchist's Guide to Historic House Museums* argue for less enshrinement of the past and more active community engagement in historic houses and period rooms, in order to create more intimacy.[64] While the FDR Historic Home hardly lives up to the high standards of inclusion and interactivity set by Vagnone and Ryan, the intimacy that is evoked mostly works through displays of original self-designed FDR wheelchairs, ramps, and fire escapes that FDR was able to use. Moreover, the museum linked to the library, which might seem like it would be less intimate, actually does offer a range of displays one can touch and play with. Even if the site doesn't seem overly successful by those standards, the combination of house and museum—and the use of references to FDR's disability—together create a sense of inclusivity and intimacy. Perri Meldon has explored in detail this specific strategy of making NPS historic house museums more engaging, not just by making them accessible on a logistic level, but also by actively uncovering disability stories.[65]

Tilden's concept of interpretation is a forerunner not only of work by public historians more focused on community and inclusion, but also of memory scholar Alison Landsberg's term *prosthetic memory*, which can refer to memories generated by experiential museum exhibitions. Largely because of Tilden's influential manual, museums and heritage sites came to think of an experiential approach as the best way to present and make accessible their material. Thus, the prosthetic memory that Landsberg analyzes is a cultural phenomenon produced in America since the middle decades of the twentieth century. Landsberg's concept is helpful in explaining how it is that Americans believe that FDR's disability was more visible during his presidency than it actually was.

Landsberg's *Prosthetic Memory: The Transformation of American Remembrance in the Age of Mass Culture* theorizes memories that operate in mass culture and are created primarily through cinema and experiential mass media such as interactive museum exhibitions. Her widely adopted term *prosthetic memory* refers to memories generated not through direct *lived* experience or *organic* family memory but through experiential representations. Such representations, she argues, create prosthetic memories; *prosthetic*, in her view, because such memories are nonorganic and interchangeable but also useful and capable of influencing the bodies they are appended to. Landsberg argues that while people realize that prosthetic memories are not real, these memories can still to some extent function as though they are real. Prosthetic memory "emerges at the interface between a person and a historical narrative about the past, at an experiential site such as a movie theater or museum."[66] Although the term *prosthetic memory* seems particularly felicitous in the context of "remembering" Roosevelt's disability, even when it was not historically well-known, Landsberg actually does relatively little to take her term seriously in the context of disability studies.

Roger Michell's movie *Hyde Park on Hudson* exemplifies how and why FDR, who himself depended on many actual and metaphorical prostheses, was so successful at producing prosthetic memories. The film capitalizes on the disability and the prostheses FDR used to offer a narrative about his role in history and uses the disability to ask the viewer to identify with FDR, employing him as a narrative prosthesis. The film's focalizer is Daisy—a nickname FDR gave to his removed cousin, friend and perhaps lover Margaret Suckley—who in the film becomes his mistress, one of his various lovers after his marriage with Eleanor Roosevelt has, at least sexually, failed. Like his wheelchair, leg braces, and other means of support, the cinematic FDR treats Daisy and other mistresses as perfectly ordinary and natural extensions of his body and entourage. They are present, also in the public view, without being given specific attention or being somehow justified or defended. Like the wheelchair, Daisy is unapologetically visible for FDR's visitors, but both presences are passed off as so natural that to inquire further would be illogical and impolite. As such, FDR in *Hyde Park on Hudson* has physical and affective appendices that are inconspicuous to the point of not being noticed, a fact he is acutely aware of, as he makes explicit in a private discussion with King George.

In *Hyde Park on Hudson*, the key meeting between FDR and King George directly follows King George pushing Roosevelt's wheelchair; the president with paralyzed legs and the stuttering king have a highly intimate personal conversation supposedly decisive for the bilateral relationship of the United States and the United Kingdom. Roosevelt is in this situation clearly the one on top, geopolitically, but primarily on a personal level. King George tries to express himself but is caught up by his stutter; he cries out, "This goddamn stutter!" in exasperation. Roosevelt coolly responds, "This goddamn polio." Roosevelt goes on to explain his personal theory that as long as he ignores his disability others will not even notice it:

> Let me confess something to you now, as you've been so honest with me. No one ever mentions the fact that I can't use my legs. It's never referred to. Not by anyone. And I used to think it was because they were embarrassed about it. [*Gets up out of wheelchair, starts "walking."*] But now I think it's because it's not what they want to see. Of course, you and I, we think that they see everything that we are. All our flaws. Our transgressions our failures. [*Laboriously moves over to desk.*] But that's not what they're looking to find when they look to us. And God help us if that ever changes. Can you imagine the disappointment when they find out what we really are?[67]

Roosevelt's words here are interestingly juxtaposed with his movements. During this speech about the benefits of avoiding discussion of his disability, he draws attention to it by trying to walk, which the paralysis makes impossible. *Hyde Park on Hudson*'s general take on Roosevelt's genius seems to be that he was a brilliant manipulator of people and appearances. Roosevelt's contemporaries in the film do not see his disability. The movie audience does; however, they see it not merely as a disability but also as an attribute that helps to show off his masculinity, flair, and the brilliance of his manipulation. The "walking" that Roosevelt does has a different meaning for the cinematic King George than for the viewer. For King George, it is a demonstration of how desperately trying to be nondisabled may actually draw more attention to one's disability than accepting it. To a modern audience, the "walking" instead suggests Roosevelt's ease with consciously projecting whatever image he needs at a particular moment. As such, the film cleverly incorporates the idea that Roosevelt's disability was viewed differently by his contemporaries in his lifetime than in the decades that followed. The film's FDR is openly and consciously passing as nondisabled (as did the historical FDR) and simultaneously puts expectations about disability in his own service, by suggesting that because of it, he is "safe for intimacy."[68] Whether the historical FDR consciously did the same thing is difficult to prove, but there are various cases where he may well have done so. Some of these cases are discussed in chapter 2, for instance his projection of his own experience of disease in the wording of his first inaugural address. This use of disability as a vehicle to intimacy may also be part of the reason why the Fireside Chats are commonly understood as intimate, despite the fact that analysis of the texts' discourse and content does not corroborate that description.[69]

The shifts in how (and whether) Roosevelt's disability was viewed demonstrate how cultural memory absorbs changing societal attitudes. But these shifts also show how Franklin Roosevelt himself, as well as other actors on his or their own behalf, have consciously tried to steer this process in specific directions. Initially, Roosevelt himself steered this process. He edited his wheelchair out of the public view, and—when he did associate himself with polio—he did so either implicitly or by framing himself as someone who remembered it but hardly experienced its effects on his life in the present, and was working to help others "achieve" the same. From Roosevelt's death through the 1970s, family, friends, and associates of Roosevelt portrayed his disability as a "blessing in disguise" that strengthened his character and readied him for the presidency.[70] In the 1980s, Hugh Gallagher published his influential analysis arguing for seeing disability as a key part of FDR's identity. Disability rights activists began to employ the FDR icon as their mascot, which was a key ingredient to FDR's wheelchair becoming even more central to his public image.

Roosevelt rhetorically cast himself as a source of support for a "stricken Nation," albeit obliquely and without direct reference to himself or his wheelchair. As Roosevelt's disability has become more prominent in the decades following his death, the FDR icon has come to function as a source of support for the nation by acting as a narrative prosthesis, a metaphor for the nation's ability to "conquer" adversity, a topic explored in the next chapter. A framing of the disability and wheelchair as crucial to FDR's success as president has become dominant and explicit. Inspired by movies and memorials that portrayed the wheelchair, spurred on by the disability rights movement, many people have constructed prosthetic memories of FDR in his wheelchair.

CHAPTER SIX

Understanding FDR as a Cultural Icon

Parents to the Nation

In the preface to her paradigmatic biography, *No Ordinary Time: Franklin and Eleanor Roosevelt, The Home Front in World War II*, Doris Kearns Goodwin compares the United States during World War II to Franklin and Eleanor Roosevelt. She notes that they shared "the sense of a cause successfully pursued through great difficulties, a theme common to America itself and to the family which guided it."[1] Goodwin suggests both that the Roosevelts were able to "guide" America because of their personal knowledge of "great difficulties" and that the later reputations of both family and nation hinged on the greatness of the difficulties confronted. In various later literary and cinematic FDR representations as well, FDR is treated as premediating the United States at war and, therefore, able to guide the United States through it. This recurring metaphor has been important to FDR's continued relevance as an iconic figure representing the United States in cultural memory because it speaks to a central part of American national identity: the ability to overcome difficulties.

Goodwin's phrase "the family which guided it" firmly places Eleanor Roosevelt as having been in an adjunct position in leading the United States. And indeed, Franklin and Eleanor Roosevelt, in autofabrication as well as remembrance, have been extremely successful as the nation's projected parents. Many fictional and documentary portrayals of Franklin and Eleanor Roosevelt have emphasized their role as parental figures to the United States.[2] As a result, FDR—who, as discussed in the previous chapter, was perhaps not the most obviously macho war president due to the stigma attached to his disability—has been represented over the years as a paternal war president.

Goodwin's biography weaves together the Roosevelts' private and public lives, opening with what in a film would be a parallel projection of the German occupation of Europe in 1940 and FDR's illness with polio in 1921. Thus, Goodwin consistently interprets the home front as being both "national American" (the battlefield) and "domestic" (the intimacy of the Roosevelts' household). Goodwin suggests throughout that the Roosevelt home directly reflected America as a whole, and she casts the family as an allegory for the nation and all its citizens.

No Ordinary Time consistently uses the first names of its narrative's *dramatis personae*. It often stages Eleanor Roosevelt as the narrator, since the personal, familial side of the narrative relies heavily on ER's autobiographical writings. As the use of first names already signals, the biography is intensely intimate. It strongly links private events in the Roosevelts' lives to American engagement in the war. For example, Goodwin frames the Japanese attack on Pearl Harbor with an elaborate discussion of the deaths of FDR's mother and ER's brother in the months prior to December 7, 1941. She devotes a great deal of attention to the personal memories and grieving processes of both FDR and ER, suggesting that both worked concertedly on preparing for the war they realized was coming in part to alleviate their grief. For example, Goodwin quotes a comment that ER made about herself in her memoir: "I think it was in an attempt to numb this feeling that I worked so hard at the Office of Civilian Defense that fall."[3]

Goodwin's intimate portrayal speaks to public fascination with FDR's personal life; a fascination that relates to FDR's role as an important cultural icon, a figure with whom the American public identifies. Americans who identify with Roosevelt, or think of him as representative of key American values and narratives, do so in different ways. Roosevelt has managed to cater to the needs of a broad diversity of Americans in the image he offered of himself, and in relating this image to larger national self-perceptions. In the years since Roosevelt's death, various cultural representations have continued to contribute to his iconification in ways that have shifted over time—something FDR's public image allowed for from the start. Another reason why FDR became an American icon is the unmatched and unprecedented fact that he was elected president four times. This in itself meant that he was part of an unusually wide range of contexts, and took on different roles—and, in cultural memory, different meanings—in each of those.

Icon in the original Greek means *image*. Here, I primarily use *icon* to mean *foundational mimetic image*, as Catherine Sousloff has called it, which—in the case of cultural icons—is fundamentally representative of a culture.[4] I also draw on art historian Martin Kemp's framing of icons as images that have taken on meaning beyond their original context and that consistently "accrue legends," often around the belief that the icon "involve[s] some kind of secret." As Kemp argues, iconification implies the transgression of parameters and transplantation of themes to often far-flung contexts.[5] In textual narratives (such as those that I examine in this chapter), iconification can take place through allegory, which allows narratives to "travel" between different contexts and levels of meaning.

I deemphasize the visual element of icons here to stress instead that, to the culture in which a cultural icon exists, the cultural icon is a "vessel" for identity questions.[6] Thus, I define a cultural icon as a person (or artifact) that is identified by members of a culture as representative of that culture. In the process of identification, *icons* are judged by the extent to which they can be seen as authentic proxies of that culture. The way in which the icon relates to the cultural identity represented is variable and open to change. Indeed, the extent to which a cultural icon can be imbued with new meanings and operate in new contexts is a measure of its success. Since cultural memory hinges on the needs of different groups in the ever-evolving present, this flexibility of an icon is essential to its survival.

FDR is an unusually fruitful cultural icon, especially to represent the nation and state. He is open to various kinds of representations: for example, as father figure, husband, wealthy patron, and polio survivor. People also identify with FDR in a variety of modes. Some might see themselves in him, while others perceive him as embodying the nation or the Democratic Party. These representations all connect past and present in one way or another, leading to a multitude of potential configurations of Roosevelt narratives in cultural memory. The Roosevelt icon lends itself to the projection of prosthetic memories (or memories that people acquire not through lived experience but through experiential media). In such memories, the Roosevelt icon becomes a material metaphor, the receptacle for collective problems and memories that cannot comfortably be addressed directly.

It is no surprise that presidential icons usually first develop in the realm of national narratives and patriotic remembrance. In the case of textual narratives, figures are iconified through allegory—metaphor extended into narrative. Just as a metaphor "treats something as something else," an allegory is a text with a symbolic secondary narrative.[7] FDR is often—as one might expect—implicitly or explicitly allegorized to represent the United States and its ideology, particularly in the setting of World War II. Franklin Roosevelt appears as a character in many films and novels, most of which are either primarily or also about World War II. Although he is often a minor character representative of authority and the highest level of decision-making, his character is usually developed narratively at least to some extent. Such literary and cinematic texts use historical elements and attributes from Roosevelt's life. As a rule, these texts lend themselves to being read as allegories or vehicles for a national American narrative.

By examining such allegorical texts, this chapter analyzes the ways that Franklin Roosevelt can be understood as a cultural icon. The chapter focuses on the remembrance of World War II and the "Greatest Generation," showing how the FDR icon is understood to be an embodiment of that generation and pinnacle of American morality as well as a symbol of American corruption. Various twenty-first-century films employ Roosevelt's disability as a "narrative prosthesis" to propel stories that understand the United States' historical or current-day role in the world as empowered by its tolerance for and refusal to exclude wounded heroes. I close read *Hyde Park on Hudson* and *FDR American Badass!* (both 2012) to show how this dynamic works. Finally, I analyze two novels that use FDR as an allegorical figure, showing how both allegorization and the understanding of FDR as a metaphor contribute to his role as a cultural icon.

FDR has come to occupy his role as one of the most iconic US presidents first and foremost as a result of his role in World War II. Be it as the *primus inter pares* of the Greatest Generation or as the eager interventionist who was proven right by the attack on Pearl Harbor, FDR is remembered as embodying the United States at war.

The Glorification of the Greatest Generation

The last decades of the twentieth century and the first of the twenty-first have seen a shift in popular interest away from leadership narratives toward the experiences of common people and communities. John Bodnar asserts in *The "Good War" in American Memory* that "the public performance of the victory in the 1990s had privileged romantic myths about ordinary individuals more than the contributions of wartime leaders like Franklin D. Roosevelt."[8] Contrary to what Bodnar seems to argue, Roosevelt characters have continued to be central to cultural artifacts representing World War II. I argue here, extending chapter 2's discussion of FDR's synecdochic and metonymic voices, that this is because FDR lends himself exceptionally well to working as a cultural icon. Roosevelt representations continue to be successful, as I will show, because they activate and enable particular remembrance practices, employing the FDR icon in various ways, contingent on the needs of the present in which the representation is used.

There are many examples that back up Bodnar's claim about ordinary individuals, including Studs Terkel's successful oral history, *"The Good War": An*

Oral History of World War Two, journalist Tom Brokaw's best-selling *The Greatest Generation*, and Ken Burns's seven-part documentary *The War*, which narrates the war from the perspective of four paradigmatic American communities.[9] Each of these mainstream and successful cultural artifacts are part of the mode of privileging "romantic myths about ordinary individuals," Bodnar describes. If FDR comes up in such texts, it is often as a common man himself, who happened to be called upon to fulfill the role of president. It is easy to read the FDR Memorial in Washington, DC (1997) in this manner: it portrays Roosevelt both as a common man himself, and as someone surrounded by other ordinary individuals, in the shape of sculpted human figures—more a representative pars pro toto than an elevated leader like Jefferson or Lincoln in their Washington memorials.

Such synecdochic representations of Roosevelt treat him as a randomly chosen individual, "your typical American," but not as a metaphor for America as a whole. Essentially, the movement toward the social history of the people mirrors FDR's successful rhetorical embodiment of the common man. His public image is—however ironic it may seem, given Roosevelt's privileged upbringing—joined to his foregrounding of the plight of "the forgotten man." Even though that phrase is taken from the context of the New Deal, it sits well with the post-1970s popular interest in "people's history": bottom-up, revisionist history, with Howard Zinn as its main proponent in the United States, and the History Workshop movement in the United Kingdom.

While Tom Brokaw is by no means a postmodern or left-leaning oral historian—his mode is that of the documentary maker, even if *The Greatest Generation* is a book—he, too, invokes Roosevelt explicitly to pull together the experiences and popular perception of countless common Americans whose war stories he tells. He cites Roosevelt's famous and endlessly echoed epigram from his June 27, 1936, renomination acceptance speech: "This generation of Americans has a rendezvous with destiny."[10] He then continues the generation trope in his introduction: "I am in awe of them, and I feel privileged to have been a witness to their lives and their sacrifices. There were so many other people whose stories could have been in this book, who embodied the standards of greatness in the everyday that these people represent, and that give this generation its special quality and distinction. This is the greatest generation that any society has produced."[11]

Here, Brokaw stresses the random selection of the people whose stories were included; many others would have qualified, too. He also revives and interprets Roosevelt's "rendezvous with destiny" maxim, making a strong claim that he is not shy or cynical about: that this generation was the greatest that any society has ever produced. The book's premise is that, while Europe was bogged down in Nazism, communism, and old-world imperialism, America became the dominant world power thanks to its freedom, democracy, and the moral uprightness and bravery of its people. America was then honor bound to share these attributes worldwide. In this context, World War II remains an important moral touchstone, with a clear-cut opposition between good and evil that escapes relativism, as Michael Rothberg discusses as length in *Multidirectional Memory*.[12]

Thus, the war also provided Roosevelt with a logical and heroic place in history. He was an individual who represented the generation as a whole; at the same time, he also served as an eminent receptacle, able to accommodate, communicate, and give weight to others' stories. While the war setting provided Roosevelt with a stamp of moral righteousness and lasting remembrance, he was the one who positioned himself to be able to fill so many different roles as a cultural icon.

Brokaw, like Burns and Terkel, tells the stories of a number of individuals, each of whose experiences stand in a synecdochic relation to the American experience as a whole. Like Burns but unlike Terkel, he suggests that those stories in sum "embody the standards of greatness" of American society and culture during World War II: collectively, they represent the nation over and above the sum of its parts. Thus, *The Greatest Generation*—through a title that provides an indexical link with FDR—sets out to represent the nation through portraits of regular people. However, it includes war narratives of a number of "Famous People,"[13] most notably President George H. W. Bush. Bush actually resists Brokaw's suggestion that his narrative represents the American experience in a much larger sense, saying that by serving in World War II, he was just a "tiny part of something noble."[14] Bush also suggests that the war taught Americans something new about themselves: "In a way, America came to know itself better through this common experience."[15]

Robert Burgoyne's *Film Nation: Hollywood Looks at U.S. History* argues that Hollywood film, too, has moved, from mainstream heroic historical narratives undergirding American grand narratives toward narratives that allow for narration "from across" and negotiation with perspectives from "outside" or "below": "Recent historical films can be seen as part of the ongoing revisionary enterprise of the late twentieth century; they reenact the narrative of nation in terms of its tributaries, in terms of stories of ethnic, racial, and gender struggles to reshape the national narrative, and to make the experiences of marginal groups a 'formative and necessary part of the story.'"[16]

We may see this "ongoing revisionary enterprise" as reflective of the growing interest in synecdochic people's histories and in the plights of those marginalized by the grand narrative. Those late-twentieth-century films do represent historical narratives as stories of nationhood, Burgoyne concludes: "Despite highly critical messages concerning the national past, the films that form the core of this study preserve and revivify some of the basic tropes of traditional narratives of nation—the image of a mystic nationhood that is revealed only on the battlefield, for example, or the importance of warfare in molding a sense of ethnic and national community."[17]

Although they may express some critical messages, Burgoyne suggests that these films are actually similar in key ways to their older, more explicitly nationalistic counterparts. Their synecdochic portrayal of members of marginal groups eventually does "revivify basic tropes of traditional narratives of nation" that are centralized to narrate narratives of nation. In a dynamic that Burgoyne's analyses find again and again, complex historical narratives preserve allegorical "narratives of nation," even when they allow for non-dominant synecdochic elements "from across" the rift (between the dominant mainstream and the margins of society). Like *The Greatest Generation*, many of the films Burgoyne analyzes suggest that experiences of war and battle lead to a "mystic nationhood" in which the whole is larger than the sum of its parts. This mystic nationhood is the narrative outcome of collectivized individual war experiences, as told in historical narratives. Such narratives frequently feature white male figures (like Forrest Gump, one of the characters Burgoyne analyzes in depth, or like George Bush, in Brokaw's case). White male figures thus play a key role in creating dominant narratives of nationhood through war experience.

FDR himself was a privileged white male but—through his disability—is also associated with marginal positions "from across." In cultural memory, he is thus able to occupy both dominant and marginal positions. FDR embodies the nation as a whole but also implicitly endorses—and provides an indexical connection to—synecdochic narratives of individuals outside the circuits of power.

FDR as a Material Metaphor for the United States at War

In discussing FDR's disability in chapter 5, I introduced the notion of *narrative prosthesis*, a term coined by David Mitchell and Sharon Snyder. They argue that narratives in almost any culture are, more than readers tend to notice at first sight, rife with disabled characters who deviate from the norm and are regarded as aberrant and less than complete. This pattern is, they show, near-universal and also exists, I would add, outside of expressly literary narrative. Such characters have two main roles: "people with disabilities function in literary discourse is primarily twofold: disability pervades literary narrative, first, as a stock feature of characterization, and second, as an opportunistic metaphorical device. We term this perpetual discursive dependency upon disability *narrative prosthesis*."[18]

As is usual in the field of disability studies, Mitchell and Snyder understand the dominant perception of disability (as signaling imperfection, or as the ominous absence of ability) as a cultural construction communicating a significant point about the mainstream, ableist culture. First, they argue that the disabled individual, unlike the run-of-the-mill nondisabled person, socially "requires" a narrative justification and therefore inspires storytelling. Such stories often end with the punishment or restoration of the protagonist to the nondisabled norm. Second, they point out that disabled bodies function as metaphors: "physical and cognitive anomalies promise to lend a 'tangible' body to textual abstractions; we term this metaphorical use of disability the *materiality of metaphor*, and analyze its workings as narrative prosthesis."[19] The implication of this theory is that FDR characters and their "conquest" of polio as portrayed in these films are materialized metaphors for something else: I will argue, for the United States as a wounded nation.

To explain these processes, Mitchell and Snyder analyze Sophocles's *Oedipus*. Presumably because of his own experience with having a limp, incurred as a result of his father's abandonment in his infancy, Oedipus can solve the Sphinx's riddle by answering "the man who walks with a cane."[20] Later, his self-blinding coincides with the moment he becomes a seer, both literally—he understands what has happened—and in the sense that he becomes an interpreter of what the people without disabilities do not normally perceive. Mitchell and Snyder also draw attention to other treatments, and nontreatments, of Oedipus's disabilities in the plays. For instance, they note that critics usually disregard the practical impact of his limp but highlight the trope of the physically disabled as extra able in a metaphorical sense. This element also seems especially relevant in Roosevelt narratives. In the same way that Oedipus could foresee because he could not literally see, the narrative perception of FDR's inability to walk has become an element that uniquely enables him to "lift the nation from its knees."

Oedipus and FDR share, in addition to their hardly visible yet important disabilities, their position as supreme leader. Historian Ernst Kantorowicz theorized the now classic double act of embodiment performed by medieval kings as on the one hand a "body natural," a tangible and vulnerable physique, and on the other a "body politic," which in the Middle Ages meant that political power was located absolutely and by divine order in the king.[21] Later critics expanded this distinction of "the King's two bodies" to include political leaders who were neither royalty nor medieval leaders, because it is a fruitful way of thinking about a leader as both an individual body and the embodiment of a larger institution.

This terminology has also been applied to FDR and particularly to the issue of dealing with his disability: for instance, by Davis Houck and Amos Kiewe in *FDR's Body Politics: The Rhetoric of Disability*, by Frank Costigliola in "Roosevelt's Body and National Power," and by Sally Stein in "The President's Two Bodies." Such texts tend to suggest that either the public perception or the autofabrication of FDR's body politic was informed by his disabled body natural. However, they hardly touch on the role of cultural memory in this process; the focus of the present section. I use Mitchell and Snyder's approach to the representation of disability in literature as *narrative prosthesis*, applying the notion to cultural texts and the narrative texture of historical events rather than to literary texts. I also use their concept of the "materiality of metaphor" to argue that the FDR icon, because of Roosevelt's disability, is unusually fit to engender *prosthetic memories*.

The memory of Roosevelt's disability is primarily a prosthetic one: a historical fact, but one that few people during his presidency knew about in any detail and that doesn't function as an actual memory. Its historical relevance seems hard to understand in hindsight, except as a prosthetic device, a material metaphor, to address other things. The fact that it is Roosevelt's *disability* that enables the icon to function so well in inspiring prosthetic memories is crucial. The FDR icon is itself often a narrative prosthesis in Mitchell and Snyder's sense: a narrative device to justify storytelling that is culturally needed because it fills a gap, as well as a material metaphor for the brokenness and healing that occurred on a national level.

FDR: American Badass!

Many narratives of Roosevelt's "overcoming" his disability carry an implicit narrative of America overcoming devastating losses and challenges, such as the attack on Pearl Harbor. An almost embarrassingly simplistic example is the 2012 movie, *FDR: American Badass!*, in which FDR contracts polio because he is bitten by a Nazi werewolf. The poison paralyzes his legs but spurs him on first to become US president and then—singlehandedly, with the use of various hypermodern and hypermasculine war machines, particularly the "Delano 2000" wheelchair-tank hybrid—to defeat the Axis powers. *FDR American Badass!* presents FDR's disability as a virtue, a mark of martyrhood that gives him the status of a war veteran. As the survivor of an alien infestation by a virus, an invisible enemy threat that is looking to infect and terrorize the United States from the inside, the *Badass* FDR appears as a leader to a far more modern and technologized America. I do not argue that *FDR: American Badass!* is or intends to be a political commentary—the producer in an interview assured me that it does not mean to be—but in its very triviality, the film responds to fears and threats that still exist.[22] These are, no doubt unintentionally, projected onto the past: the Nazis become werewolves, and Roosevelt (with his superpower wheelchair) becomes the epitome of swaggering yet morally righteous American proactiveness.

Robert Burgoyne in *Film Nation* discusses the opportunistic use of prosthetic memory, "memory" acquired through immersive experiences of mass-mediated texts (such as film). Landsberg somewhat naively describes prosthetic memory as "useful" for its ability to allow memory to be shared across cultural groups and ethnicities. Burgoyne terms this opportunistic use "prosthetically enhanced memory": "It is my argument that, rather than viewing prosthetic memory in the positive sense of creating an interface with "past lives, past experiences, past bodies" so as to ground individual subjectivities "in a world of experiences larger than one's own modal subjectivity," *Forrest Gump* revises existing cultural memory in such a way that it becomes prosthetically enhanced."[23]

He argues that *Forrest Gump* prosthetically enhances American cultural memory, showing how the movie turns the American past Gump lives through into a nostalgic celebration of the 1960s and 1970s. As he points out, it removes or glosses over the traumatic events of those decades—literally running past, but not addressing, gender issues, racial struggle, and other problematic elements. The use of prosthetic memory as beatifying enhancement of a troubled past is far removed from the interpretive enhancement Freeman Tilden called for in chapter 5. Tilden and the NPS aim for academically founded and evenhanded interpretation, even if staff at national heritage sites might in fact sometimes narratively improve the past. *Forrest Gump*, however, lays no claim to historical correctness, even if its success relies on a sense that it does represent a shared past.

Burgoyne, like Landsberg, seems to overlook the role of disability in the prosthetic enhancement he calls attention to. The result is that he considers "prosthetic enhancement" as a theoretical lens without attending to the actual prosthetic devices used in the film: essentially the mistake Ott warned against in the introduction to *Artificial Parts, Practical Lives* discussed in chapter 5. Forrest Gump, the movie's focalizer and protagonist, is severely disabled as a child. He uses leg braces because of a back problem that magically dissolves into an ability to run unusually fast, and he has an IQ of 75. His commander and later friend and colleague Lieutenant Dan loses both his legs in Vietnam. Although these disabilities, the prosthetics they require, and the characters' special abilities obtained through them are crucial to the film's plot, as well as to the manner in which it works to generate a prosthetically enhanced view of the American past, Burgoyne's chapter on prosthetic memory in *Forrest Gump* does not address these matters. He does not attend to the fact that Gump's leg braces start off the narrative or that his learning disability provides the guileless innocence that carries it forth, as, for instance, disability scholar Angela Smith has done.[24] Burgoyne is right that "the film evokes the cultural encyclopedia of the sixties and seventies chiefly in order to construct a virtual nation whose historical debts have all been forgiven and whose disabilities have been corrected." However, because a disabled main character is employed to "correct" the "disabilities" of a nation, the film—perhaps inadvertently— adopts a problematic perspective on disability.

FDR: American Badass! elucidates well how common such functional utilization of a disabled main character is in achieving the effect that the country is presented as "healed," because one person's disability has been addressed. Its trailer cuts intriguingly between various scenes in the movie. Starting with footage of the film's representation of World War II—Roosevelt going to war in Europe, personally and singlehandedly—one then hears him declare in front of his airplane, "The only thing we have to fear is . . ." But before this famous maxim is finished with "fear itself," the trailer cuts across to a shot of FDR (Barry Bostwick) addressing a crowd from his wheelchair and jokingly referring to his paralysis as "Marco . . . Polio." Thus, we hear, "The only thing we have to fear is . . . (Marco) Polio . . ." and then ". . . fear itself!" Roosevelt's polio is effectively connected to World War II through his body; polio is treated as if it were the war, projected onto FDR's physique. This doubling is central to the movie. Roosevelt in the movie contracts polio in an encounter with what turns out to be a Nazi werewolf in the 1930s (rather than in 1921). The disease acts on his body as the war acts on the United States as a nation: paralyzing but simultaneously inspiring courage and needed impetus to move forward in destroying the Nazi threat. Roosevelt's by now celebrated adage about "fear itself" historically spoke to the fear that led to the economic and financial paralysis of the country in 1933. In the movie, it refers on one level to the need for national bravery in the face of Axis attack, and on another to Roosevelt's personal angst and laconic pluck in the face of a terrifying disease.

Roosevelt's personal mishaps work as a material metaphor for an America at war: FDR in the film embodies America both in its suffering from and conquest of the Axis powers. Of course, *FDR: American Badass!* does not make an outright claim to historical accuracy. Rather, it stands in the tradition of *The Naked Gun* movies: intentionally silly, visibly low-budget, yet clearly made with love. Nevertheless, it does negotiate with the past, aestheticizing it and making it harmless through the use of Roosevelt's disability. It is important, in that respect, that its producer, Ross Patterson, made it for a high school audience, with the explicit aim to "make FDR seem cool."[25] FDR becomes a kind of "supercrip" masculinity, whose masculinity and disability mutually reinforce each other—a theme often seen in pedagogies of militarization.[26] Patterson did aim to some extent to interpret FDR, but the product is prosthetically enhanced through its use of FDR as a narrative prosthesis.

Pearl Harbor

FDR American Badass! is not a mainstream Hollywood movie; it was made in Hollywood but not by one of the major studios. A more subtle and more widely distributed example of a film that narrates the national trauma of Pearl Harbor through FDR's body is Michael Bay's *Pearl Harbor* (2001). Released in the year of the sixtieth anniversary of the Japanese attack on Pearl Harbor, and months before the terrorist attacks on 9/11, it became a box office success and an Oscar winner in the months after. Although the movie was viewed by many in the shadow of 9/11, it was produced and made most of its revenue—a gross of just under $200 million against an estimated budget of $140 million[27]—during the last triumphalist months of the long 1990s (1989–2001), in which the United States was the unchallenged world hegemon.[28] Although it features an important FDR character, it is a film about the heroism of common American fighting men, like *The Greatest Generation*, *The War*, or *Saving Private Ryan* and other cultural representations of World War II from about the same period. However, the Roosevelt character is important: it introduces, alongside synecdochic individuals representing America, an iconic one who embodies it.

Pearl Harbor remains, as Emily Rosenberg argues in *A Date Which Will Live*, "one of the most emotive icons in American culture," a "dramatic story" that has been "told and retold in thousands of print and visual representations" and "invoke[d] . . . in variable, even inconsistent, contexts."[29] Narratives of Pearl Harbor are told and retold infinitely in a limiting and repetitive loop. The film *Pearl Harbor* breaks away from this repetitive recounting of a traumatic experience by metaphorically projecting the attack onto FDR's body. The film uses FDR as a prosthetic figure who lifts the attack on Pearl Harbor out of its position of unresolved narrative inertia.

The historical Roosevelt understood that the Japanese attacks on Pearl Harbor and other American bases on December 7, 1941, would loom large in American memory. In his historic address the next day, FDR called it "a date which will live in infamy" and asserted: "Always will our whole Nation remember the character of the onslaught against us."[30] "Pearl Harbor" has indeed ever since remained a key "emotive icon in American culture": for instance, as the first point of reference to be invoked following September 11, 2001. There is a stark contrast between the habitual self-impression of the United States as proactive and shrewd, and the devastation caused by the surprise attack at Pearl Harbor. Some of the cognitive dissonance at the time was dissipated, Rosenberg convincingly argues, through the—much older—trope of the United States as a "sleeping giant," an innocent and benign but extremely strong superpower, awakened by a "dastardly attack," as FDR termed it in his Pearl Harbor speech (December 8, 1941).

The Sleeping Giant metaphor also comes up in *Pearl Harbor*, when a Japanese general just after the raid expresses his fear that "all we have done is to awaken a sleeping giant." However, the main mechanism in the film that makes Pearl Harbor bearable as an event to be incorporated into the American narrative is the Roosevelt character, who functions as a material metaphor both to make the attack on Pearl Harbor fathomable and to instigate a strong response. The film's primary heroes, air force pilots, respond to the pain and humiliation of the attack not with words, but with a silent determination to take revenge. At a number of key moments when the shock and pain of the attacks are shown at their worst, the footage is broken off by a cut to the Roosevelt character. Thus, FDR is projected as the operative force in responding to the attack. At these moments, there is a particular visual emphasis on his wheelchair, which becomes a metonym for both the devastating effect of war and the possibility of addressing the impact of external siege by hypermasculine technological prosthetic devices.

Pearl Harbor utilizes Roosevelt's wheelchair in precisely this manner. His first entrance, showing the wheelchair before its occupant, already signals that the president's disability is attributed an important role in the film, however tentatively it is related to its subject and action. In the same scene, introducing the narrative of the decision-making officials, Roosevelt opens the meeting by saying: "I'm afraid I'm in a bad mood. Churchill and Stalin are asking me what I'm asking you. How long is America going to pretend the world is not at war? But our people think Hitler and his Nazi thugs are Europe's problem."[31]

That is also clearly what the present chief officers think at this stage, but Roosevelt sees ahead. He characterizes the enemy in terms of a spreading infection, made worse by America's petrified denial of its global contagiousness. Thus Roosevelt, together with the film's audiences—who, presumably, know largely what happened during World War II—recognize the threat of contagion. As a figure in and from the past who is, interpreted through a kind of discourse that suits the present, his character makes the past accessible for audiences in the present. The film already foreshadows the resolution of the conflict at the moment America is still at its most defeated.

Further into the film, following dramatic footage of the Pearl Harbor attack—including a series of shots of lost or to-be-amputated limbs—Roosevelt is wheeled toward a messenger whom he asks "How bad . . . ?" This cut and Roosevelt's question, suggesting that he, too, is somehow a direct physical victim of the attack, conjures up a link between his disability and those anonymous Pearl Harbor veterans. The film visually suggests that Roosevelt embodies the United States as a beleaguered nation. The scene implicitly evokes a sense that Roosevelt is the ideal man for this job because he is experienced, if not directly as a war veteran, then at least as someone who knows what it means to be the bodily site for a fight between good and evil, as contagion narratives are often framed. As such, his particular narrative of dealing with disability is an apt placeholder for what is too devastating about Pearl Harbor to address head-on. This visual subtext is at odds with the conviction, expressed by FDR in the movie, that trauma is best confronted frankly and straightforwardly. Roosevelt indeed does face the attack head-on in *Pearl Harbor* but on the visual level of actively confronting the loss at Pearl Harbor; the movie itself does not.

The more manifest triumphalist narrative, however, is later elaborated on, first by the combination of Roosevelt's famous war speech (cited above) in voiceover, with more extensive and dramatic footage of Pearl Harbor, connecting the sheer atrociousness of the trauma to the reassuring and fearless voice and message of FDR. This documentary-style interlude repeating words and visual images that remain highly familiar in cultural memory, is followed by another scene of a meeting between FDR and his military chiefs of staff. Again, Roosevelt is portrayed as eager to fight back and show America's spirit. Again, body metaphors are used to connect, or indeed metaphorically replace, Roosevelt's body with that of the nation, for instance, when FDR invokes a boxing expression: "We are on the ropes, gentlemen." This casts the United States and Roosevelt personally as being in the same position of being nearly beaten down physically and mentally, with the difference that Roosevelt has already had time to recover from his injuries, at least psychologically. This is an experience the rest of the nation—evoked here by the military leaders surrounding him—clearly have not yet had, as their panicked response in the meeting signals. In a charismatic and meditative monologue Roosevelt says: "Gentlemen, most of you did not know me when I had the use of my legs. I was strong and proud and arrogant. Now I wonder every hour of my life, why God put me into this chair. But when I see defeat in the eyes of my countrymen, in your eyes right now, I start to think that maybe He brought me down for times like these, when we all need to be reminded who we truly are, that we will not give up or give in."

The scene ends dramatically when, in answer to this speech, one of the generals says, "what you're asking can't be done." Roosevelt, refusing all help, gets up out of his wheelchair, and replies: "Do not tell *me* it can't be done!" Here, the cinematic Roosevelt implies that it is precisely his disability that has caused him to be mentally prepared and equipped, unlike the others, for a crisis situation like this. The primary meaning of "in this chair" is "in this wheelchair," but it could also be taken to refer to "this position" or, indeed, "in this throne." This language conflates the office of the presidency with being disabled, underlining that the two are united in one person, and stressing the divine interference at work here. As such, Roosevelt's body politic takes on the trauma, taking it over from the nation as a collective. When the cinematic Roosevelt says, "Maybe He brought me down for times like these, when we all need to be reminded who we truly are," he implies that being "brought down" by polio is, after all, an empowering experience, strengthening him perhaps not physically but psychologically, to be able to buck up a nation under duress. The scene's own drama and its dramatic juxtaposition to the shocking Pearl Harbor footage that precedes it produces a structure in which Roosevelt is an obvious metaphorically embodied locus of Pearl Harbor. In that material metaphor, Roosevelt's courageous move out of his wheelchair foreshadows the future of America. From being "on the ropes," the nation will—like Roosevelt—move on to become more powerful than ever.

Roosevelt's literal standing up and his resistance to the idea that "it can't be done" are, however, also troubling. Physically, the cinematic Roosevelt cannot really stand independently. His refusal of help makes the gesture more powerful but simultaneously exposes his psychological as well as his physical vulnerability. One of the widespread narratives surrounding Roosevelt's illness and his process toward the integration of the disability in his life is that he utterly refused to acknowledge that he would not walk again. Gallagher and other chroniclers of Roosevelt polio narratives have regularly repeated how in social situations FDR often professed that "with a year or two more of progress he would be able to discard his braces and walk unassisted." Even in private, he kept assiduously practicing to walk in ways that were realistically unattainable given the permanent condition of his leg muscles.[32] These scenes in *Pearl Harbor* imply that the United States was in denial after Pearl Harbor, just as FDR himself was in denial. The film exposes the nation's vulnerability through FDR's, an obvious example of how he functions as a material metaphor. This effect, which seemed willfully produced in *FDR, American Badass!* in this case seems unintentional.

Hyde Park on Hudson

A third film, *Hyde Park on Hudson*, suggests that Roosevelt's silence about his disability was an intentional media strategy. The film itself is surprisingly silent about unpleasant aspects of American history in the war years. The film pointedly avoids making any references to Pearl Harbor, for instance—a movement similar to FDR's silence about his disability. Of course, the narrated royal visit took place in 1939, well before Pearl Harbor or any concrete threat from the Pacific on American soil. But the fact that the film does not refer to it in any way nonetheless stresses America's role in the war as primarily a matter of disinterested moral superiority, diverting attention away from its beleaguered state in 1941. In that context, it is interesting that the final voiceover is explicit about Roosevelt's own wish to repress the presence of bad news in his private life. Describing the illness and death of his secretary and former mistress Marguerite LeHand, the narrator says: "When she fell terribly ill, he paid for everything. He even changed his will, giving her half should she outlive him. But to the surprise of nearly everyone, he did not visit her once in the hospital. I asked him why. 'It's a terrible fault of mine,' he said. 'I find it too painful to be around illness.'"

In spite of the film's own ominous silence about the dramatic attack on America two years after the British royal visit, it does focus on Roosevelt's attempt to negate the existence of disease in his life. On the one hand, he does what he can, materially, to exorcise it; and on the other, he refuses to engage with it on an emotional level. Roosevelt's feeling that being "around illness" is "too painful" mirrors the viewer's sense that it is too painful for the film to address Pearl Harbor. In the film's final sequence, the audience sees FDR being carried and lifted into his car by assistants. After having installed himself, he says, "Ok boys, take it away!" to press photographers, who then start taking pictures of him. Here, too, Roosevelt indirectly denies imperfection. The narrator ends: "A year passed. And then another. And another. I watched him grow tired and frail and ill. He tried to hide this from everyone. He knew how to do that. From everyone but me. Everyone still looking to him. Still seeing whatever it was they wanted to see. In a time, not so very long ago, when the world still allowed itself secrets, Franklin Roosevelt was mine."

The narrator presumes to know Roosevelt's full story, filling in the void that he leaves in his silence about his inadequacy. She assumes the role of addressee of an implicitly told story. Both this movement and the sense of privilege involved mimic the American tendency, noted by Robert Burgoyne in *Film Nation*, to fill silence with a prosthetic narrative (a narrative that suits one's own purposes). Like Roosevelt, *Hyde Park on Hudson* gives viewers "whatever it [i]s they want to see"—in this case, heroic but nonconfrontational characters in a pastoral setting, far removed from the war in England. The film belies the narrator's claim that the world no longer allows itself secrets.

Landsberg's understanding of prosthetic memory as useful in overcoming antagonism between groups in society—because they can share prosthetic memories regardless of background—thus parallels FDR's treatment of his own narrative. In FDR's case, his very silence allows people (the narrator in this film, biographers, etc.) to come up with "prosthetic" narratives. Neither Landsberg nor Roosevelt acknowledge that there is a difference between disabled people and others in culturally perceived and real ability to use prosthetics. In the same way that an actually disabled person would probably use a wheelchair, or other prosthetic device, differently than an actor who "just plays the role," FDR was trained not just in using a wheelchair but also in letting people make of him what would serve them (and thus him) best. The disability and wheelchair narratives are apt because they provide room for prosthetic memories to diverge in their interpretation of how FDR embodies the United States without seeming to do so. Disability, together with prosthetic devices and structures, require and connote a strong interdependency between person and context, that works on a practical level but also on the level of narrative and ideology. They stress America's technical prowess but also retroactively (by highlighting FDR's illness and physical vulnerability) include the disintegration of the body natural.

Deflating Triumphalist Narratives: *The Plot Against America* and *The Golden Age*

Although *Hyde Park on Hudson* focuses on some of FDR's inadequacies and sly manipulations, for the most part, the films discussed here treat FDR in a highly laudatory way, as indeed an emblem of American patriotism and bravery during World War II. In contrast, the two novels that I analyze next—Philip Roth's novel *The Plot Against America* and Gore Vidal's novel *The Golden Age*—puncture the dominant narratives detailed above. *The Plot Against America* makes readers rethink the very concept of the "Greatest Generation," while *The Golden Age* invites readers to question FDR's virtuous image.

The Plot Against America

Philip Roth's novel *The Plot Against America* is a particularly rich case study that employs FDR as an allegorical figure with a crucial role in shaping the United States in cultural memory. This is a counterfactual historical novel in which Roosevelt is not reelected in 1940 but beaten by staunch isolationist and champion aviator Charles A. Lindbergh. The iconic Lindbergh, like FDR, can function as a bridge between a remote past and the present because of his technological modernity and focus on the future: he is a pilot, uses modern media, and campaigns personally, using aspects of his private life. Lindbergh's political convictions—in particular, his association with the America First movement and phrase—seemed less amenable to modernization when the novel was published but have, since 2016, gained renewed resonance as well. *The Plot Against America* portrays Roosevelt as particularly amenable to allegorization, while exposing the fragmentation of America by focusing on anti-Semitism and sympathy for Germany: the sharp edges of the triumphalist narrative.

The issue of Roosevelt's—and the United States'—role vis-à-vis Jews and the Holocaust in Europe in the 1930s and 1940s is hotly debated in historiography. The most incisive study of the topic is Richard Breitman and Allan Lichtman's *FDR and the Jews*, which distinguishes four phases that FDR passed through during his presidency in the evolving American social and political context. During his first term, they argue, it was politically risky for Roosevelt to engage too deeply with "the Jewish question," as doing so was wont to raise resistance among large parts of society, still haunted by the traumas of World War I. Then, between 1936 and 1939, FDR regularly met with Jewish leadership in the United States, supported measures to make it easier for European Jews to enter the United States, and pressured Britain to continue allowing Jews to flee to Palestine. This was followed by another period of silence from FDR on the issue, presumably out of fear of arousing anti-Semitic backlash from isolationist opponents, until 1943, when rescuing European Jews became a central aim of the Allied engagement in Europe. All in all, it seems that FDR, who was extremely popular among Jews, could at times be considered a bystander to the Holocaust but also that he did more than any other potential president probably would have done.

The Plot Against America portrays FDR's attitude to Jews (and their strong support of him) as representative of the dominant liberalism in the United States, and his absence as a great threat to that spirit. Thus, Roth's book glorifies FDR, while also showing what might have happened. Because of FDR's common role as an icon of the United States in World War II, it is easy for contemporary audiences to forget that there was no predetermined outcome. Roth takes FDR to be more of an embodiment of the United States than a synecdochic representative. By showing what might have happened had FDR not stayed on as president in 1940, Roth belies the "Greatest Generation" rhetoric of Tom Brokaw and others. The fact that Roth negates such rhetoric in his fictional account by exploring the consequences of removing FDR from office attests to the strength of FDR's character as allegorically upholding the discourse of American moral righteousness.

In Lindbergh's 1940, American fascist tendencies are increasingly abounding, to the detriment of main character and focalizer, the secular Jewish child Philip Roth. This novel takes Roosevelt out of the locus of power, asking what might have happened if he had not then embodied America. As a result, the novel should indeed be read as a plot against America's heroic reading of itself: a country where anti-Semitism and racism in general were actually painfully close to the isolationism of more than half of its population in 1940. Roosevelt is thus cast as the allegorical figure holding together both a nation and its congratulatory self-perception in cultural memory. The novel extracts FDR from his historical context, leaving that context an ideological ruin.

Although Franklin Roosevelt is a looming absence in Roth's counterfactual novel, he is represented in relative detail: many of the very personal Roosevelt trivia in the child Philip Roth's awareness are still part of cultural memory and have become more so through the publication of this novel in 2004. *The Plot*

Against America does not only honor old Roosevelt myths but uses them to frame its narrative and bridge the gap between the family history of its child protagonist and world history. Its plot intervenes in history in the most literal way possible: it is a fictional autobiography in which Franklin Roosevelt is beaten in the 1940 elections by Charles Lindbergh. The novel's basic plot revolves around the anti-Semitism young Philip's family is subjected to as soon as Lindbergh, and not Roosevelt, has become president. It is important to note that, while Roth changes the course of history, he is very reticent in changing any actual historical facts other than who became president in 1940. Thus, the isolationist and anti-Semitic things Charles Lindbergh is quoted as saying, he did say in reality, though not of course as president or presidential candidate as he does in the novel. Roth incorporated an extensive list of historical sources and data as an appendix, so as not to create any confusion about what happened historically and what was added by him.

The novel shows how young Philip's knowledge of Roosevelt's personal life helps him to feel represented by his president and helps him to reduce the world to a scale he can cope with. Philip's experience mirrors that of twenty-first century readers: Roosevelt functions as a vehicle for grasping a time and political context that is otherwise incomprehensible. Early on, Philip introduces himself as "a third-grader a term ahead of himself—and an embryonic stamp collector inspired like millions of kids by the country's foremost philatelist, President Roosevelt."[33] Stamps remain important throughout the novel, linking the child, whose identity and personal history is profoundly reflected in his stamp album, with national history, and literally bring it down to his scale and level of comprehension. Thus, the pictures on the stamps—for instance, of American national parks—symbolize for Philip his attachment and belonging to the United States. His later nightmare that each national park picture is overlaid with a giant swastika symbolizes the alienation and exclusion from his home soil he experiences as soon as the atmosphere changes after Lindbergh's election. Similarly, the fact that no US stamp has yet been issued portraying a Jew significantly brings the level of latent anti-Semitism in America home to Philip and the reader. The fact that he cannot part with his stamp portraying Charles Lindbergh in his airplane Spirit of St. Louis suggests even to himself that he, too, despite Lindbergh's overt anti-Semitism, still harbors admiration for the strength and visual attractiveness Lindbergh exudes.

In many ways, Charles Lindbergh in *The Plot Against America* can be read as a foil for Franklin Roosevelt: the fictitious Lindbergh is in some ways obviously very different from FDR, but in other ways actually very similar. Many of the successful media strategies that Lindbergh uses in the book, such as literally appearing out of the blue—dropping from the sky—are actually strategies that Roosevelt also used, famously in 1932 when he flew to Chicago to personally accept his nomination for the presidency by the Democratic National Convention. Lindbergh's attractive media presence, his communicative genius, and his strong personal link with innovation and modernity are reminiscent of FDR. Part of the effect is that the novel suggests that these elements—which also served the charismatic European dictators well—were perhaps as decisive in the reelection of FDR in 1940 as his internationalism. Like FDR, Lindbergh in *The Plot* works hard to personalize the presidency, that is, to use elements of his private life in a public manner to garner sympathy. For instance, Lindbergh's public dealing in the novel with the loss of his son through a kidnapping is comparable to Roosevelt's process of dealing with the aftereffects of polio. Both are presented as losses that have made the president a stronger person who can empathize with others' suffering. Equally, the active role Lindbergh's wife Anne Morrow takes as writer and publicly visible First Lady is reminiscent of Eleanor Roosevelt's position during and after Franklin Roosevelt's presidency.

The novel makes other indirect but obvious references to Roosevelt: for instance, through Philip's cousin Alvin, who, when Lindbergh becomes president, joins the Canadian army and loses his leg fighting in England. He must struggle throughout the rest of the novel, not only with learning to walk using an ill-fitting prosthesis, but also with his own anger and frustration about his fate, and the stigma attached to disability by himself and others. In a similar manner, radio reporter Walter Winchell, who later in the novel becomes presidential candidate, represents and foregrounds the massive social and political power of radio. Historically, Winchell was, like FDR, one of the first public radio figures to develop a successful and charismatic radio style. He was also politically similar to Roosevelt and thus an obvious choice to replace Roosevelt in his fictional absence. Through shifting such defining characteristics of FDR onto other characters in the novel, Roosevelt remains conspicuously present through his best known personal and public emblems.

The novel insinuates that without FDR, America might have become fascist, or at least, that the FDR icon allows Americans in the present to believe that fascism was no factor in 1940s America. In his essay "The Story Behind *The Plot Against America*," Roth acknowledges that it remains important, significant, and by no means coincidental that America did not become fascist when other countries did. Rather, he argues that it could have happened more easily than one tends to think with the benefit of hindsight:

> I imagined something small, really, small enough to be credible, I hoped, that could easily have happened in an American presidential election in 1940, when the country was angrily divided between the Republican isolationists, who, not without reason, wanted no part of a second European war—and who probably represented a slight majority of the populace—and the Democratic interventionists, who didn't necessarily want to go to war either but who believed that Hitler had to be stopped before he invaded and conquered England and Europe was entirely fascist and totally his. Willkie wasn't the Republican to beat Roosevelt in 1940 because Willkie was an interventionist himself. But if Lindbergh had run? With that boyish manly aura of his? With all that glamour and celebrity, with his being virtually the first great American hero to delight America's emerging entertainment society? And with his unshakeable isolationist convictions that committed him to keeping our country out of this horrible war? I don't think it's far-fetched to imagine the election outcome as I do in the book, to imagine Lindbergh's depriving Roosevelt of a third term.[34]

So, what *The Plot Against America* essentially does is bring out, in various ways, the contingency of history. In doing so, it also exposes the way in which icons like FDR tend to be employed to make what we study as history seem more inevitable than it really was. Casting Lindbergh as the World War II president instead, Roth brings out the isolationist and anti-Semitic tendencies that did also exist in the United States at the time, not so much because of what Lindbergh in the novel actually does, but because he releases preexisting popular sentiments. In that sense, the novel dispels or at least questions the popular historical plot that America's "Greatest Generation" was simply good and righteous during the "Good War." In this manner, the novel engages in the memory wars about who gets to tell what story of America's role in the World War II. It does so not by criticizing Roosevelt, but rather by exposing the implicit effect of most uses of the Roosevelt icon, which allow one to believe in a purely heroic United States, in which any brokenness only contributes to its moral uprightness and determination.

Some of the conservative responses the novel received were predictably rabid. Bill Kaufmann, for instance, calls the book "a repellent novel, bigoted and libelous of the dead, dripping with hatred of rural America, of Catholics, of any Middle American who has ever dared stand against the war machine."[35] Taki Theodoracopulos writes: "One cannot suspend disbelief, as fiction requires, when a hero like Lindbergh is besmirched, no matter what Roth says about not trying to send a message. One cannot suspend disbelief when it was American farm boys who died fighting those who were murdering Jews."[36] Although these authors point to an ethical problem inherent in fictionalizing historical characters, Roth's efforts to detail historical events in the novel effectively dismiss their argument. Moreover, the point is not so much that the novel denies America's heroic role in the war, but rather, that it says something about the clear-cut celebratory quality the past tends to assume in the process of becoming "History." Calling to mind Walter Benjamin's storm and chaos in the Angel of History vignette, Roth writes: "Turned wrong way round, the relentless unforeseen was what we schoolchildren studied as 'History,' harmless history, where everything unexpected in its own time is chronicled on the page as inevitable. The terror of the unforeseen is what the science of history hides, turning a disaster into an epic."[37]

Roth, however, in *The Plot Against America*, also does "turn a disaster into an epic" by providing a plot and a consistent narrative, even if that narrative exposes unpleasant traits of 1940s American society. In doing so, Roth shows how a connection with FDR couches historical events more firmly into triumphalist American war memory. However, the way in which Roth tries to reconnect past and present, fiction and history by reinstating FDR in the novel is highly problematic. In terms of plot, it is by far the most contrived and the least credible moment; the need to provide closure and a return to the historical course of events is clearly problematic after the novel's extensive investment in an alternative. The removal of the FDR icon is employed in *The Plot* to expose festering American anti-Semitism in an era whose moral imperfections have been forgotten, in part through FDR allegories. When Roth tries to reinstate the FDR icon as the nation's embodiment, he is not wholly successful; he has not cast FDR, after, as representative of the Greatest Generation. Indeed, *The Plot* suggests that the Greatest Generation as such did not exist, and that FDR acted as a last barrier between the United States and Nazism.

The Golden Age

Gore Vidal, in *The Golden Age* (2000), the last of seven novels that together make up the Narratives of Empire series, also deplores the corruption and fragmentation of American politics. *The Golden Age* ironically deflates the maneuvering of FDR in a way that is almost sadistic to heroic FDR remembrance. Vidal was a Democrat but also eager to deflate mythologized heroes as a historian, although he used fiction to allow himself leeway for speculation that he would not have had in historical research. In *The Golden Age*, a corrupt and power-mongering Roosevelt invites the Japanese attack on Pearl Harbor and deviously engineers his reelection in 1940. The novel describes the years 1939 to 1954 from the perspective of fictional Roosevelt friend Caroline Sanford and her nephew Peter Sanford. While the focalization is supposed to be sympathetic, it is also critical and aware of the hiatus between Roosevelt's public image and his individual character and manipulation. Caroline, for example, reflects on the fragility of her Roosevelt connection: "The nation was littered with former Roosevelt intimates who had been found unusable."[38] Through such comments on FDR's disloyalty to "unusable" friends, Gore Vidal, though a staunch Democrat, resists hagiographic interpretations, favoring to represent Roosevelt as he assumes FDR was seen by contemporaries in Washington.

Through the eyes of Caroline and Peter, Vidal also offers a glimpse no historical monograph could give on the relationship between Franklin and Eleanor Roosevelt:

> Eleanor had been late in joining them. "There has always been something odd about my blood. But the doctor says there's nothing really wrong." As the President wheeled himself past her, he gave her a friendly slap on the bottom. "But what did he have to say about this big fat ass of yours?" Without a pause, Eleanor had said "I'm afraid, dear, you were never mentioned." Even the President had laughed, with every appearance of heartiness; and Caroline had glimpsed another aspect of the Roosevelt relationship. It was the shy Eleanor who held the knife and so was the one to be feared.[39]

Although this passage portrays Eleanor Roosevelt as witty and endearing in a way, it also suggests that it is really ER who—despite appearances—holds power in the relationship. Elsewhere too, it becomes clear how deeply ER is engorged in wielding power over, with, and in lieu of her husband: "Peter was awed by the millions of votes these three men represented; and he watched, again with awe, as Mrs. Roosevelt put her lions through their paces. She spoke to them in a low voice; they listened closely. This was brute power and she was now exerting it."[40]

Although Eleanor Roosevelt is here entirely on top of the party bosses she is commanding, she is also tainted both by her association with them, and by her exertion of power she has not democratically won. Both these passages eroticize ER by representing her as the one holding the whip. In the first instance, this belittles FDR, while in the second, it contributes to his re-nomination in 1939; in both cases, she is the decisive player, not FDR.

Throughout, the novel goes out of its way to debunk Roosevelt's positive and inflated public image and expose the manipulative performance of power. In doing so, Vidal punctures the imperial and glorifying cultural memory of FDR. At the same time, he presents the loss of integrity in politics as regrettable. The FDR icon in this instance is not the heroic representative of a glorious past, legible for Americans in the present and contributing to historical justification for American overseas interventions in conflicts. Rather, Vidal brings out the pettiness and deceitfulness of the historical FDR. Though writing fiction, Vidal does claim a form of historical veracity, leaving the iconic figure disappointingly fallible and unattractive. *The Golden Age*, thus, actually leaves the image of the Greatest Generation unharmed but shows how its usual champion in fact might not deserve his place in cultural memory.

The Golden Age is on some level a conspiracy novel: its plot revolves around Roosevelt's advance knowledge—indeed, conscious provocation—of the Japanese attack at Pearl Harbor. The title refers to the 1940s as a pinnacle moment for America as a central power in the world but also back to the eighteenth century, when the United States came into its own domestically, as an independent former European colony. It refers back to Vidal's earlier novel *Burr*, another counternarrative in which he argues that Thomas Jefferson had illegitimate offspring with his female slave Sally Hemings. Vidal suggests that his novels present the other side, the unheard and unwanted narratives of American history. *The Golden Age* is an ironic reference to undue credit given by officially sanctioned history. The title is also reminiscent of "The Gilded Age."—a term for roughly the 1870s and 1880s, coined by Mark Twain and Charles Dudley Warner in their novel, *The Gilded Age, A Tale of Today* (1873), that satirizes the greed and corruption of politicians. The Gilded Age is their ironic name for the era following the Civil War, marked by seeming success and growing wealth but actually characterized by poverty, immigration problems, and raging corruption. *The Golden Age* reads the 1940s similarly as a supposedly glorious era that is in fact fundamentally—through FDR himself—permeated with corruption. Finally, *The Golden Age* implicitly claims to also be "A Tale of Today." Published in 2000, it is a product of the previously mentioned long 1990s, in which the United States was the unchallenged world hegemon. This period was also superficially a golden age, though in fact plagued by internal and external conflict and impending danger.

Vidal, rightly or wrongly, attempts to lay bare mechanisms of power, politics, and iconification which, despite the vindictiveness of his tone, he essentially seems to deplore. However, by writing a counternarrative that effectively supports a popular conspiracy theory, he also taps into a long Republican tradition of mistrusting and discrediting FDR. In his afterword to the novel, Vidal writes: "It was well known in the whispering gallery of the day that FDR had provoked the Japanese into attacking us. In fact, our pre-eminent historian, Charles A. Beard, was on the case as early as 1941 with *President Roosevelt and the Coming of War*. Needless to say, apologists for empire have been trying for fifty years to erase him."[41]

The whispering gallery in Washington, DC, is indeed the key location in which *The Golden Age* is set, and the novel speculates about what it is one might have heard there. However, the conspiracy narrative Vidal presents is also one that has been repeated like an incantation in Republican circles ever since. The notion of a whispering gallery thus assumes a new meaning. It is not just a place where one hears whispered the truth that never makes it into the history books but also one in which repetitive sounds create a rhythmic babble, a right-wing antithesis to the similarly ritualized tale of the "apologists for empire" whom Vidal here upbraids.

Conspiracy narratives about Pearl Harbor have indeed flourished since the early 1940s, eerily echoing one another.[42] Although such accounts are plenty and are often successful through many reprints, they are essentially very similar in narrative structure, phrases, and tone. In these books, the same sequence of events is conjectured to have taken place as Vidal lets occur in his novel. These are counternarratives: not only in the sense of narratives that go against the dominant reading but also in the sense that they defy further narrativization. They cast FDR as an icon of essentially undemocratic and thus un-American Democratic machinations.

The Golden Age, however, is different from these echoic whispering gallery arguments, not only because it is a novel, but because the novel is mildly sympathetic of FDR even while it exposes him as an Emperor-like leader with imperial ambitions not unlike Hitler's and Mussolini's. Vidal does not reject politics itself but its corruption. In contrast, most other conspiracy theories, over and above disliking a big government imperial president like FDR, express a wholesale mistrust of all politics and the state as such. As a result, they do not deplore but actually relish the demolition of FDR as a hagiographic icon of Americanness. The fact that FDR continues to function as a gratifying icon to hammer on, however, speaks to the icon's flexibility in allowing for a range of different kinds of allegories.

Roosevelt serves as a ruin that continues to invite ritual destruction. For FDR conspiracy theorists, any claim that something or someone is like FDR (or like the New Deal) invokes a kind of automatic rejection: an intriguing example of what Michael Rothberg terms *multidirectionality*.[43] Practically any government involvement can be interpreted as yet another version of FDR's double-dealing (as conspiracy theorists see it) in the case of the war engagement or the New Deal. Neither of these are the original event or political decision that "triggered" it, but they are key notes in an incantation—sung by the neoconservative movement in the 1980s, and more recently by the Tea Party—that is itself part of the fabric of American society.

FDR as a Cultural Icon for the United States

This chapter has fleshed out how FDR became a cultural icon for the United States, particularly in the context of World War II, by examining the metaphors and allegories that were instrumental in the process. An easy complement to the portrayal of the Roosevelts as "parents to the nation" has been the popular notion of the "Greatest Generation," since Roosevelt is often viewed both as an exemplary individual member and as an embodiment of this generation.[44] The relationship between FDR and the Greatest Generation came up in one form or another in each of the three films and both of the novels discussed. Each of the films hinges, albeit in different ways, on the comparison between a wounded America and a disabled president. The films cast FDR as a material metaphor for the United States, utilizing him as a narrative prosthesis that justifies the storytelling. The novels, on the other hand, show how the metaphor can easily break down. *The Plot Against America* holds on to the dominant story of FDR's heroism but shows the Greatest Generation as less morally unflappable than it may seem in hindsight. *The Golden Age*, in contrast, retains the positive image of the Greatest Generation but presents FDR as less saintly than most cultural texts do.

The films I have discussed are examples of mass-mediated narratives about FDR that function as prosthetic memories to their audiences. In each of these films, concrete narratives of Roosevelt's disease and disability (involving actual prostheses, such as wheelchair, crutches, and leg braces) demonstrate what happens on a conceptual level: FDR's disabled body becomes a material metaphor for the wounded nation. The silences kept by Roosevelt and his staff have provided room for filmmakers and their audiences to interpret traumas that they overtly attribute to Roosevelt as actually standing in for more collective ones. Roosevelt's silence about his wheelchair in particular means that it has come to lend itself well as a prosthetic site where other trauma narratives can be adapted. This process is indeed useful, but not in the laudatory way Landsberg suggests: it is useful instead as a band-aid or a cover, a means to create a sense of wholeness without actually addressing the trauma at the heart of the matter. The use of material metaphor as band-aid can also hide other difficult issues, such as the potentially explosive opposition of interests. In a national context in which American identity as a widely shared concept risks falling apart, such bland FDR remembrances perhaps help the nation to retain a sense of wholeness and avoid conflict. If so, Roosevelt would probably have been happy with the current emplotment of his disability, however secretive he may have been about it at the time.

Through both allegory and narrative prosthesis, FDR functions as an icon for several aspects of (or takes on) American identity. These aspects include the canonical belief that with grit and courage, dreams can come true regardless of circumstances; that hardship should primarily be understood as a test of character; that fairness and democracy must prevail; and that the United States has been assigned exceptional abilities and a special role in helping democracy prevail. In both of the novels discussed, FDR is an allegorical figure who either bears up a positive story of the United States' role during the war (*The Plot Against America*) or exemplifies the corruption of those in power in a context that is popularly remembered as "great" and generally selfless (*The Golden Age*). In the films discussed, FDR functions as a material metaphor for the United States, both at the time in which they were set and in the present of their making.

In fictional works, a material metaphor is often a narrative device: a character's literal crutch, often bearing up the storytelling itself. But such works, especially films, can themselves also generate "memories" that the viewers have not lived through in a literal sense, which can then become part of cultural memory. Films such as *Pearl Harbor* and *Hyde Park on Hudson* have framed FDR not just as a user of prosthetic devices but also as himself a narrative device (a narrative prosthesis) for the process of remembering the past. It is primarily through his role as a material metaphor in cultural memory that FDR functions as a cultural icon for the United States. The dominant version of FDR in cultural memory embodies, prosthetics and all, a dominant vision of the United States.

A Rooseveltian Century?

In *Time 100* of April 13, 1998, one of the most authoritative American historians, Arthur Schlesinger Jr., assertively and eloquently espoused an interpretation of Franklin Delano Roosevelt as a key player in twentieth-century world politics: "Take a look at our present world. It is manifestly not Adolf Hitler's world. His Thousand-Year Reich turned out to have a brief and bloody run of a dozen years. It is manifestly not Joseph Stalin's world. That ghastly world self-destructed before our eyes. Nor is it Winston Churchill's world. Empire and its glories have long since vanished into history. The world we live in today is Franklin Roosevelt's world."[1]

In 1998—arguably at the height of global American power—Schlesinger read four major ideologies as having vied for "our present world" in the 1930s and 1940s, each with a historic statesman as its embodiment. Nazism and Hitler; communism and Stalin; imperialism and Churchill; and finally, victoriously, freedom and democracy, with Franklin Roosevelt—the personification of America—as their proponent. Hitler's "Thousand-Year Reich" was limited to the "dozen years" it turned out to last in reality. The "ghastly" quality of "Joseph Stalin's world," up to and including its self-destruction, both highlights communism's presumably inherent harmfulness and calls to mind the ghost (or specter) associated with it. "Churchill's world," shrouded in nostalgia, has simply and passively "vanished," or floated away. The surviving paradigm for Schlesinger is Franklin Roosevelt's. As if to hammer home that that paradigm reigns around the globe, Schlesinger's final short sentence starts and ends with "world."

When I first encountered this quotation, it was 2012—no longer 1998—and things had, of course, changed. After the attacks on the Twin Towers and the Pentagon on September 11, 2001, "this" was perhaps less "Roosevelt's World" than Schlesinger had claimed in 1998. While one can debate the magnitude and nature of the paradigm change that happened between 1998 and 2012, certainly the American triumphalism of the 1990s—after the fall of the Soviet Union and before 9/11—had ended. However, it is not just the role of the

United States in the world that has changed dramatically but also the outlook of the presidency. So, at the end of this book, I think it's necessary to ask: what specific remembrance of Roosevelt's world does Schlesinger allude to, and what does that remembrance forget? If on some level the world was in fact Franklin Roosevelt's in 1998, then was this still the case in 2020? Was Donald Trump's world also Franklin Roosevelt's? Is Joe Biden's world again Roosevelt's? That last question will have to be answered later, but I will discuss the others here.

Schlesinger, in his invocation of Roosevelt's world, seems to rather easily buy into the notion of "the American Century," an expression ushered into American thought in 1941 by Henry Luce in *Life* magazine. In Luce's essay, which is essentially an exhortation for the United States to get involved in World War II, the American Century is a prescriptive term, an aspiration Luce perhaps hoped to make more attainable by making it more explicit. The article explains what elements of American culture the United States is morally bound to export globally: "What can we say and foresee about an American Century? . . . It must be a sharing with all peoples of our Bill of Rights, our Declaration of Independence, our Constitution, our magnificent industrial products, our technical skills." In Luce's formulation, which both predicts the future and lays out America's duties to the world, the term practically becomes a twentieth-century reformulation of the notion of Manifest Destiny: now that the continent has achieved its preordained destiny, the project continues in a different manner and on a novel scale. This did, to a large extent, happen, certainly in the years from 1941 to 2001, the period Andrew Bacevich has termed "the short American Century."[2]

Because I am critical of the assumption implicit in Luce's phrase—that the ideas and ideologies exported by the United States are always benign—I tend to steer clear of the expression. But I do find useful the notion of *short* or *long* centuries as popularized by Eric Hobsbawm and Ilya Ehrenburg in their work on the long nineteenth century (1789–1914) and the short twentieth century (1914–1991). The idea of a period of about a century that encompasses a specific paradigm—but that is not exactly one hundred years, from one round number to the next—can indeed be useful. Perhaps there has been something of a Rooseveltian century, starting in 1901 with Theodore Roosevelt's succession to the presidency after McKinley's death, and ending, I would argue, not in 2001 but in 2016. Theodore Roosevelt historian Serge Ricard has made the same claim in his conclusion to *A Companion to Theodore Roosevelt*.[3] Ricard specifically terms it a Rooseveltian century to stress the extent to which Franklin Roosevelt has privileged Theodore Roosevelt's imperialist model of the United States' role in the world over Woodrow Wilson's more internationalist model.

Until 2016, the claim that the current world order is Franklin Roosevelt's continued to ring true. This was because of the United States' continued cultural and military dominance in the world, because of the unquestioned power of US-supported global organizations such as the United Nations, and later the G8 and G20, and because of the perceived universality of the Four Freedoms and the Declaration of Human Rights. Sixteen years after Schlesinger made this claim, Ken Burns's *The Roosevelts: An Intimate History* in 2014 effectively resumed and revived that frame. This view of Rooseveltian America as the world's moral high ground also fits perfectly with the ever-popular view of the United States continuing to occupy the pedestal John Winthrop put it on when he pronounced his colony a "City upon a Hill" in 1630. Following a tradition started by Winthrop, Schlesinger's "the world we live in today is Franklin Roosevelt's world" reinforced the idea that the United States, embodied in this case by Franklin Roosevelt, was the world's moral focus.

Luce—in his moral exhortation to spread American ideas—uncritically embraces the position (shared in part by Schlesinger) that all ideas and ideologies the United States exports are positive, or are only worth mentioning in so far as they are. Schlesinger employs Franklin Roosevelt's iconic status to cement this point. He casts the United States and Roosevelt, Great Britain and Churchill, the USSR and Stalin, and Nazi-Germany and Hitler as each completely disjointed and different from the others, as if these countries' central ideological characteristics are mutually exclusive of all the others. Of course, this is not the case. There is a great deal of historical and ideological overlap between several of the six possible pairings, certainly including the United States and Nazi Germany.

Viewed through the lens of disability history, Luce and Schlesinger's celebratory line of reasoning is exactly what led both contemporaries and later historians to overlook what Mitchell and Snyder have termed the "Eugenic Atlantic." Eugenic science—as they and others have shown—was a truly transnational effort, at least between 1860 and 1950. In the 1930s, Nazi Germany picked up a wide range of theories, methods, and techniques that had been codeveloped in Great Britain, France, and the United States, and that had already been implemented in the United States. This fact is part of the "American" or "Rooseveltian" century or world, but surely not in the sense that the rhetoric by Luce and Schlesinger aims to emphasize.

The Plot Against America Revisited

Even after September 11, 2001, and the credit crisis of 2008 to 2009, Schlesinger's triumphalist interpretation of FDR's place in today's world continued to occupy a dominant strand in American cultural memory. But a glimpse of a world that is explicitly not Roosevelt's was also already embedded in one of the novels analyzed in this book—Philip Roth's *The Plot Against America*. I offer a reading of this novel in the context of the momentous events of 2016: specifically, the election of Donald Trump and the referendum in the United Kingdom to leave the European Union. A 2020 HBO TV miniseries based on *The Plot Against America* clearly emphasizes the resonances between the imagined candidacy of America First candidate Charles A. Lindbergh, and 2016 Republican candidate Donald Trump. *The Plot Against America* is seeing a revival in popularity, in large part because it presents a dystopian world that is particularly disturbing in the present political moment. Roth's book and the HBO series offer a new "use" of FDR memory: not as a glorification of all things American but as a warning of American undercurrents that have existed for a long time and that may, or already have, come to the fore again.[4]

One concrete purpose of reading, writing, and studying fiction, crudely put, is that it can offer an imaginary space for thinking through scenarios that might happen or could have happened. It is in a sense a laboratory for alternate realities. It is true that the winners write the history books, but fiction allows for other perspectives to be heard and scrutinized. Philip Roth's *The Plot Against America*—at the time of its publication in 2004, rather unconvincingly read as a roman à clef for the events of 9/11—offers an illuminating perspective on the 2016 general elections and the years of the Trump presidency. Of course, this parallel is as unintentional as any parallel with 9/11 might have been. Nevertheless, it is still worth pursuing, because Roth is onto something important in his destabilization of the notion that the Rooseveltian paradigm was inevitable, undefeatable, or entirely great. At the time of the book's publication, "The Plot" in the title was easily taken to mean "the conspiracy" against America. But since the book is hardly about a real conspiracy from the outside against an innocent America, I would suggest "the plot against America" should be read as "the story" or "the narrative" against America's inflated and self-congratulatory image of itself. *The Plot Against America* is a fictional history that "reads" America against the grain. It offers a counternarrative to the American belief, voiced by Schlesinger, that while Europe was in the 1930s and 1940s overrun by Nazism, communism, and the dregs of colonial imperialism, America was the world's beacon of freedom and tolerance and its arsenal of democracy.

As discussed in chapter 6, *The Plot Against America* revolves around a fictional scenario: instead of Franklin D. Roosevelt, the novel portrays Nazi-friendly Charles Lindbergh being elected president of the United States. In reality, Charles Lindbergh was the aviator who first crossed the Atlantic Ocean during a solo flight in 1927. A blue-eyed, all-American hero who fanatically advocated American isolationism, Lindbergh was a fan of Adolf Hitler and had openly anti-Semitic views. He was spokesperson for the isolationist America First Committee in 1940 and 1941. While Lindbergh never actually ran for president, the Republican Party did consider the option. At the America First rally that escalated most severely—incidentally, on September 11, 1941—Lindbergh said about American Jews: "Their greatest danger to this country lies in their large ownership and influence in our motion pictures, our press, our radio, and our government." He thus publicly cited an anti-Semitic trope of Jews dominating finance and media in a conspiracy against Americans "of honesty and vision."

In Roth's novel, Charles Lindbergh does decide to run for president in 1940. Campaigning from his very own airplane—much like Trump did during the 2016 campaign—the fictional Lindbergh wins the elections with speeches that the historical Lindbergh used a year later and is inaugurated as president early in 1941. This isolationist swing in Roth's novel leads to an enormous surge in anti-Semitic sentiment among Americans. In reality, the United States, of course, did not make this swing, although probably more than half of the American population did at one point oppose American involvement in World War II. In the novel, Lindbergh's Nazi-sympathizing rhetoric unleashes massive violence against Jews; the secular Jewish Roth family and particularly their neighbors, the Wishnows, are among those targeted. While it is clear that Roth's Lindbergh himself would not encourage anyone to lynch Jews, he does, through his rhetoric, implicitly give permission to the expression of virulent anti-Semitism. This is a point that the HBO series stresses, presumably because of its resonance with Trump's handling of neo-Nazis among his sympathizers.

Even though *The Plot* is fiction, Roth is, in effect, showing us how much anti-Semitism there really was in the United States in the 1930s and 1940s (and well into the 1960s). In hindsight, and with the cultural memory of America's heroic role in World War II, it may seem as if the United States was always on the right side of history. But the novel suggests that just below the surface, all the social and cultural forces to incite the exclusion and even extermination of Jews were present in the United States, as they were in Europe, although they did not come to the fore. Although the novel does not explicitly focus on eugenics, or the Eugenic Atlantic, it is actually fairly cognizant of the role disease and disability play in the transatlantic nightmare that comes home to the child Philip's Newark neighborhood. Philip's cousin Alvin, having lost a leg, returns from voluntary military service in Europe with the Canadian army, and all but drowns in his struggle to come to terms with this. It is after the father in the Wishnow family has died of cancer (or, it is rumored, suicide) that the Wishnows are especially targeted by the anti-Jewish regime. This targeting consists of their forced relocation to a rural area in Kentucky, essentially an attempt to reeducate them to be healthier and more like white Americans. The novel also points to the transatlanticism that characterized eugenic science: Lindbergh owes his heroism to his literal transatlantic flight and intellectual rapport with Nazi-Germany's leadership.

Roth has stressed that he did not mean his novel to be a historical analogy. While there are striking parallels—not just between Lindbergh and Roosevelt but also between Lindbergh and Trump—the differences are always much greater. Nonetheless, it seems meaningful that Roth's foil for Franklin Roosevelt, Charles Lindbergh, was the spokesman for the America First Committee. "America First" was a rallying cry that was steadily ignored by post-war US presidents across the political spectrum—hardly remembered except as a minor counterpoint to the drive of dominant history—but it came to the forefront of attention again through Donald Trump's inaugural address in January 2017.

Charles Lindbergh and Donald Trump are products of different historical contexts, but they embody the same xenophobic isolationist movement within American political culture. Roth clearly shows that this movement does not come out of the blue, even if swooping out of the blue is a visual style shared by Lindbergh and Trump (and by FDR, for that matter). Like Roth's Lindbergh, Trump has brought to the surface—and given permission to—huge shifts in what many people allow themselves to do and say when it comes to excluding minorities. There is a fair amount of evidence that, in his private life, Roosevelt was wont to make anti-Semitic jokes, and he no doubt held prejudices about Jews (as he did about other cultural and racial minorities). However, in the early years of World War II, he did not give permission for the anti-Semitism that existed to be publicly expressed. If we take seriously the alternative posed in *The Plot*, it becomes clear how important that may have been in shoring up anti-Jewish violence. In the United States, as in Germany, the war industry's grinding into gear eventually ended the Depression, but in the United States the power of mass industry did not inspire industrialized genocide.

The US intervention in the war in Europe makes it easy to forget that discrimination, forced sterilization of those deemed "unfit," racial segregation, and anti-Semitism were common in the United States at the time. Even so, the America First Committee was suspect. Lindbergh's speech in Des Moines on September 11, 1941, was widely considered to be outrageous, although it put forward a view that was fairly widespread. The same political current, still eagerly invested in aggressively scapegoating specific ethnic and religious minorities, came to the surface again in 2016 and still employed the phrase "America First." The big difference lay in the fact that this time, the actual president ushered in this movement, triggering and making visible undemocratic and racist forces that during the 1940s had remained largely invisible. The president's role became abundantly clear during the "Unite the Right" rally in Charlottesville on August 11 and 12, 2017, and on the many occasions when Trump has invited— and smilingly nodded during—choruses of supporters demanding to "lock up" political opponents, particularly when female and/or nonwhite.

I would not argue that Philip Roth predicted the rise of Trumpism. But— within the laboratory space of narrative fiction—*The Plot Against America* did consider, well before it happened, what a Trump-like figure could do as president. Of course, if we heed Roth's interpretation and its parallel with the present, then it follows that the world we have lived in after 2016 was no longer Franklin Roosevelt's world.

The national moral of being an example for the world, once voiced by John Winthrop, was repeated often by presidents who considered themselves "Rooseveltian." This included Ronald Reagan, who explained his vision of the city upon a hill as "a city with free ports that hummed with commerce and creativity, and if there had to be city walls, the walls had doors, and the doors were open to anyone with the will and the heart to get here." The moral imperative that presidents until Trump have embraced was to be open to the world, both in terms of receiving and sending out people, goods, and values. Donald Trump simultaneously echoed and forcefully rejected this idea in his inaugural address: "We assembled here today our issuing a new decree to be heard in every city, in every foreign capital, and in every hall of power, from this day forward: a new vision will govern our land, from this day forward, it's going to be only America first."

Trump's rhetoric is a departure from Roosevelt's vision of the United States as a world-leading actor on the stage of international politics, invoked many times in the decades since. A perspective similar to Roosevelt's was borne out in the many uses of the moral and military success of the American intervention in World War II as an argument in favor of American intervention in conflicts overseas in the second half of the twentieth century and the first fifteen years of the twenty-first. During the second half of the twentieth century, and the first fifteen years of the twenty-first, foreign-policy hawks have often used the moral and military success of the American intervention in World War II as an argument in favor of American intervention in conflicts overseas. Former Bush speechwriter David Frum's coinage "Axis of Evil," for instance, consciously echoed the "Axis powers" of World War II, drawing a parallel to rhetorically justify the War on Terror. Frum wrote about this in his book *The Right Man: The Surprise Presidency of George W. Bush*: "By identifying the Iraqi and Iranian regimes with the Axis of the 1940s, Bush was challenging all those European governments that had denounced the rather pallid menace of Jörg Haider in Austria to join him in confronting the transplanted fascism of the Islamic world."[5] Politically speaking, the association between fascism and the Islamic world made no sense. But in rhetorical terms, "Axis of Evil" did sound like the Axis powers from World War II, and the term offered a logical extrapolation of the endlessly echoed parallel between Pearl Harbor and 9/11. In both cases, the contrasting body was "the free world," an international coalition led by the president of the United States. Within this frame, Franklin Roosevelt continued—until Trump's inauguration—to operate as archetype and blueprint for modern American presidents with enormous domestic and international authority.

Reading Schlesinger against the Grain

Schlesinger's statement, which he made without any sense of irony, invites reading against the grain in another sense. By putting Hitler, Stalin, Churchill, and Roosevelt next to one another in his comparison, Schlesinger actually highlighted not just the contrasts but also the similarity between these leaders. The anaphora—presumably intended to point out that these four leaders, with their radically different ideologies, were competing for the same ground (often literally)—actually stresses that similarity. However different their ideologies were, Hitler, Stalin, Churchill, and Roosevelt had worldviews that were, to some extent, comparable aesthetically and in practical terms. Although their utopian ideals differed a great deal, they each believed that the organization of society—perhaps even of the world—was one vast project demanding a large-scale and integrated approach. Their aesthetics took different forms, but grand architectural and infrastructural projects were on each of their agendas, and their approaches to the mass media also had much in common. One reason why FDR was so quick to grasp how serious the Nazi threat to European and world peace was that he knew Germany well; he had attended public school there in his childhood. FDR had an unusually profound understanding of, though no political affinity with, Hitler's worldview.

While their politics were fundamentally different, there existed real overlap between FDR and the other three leaders' autofabrication styles, particularly in their visual and aural rhetoric and their use of modern mass media. FDR, like Hitler and Stalin, believed in developing unprecedentedly large employment programs, often creating enormous bureaucratic and infrastructural apparatuses. He was also convinced of the suitability of film, social realist poster art, and radio addresses for government communication and propaganda. Churchill and FDR both had intimate, personal, and persuasive radio styles. While Churchill's colonial imperialism was indeed outdated, the more Rooseveltian, still-current American forms of cultural diplomacy and the colonization implicit in US-driven global capitalism are hardly less imperialistic in nature.

FDR Remembrance as Eugenic Erasure

The Eugenic Atlantic—termed thus by Mitchell and Snyder, after Paul Gilroy's coinage of the Black Atlantic—is another element that the United States, Great Britain, and Germany have shared historically and, in many ways, codeveloped. This element is crucial in the context of FDR memory and forgetting. Eugenic science arose in the nineteenth century both in Europe and in the United States, as part of often progressive movements to improve individual people's health and the health of the nation. One of the most fundamental ideas underlying the eugenic movement on both sides of the Atlantic was that people whose body or mind were somehow considered "defective" were to be deplored, and such biological inferiority should be mended and prevented both at the individual and on the national level. As might be expected, immigrants, the poor, women, and people who were not white (and all intersections of such categories) were far more likely to be assigned the label of defective.

Disability was in a sense the most basic category of exclusion: being brown, sexually "aberrant," or uneducated could easily contribute to one's construction as "feebleminded" or "unproductive." This exclusionary branding of some people as biologically inferior, and therefore "other," ran parallel with hierarchies established earlier between different "races": in much the same way as racial others were consistently construed as "primitive," eugenic scientists saw physically or cognitively disabled people as "degenerate" human beings. While stigma was unevenly distributed across demographic categories, the underlying assumption was that having a physical or mental disability was a defect that automatically disqualified one as a worthy member of society. The likelihood of this designation increased "naturally" when the person involved was also poor or a member of a minority group.

Eugenics was developed in the late nineteenth and early twentieth century in Europe and the United States simultaneously in a transatlantic and transnational collective effort, despite the fact that the motivation was often nationalist: to secure a healthy body politic and improve the national stock. A distinction was often made between "positive" eugenics (that stimulated specific desirable pairings, and encouraged those couples to have many children) and "negative" eugenics (that sought to prevent those deemed defective from reproducing). Negative eugenics in the United States was most clearly expressed in the enactment of compulsory sterilization laws for the "unfit" in thirty-one states from 1907 onward. Although the law was overturned in 1921 in Indiana (the state where it was first introduced in 1907) by the state's Supreme Court, the Virginia Sterilization Act of 1924 was upheld by the US Supreme Court in 1927. Later, in 1933, the first sterilization law in Nazi Germany was directly based on the US ones.[6] While initially the Nazis considered American sterilization (and anti-miscegenation) laws to be unduly harsh, these policies were adopted and, in following years, escalated into "euthanasia" programs, which in turn constituted the sites in which the Nazis developed and practiced the efficient and supposedly humane killing techniques that would later be employed in mass extermination camps.[7] American eugenics did not directly inspire mass killing, and Jews had been persecuted in Europe long before either the eugenics movement or the Industrial Revolution, but not to see the role of American eugenics laws in the early years of the Third Reich is to overlook something important.

Mitchell and Snyder, as well as Michael Rembis, argue that while the Nazis racialized eugenics (as others also did earlier and elsewhere), the transatlantic scientific and political communities largely focused on disability. The focus in the Nuremberg Trials (and among historians) has been on the genocide of Jews, Roma, Sinti, and homosexuals, and less on that of disabled people, leading to what Mitchell and Snyder call *eugenics erasure*. Transatlantic eugenic science was both so large and diffuse that it was hard to "see" as a key driving force in specific situated contexts, and, at the same time, it was relatively diverse in terms of theorization and execution (particularly in different parts of the United States). Eugenics and ableism were an intrinsic part of the Holocaust, a fact that has often been overlooked in memory and historiography. The often willfully produced failure to see and represent disability, which has come up in various ways in this book—combined with the many ways in which disabled key players like FDR passed as nondisabled—have fed into this erasure.

During his political career and presidency, FDR benefited from his many privileges, in particular because they enabled him to pass as nondisabled or to project his disability as a minor issue. Because he was himself a wealthy product and proponent of American Progressivism and not its object, he was hardly classed as "unfit" or in need of "merciful" exclusion or institutionalization. As such, the celebratory cultural memory of Franklin Roosevelt is arguably itself part and parcel of the eugenics erasure that Mitchell and Snyder signal.

Particularly telling is the way in which FDR's disability was initially obscured in memorial representations but later stressed and interpreted as the reason why FDR could "[lift] a great people back to their feet and set America to march again toward its destiny"[8] or how "in America you are measured for what you are and what you have achieved, not for what you have lost."[9] These strands of FDR's autofabrication (silencing the disability) and remembrance (celebrating it as a special quality) effectively contributed to the eugenics erasure that occurred both during FDR's presidency, and in the historiography and cultural memory of the period. Focusing on a positive remembrance of one otherwise entirely privileged man's disability can help to forget the widespread and habitual mistreatment of other disabled people in the United States and their outright murder in Nazi Germany.

Schlesinger's representation of "Roosevelt's world" is one that neither sees his disability as relevant, nor attends to the fact that the American context that produced Roosevelt's world also coproduced the eugenics that Hitler carried to its extreme. Ironically, FDR here seems to have become more than a narrative prosthesis for a particularly self-congratulatory narrative of American war exceptionalism: he is also a narrative device to assist in the cultural forgetting of the eugenic Atlantic.

So, Schlesinger's conception of "Roosevelt's World" in 1997 embraces the idea that the America First movement and American Nazi sympathies had never been a serious factor in American politics; a point that Philip Roth disputes and that the 2020 series of *The Plot Against America* emphasizes. When applied more specifically to the cultural memory of FDR and American disability history, Schlesinger's reading, which is also employed by Clinton, becomes even more untenable. By embracing FDR as an embodiment of American righteousness in treating the disabled fairly, FDR is effectively used as narrative prosthesis to gloss over the painful historical fact that Roosevelt's, Hitler's, and Churchill's world shared a deeply problematic and habitually erased eugenics history. FDR's role as an icon in cultural memory gives leeway to forget this history. When the icon is thus used, the erasure is reproduced.

FDR, a Cultural Icon

The image of Franklin Roosevelt as an icon and architect of a modern America prevails in American cultural memory in some form or another, even among haters. Several factors have conspired to lead to FDR's position as an icon of America, which I have discussed in this book. Some of these were generated in the first place by FDR himself, as a historical figure shaping his own public image and future remembrance, while others are the product of a later cultural environment that could appropriate the FDR icon to meet a particular need in the present. But mostly, these two driving factors of FDR's iconic remembrance coincide, an effect he steered toward, although sheer luck was no doubt also involved. His efforts to associate himself with modern media and technology have ensured in many cases that he seems unexpectedly contemporary in later contexts: for instance, as a president who smiles in photographs or who habitually travels by airplane. At the same time, although he actually was modern in associating himself strongly with radio, this medium was soon overtaken by television in importance. Roosevelt may thus be considered both the first modern media president and, as the first really successful radio president, a precursor to the more visual mass media that characterized the rest of the twentieth century.

In style, tone, and aims, Roosevelt may also be considered antithetical to the social media ecosystem that has taken over the realm of journalism and presidential communication since the 2010s. After all, if Franklin Roosevelt may be said to have catalyzed the formation of an American imagined community as described by Benedict Anderson—in which the majority of Americans would listen to the president at the same time through millions of radios—Donald Trump's use of Twitter constitutes an entirely different intervention in the public sphere. Arguably, Trump's tweets and his social media dressing down of political opponents (or random other people) function as means to rile up and entertain a group of close supporters while alienating "the rest." His social media messages serve to fragment any imagined community that has managed to survive into the era of partisan media networks and polarizing social media platforms.

Franklin Roosevelt was not only an important president but also an unusually successful cultural icon. He was astute at presenting himself—both to his contemporaries and to future memory—as open and visible, an approachable and authentic leader, while simultaneously veiling his less mediagenic aspects and acts. He may have learned to do this, and to shape how he was seen, from passing as nondisabled, but in any case, he was an expert at guiding attention away from the less-picturesque exertion of the executive power at his personal discretion. As discussed in the first three chapters, various factors in FDR's presidency and performance can be identified that explain his self-production as a cultural icon.

Roosevelt was particularly successful at autofabrication: the culture and environment that shaped him as an individual might not have seen in him the most viable candidate for the presidency, but that situation also provided space for him to take the initiative in defining the parameters of his position at an early stage. He then continued to assertively construct his public image. While Roosevelt geared this public image primarily toward making himself appear attractive to his audiences, this image gave a strong impression of congruence with his innate personality.

Roosevelt's constructed authenticity was coproduced by a wide range of public relations specialists, speech writers, political aides, cabinet members, and pioneers of public opinion polling. Together they created the FDR icon, both as a public image and as a voice for the nation, simultaneously representing the individual FDR and the collective national body that had elected him. FDR and his team achieved this through allowing different modalities of his voice to amalgamate: his literal voice synecdochically represented his individual body, and his collectively authored official voice metonymically constructed him as a mass-mediated persona. The enmeshing of these literal and figurative voices is indeed a concrete effect of Roosevelt's autofabrication.

FDR's collective autofabrication machine had grown out of a savvy collective effort to manage his passing as nondisabled. This autofabrication effort also influenced both future remembrance and cultural memory, mostly positively, though not always in the ways FDR may have intended. The setup of the

Franklin D. Roosevelt Presidential Library FDR built between 1938 and 1941 in Hyde Park, New York, elucidates the difference between remembrance and cultural memory. The first floor is an FDR museum, curated initially by Roosevelt himself to showcase his collections, gifts, and letters he had received. As such, it is a carefully composed selection of objects and documents that he and his staff chose for him to be remembered by. The second floor houses the archive, which contains the less curated body of FDR's presidential and personal papers. The archive, while accessible to the public, is not visited by most tourists and is not overly accessible to disabled people. The first floor offers a remembrance practice: one that has changed since the 1940s but that has always remained celebratory of FDR. Its focus is more explicitly on remembrance than when it opened; it has also become more experiential in nature. The second floor represents FDR's contribution to cultural memory: the broader, more serendipitous collection of memories and traces of the past that can feed into the further negotiation of remembrance.

Both remembrance practices and cultural memory made space for the depoliticization of FDR's cultural legacy; a depoliticization that is all but apolitical. Because FDR seemed a nonpartisan and practical searcher for consensus, he precluded a great deal of political agonism. Indeed, because FDR was so efficacious at turning cultural heritage preservation into a habitual federal engagement, since the early 1940s it has no longer seemed surprising that his own house and archive would be federally preserved and managed cultural heritage, that have instituted a range of remembrance practices. Other federally created sites also became indexically representative of FDR and therefore contributed to his position in cultural memory.

The New Deal, FDR's most important political program, has itself become so iconic that it indexes and typifies FDR more than the reverse. The phrase "New Deal" has remained popular in culture and politics. It has been imbued with new content to the point that a "New Deal" functions as a container concept indicating something novel and vast. The most recent case in point is the Green New Deal championed by New York Congresswoman Alexandria Ocasio-Cortez, which involves a comprehensive package of far-reaching measures to combat climate change, to divide its impact more equally, and to reduce economic inequality. The Green New Deal does share with Roosevelt's New Deal a progressive bent; to call it a New Deal, in this case, not only stresses the novelty of the program but also the political tradition in which it stands. Since the 1970s, the welfare state and many of the other provisions FDR foresaw in his vision for a Second Bill of Rights have steadily been curtailed. A

Green New Deal would reinvigorate those provisions through elements such as the creation of a new nationwide clean power grid.

In the decades since his death, FDR has been represented in cultural artifacts most prominently as the winner of World War II, the international champion of democracy and human rights, but also as modernizer of the welfare state and emancipator of people with disabilities. I have identified these themes as the most noticeable categories in representations of FDR in the period from 1945 until 2015. Each theme has evolved over time, mainly as a result of cultural needs for new interpretations of the past: needs based primarily on developments in the present. Nevertheless, collectively they encompass the majority of Roosevelt representations that were widely disseminated in the period of 1945 to 2016. More importantly, they each point to some of the key mechanisms by which FDR has become such a popular cultural icon in American memory.

Cultural artifacts remembering the New Deal have progressively depoliticized the Roosevelt icon—a trend FDR himself instigated. As I have argued on the basis of two diachronic case studies, this depoliticization happened in two ways, through an increasing focus on FDR as a person and away from the political aspects of the New Deal, and by creating progressively ritualistic media customs, invoking the First Hundred Days as a presidential communication and media practice without referencing their actual political impact. In representations of World War II, FDR is often given the role of an allegorical figure or a material metaphor through the emplotment of his disability.

While many knew that FDR's legs were paralyzed, very few people were aware that he used a wheelchair; the wheelchair only made its entrance in cultural memory later on. Such memories nonetheless seem authentic, because even if few people ever saw him in a wheelchair, he did use one, and in later cultural artifacts he is always portrayed with one. This artificial memory is credible in part because remembering FDR's disability and the wheelchair fulfills a cultural desire in the present. An FDR icon that relies on prosthetic devices Roosevelt employed can embody both national traumas and conquests in the cultural imagination of the United States, as well as confirm the potency of its technological solutions. If FDR was in some way a regal figure, the wheelchair was his throne, the object that empowered him and showed this power. FDR might have rightly considered the wheelchair as a risk to his vigorous and masculine public image, at the time, but it now operates as a powerful symbol of FDR's—and by extension the United States'—ability to resolve internal instability, as well as to a vigorous and virile can-do mentality.

Finally, FDR's plasticity was key to his achievement in shaping himself as a vehicle for a wide range of changing narratives in American memory. The FDR icon remains attractive because it is highly malleable and thus able to suit the needs and ideologies of many different audiences over time and in the present. Schlesinger's claim that "the world we live in today is Franklin Roosevelt's world"—a deeply troubling statement in 1998, and even more so after the end of the long twentieth century in 2016—has become difficult to sustain. Nevertheless, the power of the cultural icon lies in the fact that FDR lends himself so well to being cast as such.

Introduction · Roosevelt and the Making of an Icon

1. E.g., Schwartz, *George Washington*; Schwartz, *Abraham Lincoln in the Post-Heroic Era*; Ferguson, *Land of Lincoln*.

2. Costigliola, "Roosevelt's Body and National Power"; Kimball, *The Juggler*; Ward, *Closest Companion*; Davis, *FDR: The Beckoning of Destiny*; Burns et al., *The Three Roosevelts*; Goodwin, *No Ordinary Time*.

3. Woolner et al., eds., *FDR's World*; Leuchtenburg, *In the Shadow of FDR*.

4. This definition is loosely based on the definition Bellah et al. offer of "communities of memory" in Bellah et al., *Habits of the Heart*, 153–154.

5. Assmann, "Collective Memory and Cultural Identity."

6. Assmann, *Der lange Schatten der Vergangenheit*, 21–61.

7. Winter, *Performing the Past*, 15.

8. Rosenberg, *A Date Which Will Live*.

9. Rosenberg, *A Date Which Will Live*, 16.

10. Rosenberg, *A Date Which Will Live*, 31.

11. Frisch, *A Shared Authority*, 188.

12. Burke, *The Fabrication of Louis XIV*.

13. E.g., Holmes et al., eds., *Framing Celebrity*; Turner, "Approaching Celebrity Studies."

14. Memorializing himself was never FDR's stated aim. On its website, the NARA-administered FDR Library states its mission as being "to foster research and education on the life and times of Franklin and Eleanor Roosevelt, and their continuing impact on contemporary life," which is more neutral than "memorialize." The Roosevelt Institute, the private nonprofit partner that co-funds the museum, sets out "to honor the legacy of Franklin and Eleanor by celebrating those whose work carries their values and vision forward today."

15. Hufbauer, *Presidential Temples*, 41.

16. Nielsen, "The Perils and Promises of Disability Biography," 21.

17. Nielsen, "The Perils and Promises of Disability Biography," 23.

18. Ott, "The Sum of Its Parts," 9–10.

19. Scotch, "Medical Model of Disability," 602.

20. Linker, "On the Borderland of Medical and Disability History;" Kudlick, "Social History of Medicine and Disability History."

21. Wilson, "Passing in the Shadow of FDR," 14.

22. Longmore, *Telethons*, xvii.

23. O'Ryan, *The Making of Jorge Luis Borges*, 7.

24. Peirce, *Collected Papers, Vol. 2, Elements of Logic*, § 276–280, 157–158.

25. Kemp, *Christ to Coke*, 3.

26. Kemp, *Christ to Coke*, 3.

27. Badger, "The New Deal Without FDR," 250.

28. Garland-Thomson, *Staring: How We Look*, 9.

29. Garland-Thomson, *Staring: How We Look*, 9–10.

30. Badger, "The New Deal without FDR," 251.

31. Clark, *The Last Campaign*, 50–53.

32. Albee, *Home of Franklin D. Roosevelt*, 6.

33. I discuss this at length in a book chapter in Dutch: Polak, "Roosevelt in Zijn Eigen Museum."

34. "'One Definite Locality.'"

35. Siebers, "Disability as Masquerade," 16.

36. Meringolo, *Museums, Monuments, and National Parks*, 110–111.

37. "About the Roosevelt Institute."

38. Clark, *The Last Campaign*, 39.

39. Roosevelt, "Remarks at the Dedication of the Franklin D. Roosevelt Library, June 30, 1941."

40. Kafer, *Feminist, Queer, Crip*, 3.

41. Titchkosky, *The Question of Access*, 56.

Chapter 1 · *"I am a juggler"*

1. Roosevelt, "Fireside Chat, February 23, 1942."

2. Greenblatt, *Renaissance Self-Fashioning*, 1.

3. Greenblatt, *Renaissance Self-Fashioning*, 2.

4. De Certeau, *The Practice of Everyday Life*, 59–60.

5. He did this, for example, through the New Deal, and through rehabilitation centers he set up and made accessible, but also on a more conceptual level, by showing that a disabled person could perfectly well be president or fulfill other functions that they had previously been excluded from.

6. Hobbs, *A Chosen Exile*, 154.

7. Brune et al., *Disability and Passing*, 2.

8. Arendt, *The Human Condition*, 192.

9. Burke, *The Fabrication of Louis XIV*, 1.

10. Winfield, *FDR and the News Media*, 231.

11. Smith, *FDR*, x.

12. Burns, dir., *The Roosevelts: An Intimate History*.

13. The quotations are taken from the coffee table book accompanying the series. Ward et al., *The Roosevelts*, xii.

14. Kimball, *The Juggler*.

15. Smith, *FDR*, 37.

16. Smith, *FDR*, 99–116.

17. Rossiter, *The American Presidency*, 75.

18. Morris, *The Rise of Theodore Roosevelt*, 347.

19. Boller, *Presidential Campaigns*, 72.

20. Gallagher, *FDR's Splendid Deception*, 20.

21. Ott, "The Sum of its Parts," 16.

22. Schoenherr, *Selling the New Deal*, 7; Burns et al., *The Three Roosevelts*, 121.

23. Burns et al., *The Three Roosevelts*, 142.

24. Costigliola, "Personal Dynamics and Presidential Transitions," 35.

25. Costigliola, "Personal Dynamics and Presidential Transitions," 36.

26. Roosevelt, "Address at Chicago, October 5, 1937"; also referred to as the "Quarantine Speech."

27. Roosevelt, "Fireside Chat, December 29, 1940."

28. Rosenberg, *Spreading the American Dream*, 115.

29. Cullen, *The American Dream*, 117.

30. Of course, this simplifies the ever-changing role of the United States in the global order, which particularly shifted during the 1970s. See Ferguson et al., eds., *The Shock of the Global*.

31. Fazzi, *Eleanor Roosevelt and the Anti-Nuclear Movement*, 12.

32. Borgwardt, *A New Deal for the World*.

33. Freidel, *Franklin D. Roosevelt*, 16–17.

34. Burns et al., *The Three Roosevelts*, 121; Davis, *FDR: The Beckoning of Destiny*, 224.

35. Davis, *FDR: The Beckoning of Destiny*, 274–276.

36. Smith, *FDR*, 99–116.

37. Polenberg, *The Era of Franklin D. Roosevelt*, 6.

38. Kimball, *The Juggler*, 7.

39. Goodwin, *No Ordinary Time*, 23.

40. Up until Theodore Roosevelt no one had issued more than forty executive orders per year as president, Theodore upped this to 144 and it stayed high, around 200 per year, until FDR's presidency, when it became nearly 300. The number has since declined dramatically to between 30 and 40 in the last few decades, but the function of the orders has changed, from ordering formalities to making policy. Warber, *Executive Orders and the Modern Presidency*, 128; Mehta, "Every President's Executive Orders in One Chart."

41. Quoted in Warber, *Executive Orders and the Modern Presidency*, 2.

42. Warber, *Executive Orders and the Modern Presidency*, 13; Schlesinger Jr., *The Imperial Presidency*.

43. Robinson, *By Order of the President*.

44. Smith, *FDR*, 128.

45. Roosevelt, "Annual Message of the President on the State of the Union, January 6, 1941."

46. There are varying degrees to which the Four Freedoms are quoted in isolation: at one end of the spectrum, the Franklin D. Roosevelt memorial in Washington, DC, simply lists the Four Freedoms, and at the other, the Four Freedoms Memorial in New York City quotes the speech from "In the future days" to "in our own time and generation," incorporating more of a sense of the historical circumstances that inspired Roosevelt's formulation of the four freedoms.

47. Engel, ed., *The Four Freedoms*.

48. Smith, *FDR*, 128.

49. Paterson et al., *American Foreign Relations, Vol. 2*, 179.

50. Gunther, *Roosevelt in Retrospect*, 15–16.

51. Black, *Casting Her Own Shadow*.

52. Cook, *Eleanor Roosevelt, Vol. 2*, 94–95.

53. Beasley et al., eds., *The Eleanor Roosevelt Encyclopedia*, 412–413.

54. Katznelson et al., "Limiting Liberalism," 297.

55. For example, McMahon, *Reconsidering Roosevelt on Race*.

56. Cook, *Eleanor Roosevelt, Vol. 2*, 23–24.

57. Cook, *Eleanor Roosevelt, Vol. 2*, 91. See also "NAACP History: Costigan Wagner Bill."

58. "Biography of Fala D. Roosevelt."

59. Boorstin, *The Image*, 12–30.

60. Anderson, *Imagined Communities*, 46.

61. Anderson, *Imagined Communities*, 7.

62. Levine et al., *The People and the President*, xi.

Chapter 2 · *The Collective Rhetorical Production of FDR, 1932–1945*

1. Smith, *FDR*, 92.
2. Tully, *F.D.R., My Boss*, 100.
3. For example, Houck, *FDR and Fear Itself*, 98; Rollins Jr., *Roosevelt and Howe*, 418; Levine et al., *The People and the President*, 19.
4. Cook, Foreword to *The Eleanor Roosevelt Encyclopedia*, xiii.
5. Maney, *The Roosevelt Presence*, 16.
6. Rollins Jr., *Roosevelt and Howe*, 3; Stiles, *The Man Behind Roosevelt*, 4.
7. For example, Smith, *FDR*, 82; Maney, *The Roosevelt Presence*, 16; Rollins Jr., *Roosevelt and Howe*, 63.
8. Smith, *FDR*, 92.
9. Schoenherr, *Selling the New Deal*, 1.
10. Schoenherr, *Selling the New Deal*, 40.
11. Hand, *Counsel and Advise*, 118.
12. For example, Samuel Rosenman later published *Working With Roosevelt*; Grace Tully wrote *F.D.R. My Boss*; brain truster Rexford Tugwell's entire career after 1945 was dedicated to writing political biographies of FDR; cabinet member Frances Perkins published *The Roosevelt I Knew*.
13. Freidel, *Franklin D. Roosevelt*, 66.
14. This group of "brains trusters" included FDR's former law partner Basil O'Connor, Adolf Berle, and later biographer Rexford Tugwell.
15. Rollins Jr., *Roosevelt and Howe*, 331.
16. Rollins Jr., *Roosevelt and Howe*, 329–332.
17. Stiles, *The Man Behind Roosevelt*, 166.
18. Rollins Jr., *Roosevelt and Howe*, 342.
19. Rollins Jr., *Roosevelt and Howe*, 349.
20. Sussmann, *Dear FDR*, 60.
21. Rollins Jr., *Roosevelt and Howe*, 313.
22. Rollins Jr., *Roosevelt and Howe*, 313.
23. Craig, *Fireside Politics*, 154.
24. Carcasson, "Herbert Hoover and the Presidential Campaign of 1932." Herbert Hoover was projected, particularly by the Roosevelt campaign but also, more generally, as extremely hands-off, opposing federal efforts to halt the Depression. He tried to restore confidence in the economy through speeches, which Roosevelt—like many contemporaries—perceived as counterproductive.
25. Houck, *FDR and Fear Itself*, 10–14.
26. Houck, *FDR and Fear Itself*, 130.
27. Houck, *FDR and Fear Itself*, 103.
28. Houck, *FDR and Fear Itself*, 103.
29. Houck, *FDR and Fear Itself*, 98.
30. Schoenherr, *Selling the New Deal*, 109.
31. Levine et al., *The People and the President*, 19.
32. Cited in Buhite et al., *FDR's Fireside Chats*, xvi.
33. Buhite et al., *FDR's Fireside Chats*, 5–6.
34. Carl Lamson Carmer, "April 14, 1945," quoted in Buhite et al., *FDR's Fireside Chats*, xx.
35. Levine et al., *The People and the President*, 17.
36. Roosevelt, "Fireside Chat, June 24, 1938."
37. Henry Fairlie, *The New Republic*, January 27, 1982, cited in Levine et al., *The People and the President*, 1.
38. Buhite et al., *FDR's Fireside Chats*, xv.

39. Levine et al., *The People and the President*, 1.

40. Daly, "How Woodrow Wilson's Propaganda Machine."

41. Levine et al., *"The People and the President,"* 17.

42. Levine et al., *"The People and the President,"* 1.

43. Liu, "Lacan's Afterlife," 258.

44. My translation ["Der Rundfunk hat eine Seite, wo er zwei haben müsste"], Brecht, "Der Rundfunk als Kommunikationsapparat," 130.

45. Redmond et al., eds, *Stardom and Celebrity*, 27.

46. Craig, *Fireside Politics*, xvii.

47. Levine et al., *The People and the President*, 8.

48. For example, among the unemployed, as in Fireside Chat 11.

49. Levine et al., *The People and the President*, 5.

50. Smith et al., *"Dear Mr. President . . ."* 213–214.

51. Smith et al., *"Dear Mr. President . . ."* 151.

52. Smith et al., *"Dear Mr. President . . ."* 37–38.

53. White, *FDR and the Press*, 28.

54. Roosevelt et al., *The Public Papers and Addresses*, vol. 1, 8.

55. Roosevelt et al., *The Public Papers and Addresses*, vol. 1, 8.

56. FDR to Russell Leffingwell, March 16, 1942, in Roosevelt, *Selected Speeches*, 310–311; FDR to Mary Norton, March 24, 1942, in Roosevelt, *FDR: His Personal Letters*, vol. 2: 1300.

57. Perkins, *The Roosevelt I Knew*, 110.

58. Sussmann, *Dear FDR*, 59.

59. For example, Winfield, *FDR and the News Media*, 105; Schoenherr, *Selling the New Deal*, 110.

60. Roosevelt, "Fireside Chat, July 24, 1933."

61. Roosevelt, "Fireside Chat, October 22, 1933."

62. Roosevelt, "Fireside Chat, June 28, 1934."

63. Roosevelt, "Fireside Chat, September 3, 1939."

64. Roosevelt, "Fireside Chat, February 23, 1942."

65. Roosevelt, "Fireside Chat, April 28, 1942."

66. Quoted in Levine et al., *The People and the President*, 3.

67. Tajfel, "Social Identity," 67.

68. Tajfel, "Social Identity," 72.

69. Schoenherr, *Selling the New Deal*, 148.

70. Winfield, *FDR and the News Media*, 114.

71. Schoenherr, *Selling the New Deal*, 145.

72. Schoenherr, *Selling the New Deal*, 17.

73. Winfield, *FDR and the News Media*, 109–110.

74. Winfield, *FDR and the News Media*, 114–115; Schoenherr, *Selling the New Deal*, 139.

75. Cited in Schoenherr, *Selling the New Deal*, 146.

76. Schoenherr, *Selling the New Deal*, 148.

77. Lorentz, *FDR's Moviemaker*, 34.

78. Lorentz, *FDR's Moviemaker*, 55.

79. Tebbel, *The Media in America*, 381.

80. Winfield, *FDR and the News Media*, 2.

81. Winfield, *FDR and the News Media*, 28.

82. Polenberg, *The Era of Franklin D. Roosevelt*, 44.

83. "The constant free flow of communication among us—enabling the free interchange of ideas—forms the very bloodstream of our nation. It keeps the mind and body of our democracy eternally vital, eternally young." Roosevelt, "Radio Address of the President—Herald Tribune Forum, October 24, 1940."

84. Roosevelt, "Press Conference, March 8, 1933."

85. Schoenherr, *Selling the New Deal*, 40–41.

86. White, *FDR and the Press*, 50–52.

87. Winfield, *FDR and the News Media*, 232.

88. Schoenherr, *Selling the New Deal*, 45.

89. Gunther, *Roosevelt in Retrospect*, 22–23.

90. Schlesinger Jr., *The Age of Roosevelt Vol. 2*, 558. It is striking that FDR refers to Theodore as his "cousin," here, because formerly he tended to call him "Uncle Theodore"—the closest family tie with Theodore was after all that he was Eleanor Roosevelt's uncle. FDR's promoting himself from nephew to cousin of Theodore's may have been occasioned by FDR's election to the presidency, which in a sense brought him on a par with Theodore.

91. Quoted in Holli, *The Wizard of Washington*, 64.

92. Holli, *The Wizard of Washington*.

93. Holli, *The Wizard of Washington*, 44.

94. Holli, *The Wizard of Washington*, 46.

95. Holli, *The Wizard of Washington*, 66.

96. Howe, "The President's Mail Bag," cited in Levine et al., *The People and the President*, 5.

97. *New York Times*, December 27, 1933.

Chapter 3 · Negotiating FDR Remembrance

1. Roosevelt, "Remarks at the Dedication of the Franklin D. Roosevelt Library, June 30, 1941."

2. Clark, *The Last Campaign*, 50.

3. For example, Koch et al., "Roosevelt and His Library."

4. Reynolds, "FDR's Foreign Policy," 7.

5. Reynolds, "FDR's Foreign Policy," 8.

6. Rosenman, *Working With Roosevelt*, 13.

7. Leuchtenburg, *The Supreme Court Reborn*, 227.

8. For example, Polenberg, "The Decline of the New Deal," 248.

9. Reid, *The Last Lion*, 461.

10. Hand, "Rosenman, Thucydides, and the New Deal," 334.

11. Hand, "Rosenman, Thucydides, and the New Deal," 335.

12. Roosevelt et al., *The Public Papers and Addresses of Franklin D. Roosevelt, Vol. 1*, xiv.

13. Hand, "Rosenman, Thucydides, and the New Deal," 334.

14. Hand, "Rosenman, Thucydides, and the New Deal," 335–336.

15. Roosevelt et al., *The Public Papers and Addresses of Franklin D. Roosevelt, Vol. 1*, xviii–xix.

16. Roosevelt et al., *The Public Papers and Addresses of Franklin D. Roosevelt, Vol. 1*, xiv.

17. Hufbauer, *Presidential Temples*.

18. For example, Hufbauer, *Presidential Temples*; Hyland, *Presidential Libraries and Museums*; Veit, *Presidential Libraries and Collections*.

19. Roosevelt, "Address at the Cornerstone Laying of the Franklin D. Roosevelt Library, November 19, 1939."

20. Koch et al., "Roosevelt and His Library."

21. Hufbauer, "The Roosevelt Presidential Library," 176.

22. Roosevelt, "Press Conference, December 10, 1938."

23. Koch et al., "Roosevelt and His Library."

24. Hufbauer, *Presidential Temples*, 29.

25. Hufbauer, *Presidential Temples*, 181.

26. Cover, *Narrative, Violence and the Law*, 95.

27. *Eleanor Roosevelt Papers Project*, "My Day," April 4, 1955.

28. Reynolds, *In Command of History*.

29. Beasley, *Eleanor Roosevelt and the Media*.

30. *Eleanor Roosevelt Papers Project*, "My Day," February 4, 1958.

31. Petrie, dir. *Eleanor and Franklin: The White House Years*, 01:13:00.

32. Beasley et al., eds., *The Eleanor Roosevelt Encyclopedia*, 394.

33. Black, *Casting Her Own Shadow*.

34. Roosevelt, Eleanor, "Why I Do Not Choose to Run."

35. Binker et al., "This Is What Ken Burns Neglected to Tell."

36. Assmann, Jan, "Collective Memory and Cultural Identity," 129.

37. Vansina, *Oral Tradition as History*, 23–24.

38. Aleida Assmann actually does attend to this process in considerable detail, for instance in *Der Lange Schatten der Vergangenheit*.

39. Winter, *Performing the Past*, 15.

40. For example, Schwartz et al., "Archives, Records, and Power," 172.

41. Wesseling, ed., *Plaatsen van herinnering*.

42. Rigney, *The Afterlives of Walter Scott*, 18.

43. Murray et al., *Norman Rockwell's Four Freedoms*, 35.

44. "Franklin D. Roosevelt Four Freedoms Awards."

45. Kaye, *The Fight for the Four Freedoms*.

46. Engel, ed., *The Four Freedoms*.

47. "The Four Freedoms."

48. Interview with William vanden Heuvel, August 4, 2010.

49. "About the Roosevelt Institute."

50. "The Four Freedoms."

51. Interview with Gina Pollara, August 3, 2010.

52. Pollak, "Name That Island."

53. "FDR Hope Memorial."

54. Fazzi, *Eleanor Roosevelt and the Anti-Nuclear Movement*, 49–54.

Chapter 4 · The New Deal Depoliticized in Cultural Memory

1. Schlesinger Jr., *The Age of Roosevelt Vol. 2: The Coming of the New Deal*, 3,

2. Roosevelt, "Address Accepting the Presidential Nomination, July 2, 1932."

3. Alter, *The Defining Moment*, 182.

4. Schlesinger Jr., *The Imperial Presidency*, 113.

5. Katznelson, *Fear Itself*.

6. Alter, *The Defining Moment*, 334; Roosevelt, "Excerpts from the Press Conference, December 28, 1943."

7. Badger, "The New Deal Without FDR," 250.

8. Kammen, *The Mystic Chords of Memory*, 448–455.

9. Borgwardt, *A New Deal for the World*, 6.

10. Katznelson, *Fear Itself*.

11. Breitman et al., *FDR and the Jews*, 66.

12. Renshaw, *Franklin D. Roosevelt*, 100.

13. Murray et al., *Norman Rockwell's Four Freedoms*, 60–61.

14. Kammen, *The Mystic Chords of Memory*, 452.

15. Kammen, *The Mystic Chords of Memory*, 452.

16. Roosevelt, "Remarks at Mount Rushmore National Memorial, August 30, 1936."

17. Mouffe, *The Democratic Paradox*, 108–9.

18. Mouffe, *The Democratic Paradox*, 117.

19. Davis, *FDR: The New Deal Years*, 69.

20. Badger, *The New Deal: The Depression Years*, 9–10.

21. Davis, *The New Deal Years*, 90.

22. Penkower, *The Federal Writers' Project*, 1–8.

23. Penkower, *The Federal Writers' Project*, 140.

24. "A symbol is a representamen whose special significance or fitness to represent just what it does represent lies in nothing but the very fact of there being a habit, disposition, or other effective general rule that it will be so interpreted. Take, for example, the word 'man.' These three letters are not in the least like a man; nor is the sound with which they are associated." Peirce, *Collected Papers, Vol. 4, The Simplest Mathematics*, §447, 359–360.

25. Kammen, *The Mystic Chords of Memory*, 444.

26. Kammen, *The Mystic Chords of Memory*, 444.

27. Cited in Laning, "The New Deal Mural Projects," 90.

28. Kammen, *The Mystic Chords of Memory*, 311.

29. Kammen, *The Mystic Chords of Memory*, 324.

30. Marling, *Wall-to-Wall America*, 210.

31. Marling, *Wall-to-Wall America*, 211.

32. Quoted in Mangione, *The Dream and the Deal*, 371.

33. Kammen, *The Mystic Chords of Memory*, 450.

34. Kammen, *The Mystic Chords of Memory*, 451.

35. Meringolo, *Museums, Monuments, and National Parks*, 146.

36. Quoted in Mackintosh, "The National Park Service," 54.

37. "Tomorrow," *Annie*, directed by John Huston (1982, Los Angeles: Columbia Pictures), http://www.youtube.com/watch?v=zhHjUOQdY30.

38. Cohen, *Nothing to Fear*, 267–268.

39. Schlesinger Jr., *The Imperial Presidency*, 209.

40. Alter, *The Defining Moment*, xv.

41. Alter, *The Defining Moment*, xv.

42. Louis Howe, Henry Morgenthau, Cordell Hull, Francis Perkins, Harold Ickes. Meehan, *Annie Libretto / Vocal Book*, II-3-11.

43. Meehan, *Annie Libretto / Vocal Book*, I-3-17 and 18.

44. Alter, *The Defining Moment*, 89.

45. Alter, *The Defining Moment*, 88.

46. Quoted in Alter, *The Defining Moment*, 88.

47. Badger, *The New Deal: The Depression Years*, 190.

48. Alter, *The Defining Moment*, ill. 34.

49. Heer, "Dear Orphan Annie."

50. Young et al., *The Great Depression in America*, 107, 297–298.

51. Leuchtenburg, *In the Shadow of FDR*, 167–168.

52. For example, newspaper or magazine articles with headlines like Shiller's "What Would Roosevelt Do?" or Kennedy's "What Barack Obama Can Learn From FDR."

53. Alter, *The Defining Moment*, 273.

54. Alter, *The Defining Moment*, 273.

55. Hamby, *Harry S. Truman and the Fair Deal*, vii.

56. Leuchtenburg, *In the Shadow of FDR*, 49.

57. Leuchtenburg, *In the Shadow of FDR*, 111.

58. Leuchtenburg, *In the Shadow of FDR*, 160.

59. Leuchtenburg, *In the Shadow of FDR*, 217, 278–279.

60. For video footage of the speech: http://www.youtube.com/watch?v=ToGwZFAV1Lw.

61. Rich, "For Books, Is Obama New Oprah?"

62. See for example, Linenthal et al., *History Wars*.

63. Kammen, *The Mystic Chords of Memory*, 452.

64. Kammen, *The Mystic Chords of Memory*, 450.
65. Kammen, *The Mystic Chords of Memory*, 509.
66. Hobsbawm et al., eds., *The Invention of Tradition*, esp. 279–280.
67. Powell, *FDR's Folly*, v.
68. Powell, *FDR's Folly*, vii.
69. Powell, *FDR's Folly*, 262.

Chapter 5 · FDR's Disability in Cultural Memory

1. Although there is an alternative theory that suggests he had Guillain-Barré syndrome, see the introduction and Goldman et al., "What Was the Cause."
2. Davis, *FDR: The Beckoning of Destiny*, 651.
3. Black, *Franklin Delano Roosevelt*, 146.
4. Nielsen, *A Disability History of the United States*, 100–101.
5. Gallagher, *FDR's Splendid Deception*, 53.
6. Black, *Franklin Delano Roosevelt*, 169.
7. Davis, *FDR: The Beckoning of Destiny*, 771.
8. Gallagher, *FDR's Splendid Deception*, 93.
9. Ward et al., *The Roosevelts*, 267.
10. Clausen, "The President and the Wheelchair," 26.
11. Looker, "Is Franklin D. Roosevelt Fit to Be President?" 6–10.
12. Rollins Jr., *Roosevelt and Howe*, 313.
13. Wilson, "Passing in the Shadow of FDR," 18.
14. Wilson, "Passing in the Shadow of FDR," 13.
15. Longmore, *Telethons*.
16. Longmore, *Telethons*, 16–17.
17. Longmore, "The Cultural Framing of Disability," 506.
18. Winfield, *FDR and the News Media*, 114.
19. Roosevelt, "Address to Congress on the Yalta Conference, March 1, 1945."
20. Lomazow et al., *FDR's Deadly Secret*, 187.
21. Orlansky, "Reactions to the Death of President Roosevelt," 237–238.
22. Quoted in Goodwin, *No Ordinary Time*, 80.
23. The quoted phrase here is taken from May and Hill's article "How Shall We See Them?" 604. This theme is articulated in their 1984 article about popular views on disability and regarded as a "historical image," suggesting that by 1984 it was outdated. (Although the idea that the emancipation of people with disabilities was completed in 1984 is given the lie by the glaring objectification in the article's title "How Shall We See Them?")
24. Quoted in Lippman Jr., *The Squire of Warm Springs*, 81.
25. Boettiger, "My Life with FDR," 53–54.
26. Mitchell et al., *Narrative Prosthesis*, 47.
27. Brune et al., *Disability and Passing*, 11.
28. Ott, "The Sum of Its Parts," 9.
29. Pletcher et al., "History of the Civil Rights Movement."
30. Lippman, *The Squire of Warm Springs*.
31. Gallagher, *Black Bird Fly Away*, 84–86.
32. Gallagher, *FDR's Splendid Deception*, 22–23.
33. For example, Floyd in "Hugh Gregory Gallagher's Splendid Reception," 3–4.
34. Oshinsky, *Polio: An American Story*, 11.
35. Shell, *Polio and Its Aftermath*, 200.
36. Sargent, dir., *Warm Springs*.
37. Taylor, dir., *FDR: A Presidency Revealed*.

38. Ott et al., eds. *Artificial Parts, Practical Lives.*

39. Jarvis, *The Male Body at War.*

40. Flynt et al., *One Nation Under Sex,* 126, 136.

41. Frankfurter, "The Memorial to F.D.R.," 39–40.

42. The Statue of US President Franklin D. Roosevelt on Grosvenor Square in London, for instance, was erected in 1948. It portrays Roosevelt standing, using a cane. A Roosevelt statue in Oslo, also erected in 1948, shows him seated.

43. Stein, "The President's Two Bodies," 42.

44. There are other examples of this from recent dates, for example, Edward Hlavka's sculpture of FDR standing at a lectern in Rapid City, South Dakota (2006). http://www.vanderkrogt .net/statues/object.php?record=ussd40&webpage=ST.

45. *Report to the President and Congress, 30 May 1978.*

46. Stein, "The President's Two Bodies," 44.

47. Rainey, "The Garden as Narrative," 381.

48. Lippard, "Homage to the Square," 51.

49. Rainey, "The Garden as Narrative," 382.

50. Rainey, "The Garden as Narrative," 383.

51. *Report to the President and Congress, 30 May 1978,* 6.

52. Tuchman, "The Franklin Delano Roosevelt Memorial," 98.

53. Rainey, "The Garden as Narrative," 385–386.

54. Floyd, "Hugh Gregory Gallagher's Splendid Reception."

55. Mutchler, "Roosevelt's Disability."

56. Rainey, "The Garden as Narrative," 378.

57. Quoted in Houck et al., *FDR's Body Politics,* 3.

58. Houck et al., *FDR's Body Politics,* 4.

59. Shell, *Polio and Its Aftermath,* 6.

60. Tilden, *Interpreting Our Heritage,* ix–xvi.

61. Tilden, *Interpreting Our Heritage,* 14.

62. Kafer, *Feminist, Queer, Crip,* 4–5.

63. Siebers, "Disability as Masquerade," 13.

64. Vagnone and Ryan, *Anarchist's Guide to Historic House Museums.*

65. Meldon, "Interpreting Access."

66. Landsberg, *Prosthetic Memory,* 2.

67. Michell, dir., *Hyde Park on Hudson,* 51:30.

68. This is a mechanism that Tobin Siebers has analyzed as a form of "disability masquerade" in "Disability as Masquerade," 11.

69. Lim, "The Lion and the Lamb."

70. Examples of people who portrayed FDR's disability in this way included family and friends of FDR such as Eleanor and Anna Roosevelt and Felix Frankfurter as well as theater writers like Dore Schary, who wrote *Sunrise at Campobello* (the play) and knew Eleanor Roosevelt personally.

Chapter 6 · Understanding FDR as a Cultural Icon

1. Goodwin, *No Ordinary Time,* 11.

2. Examples would include Daniel Petrie's *Eleanor and Franklin* (1977, based on the biography by Joseph Lash), the *Annie* musical film discussed in Chapter Four, and the FDR memorial in Washington, DC.

3. Goodwin, *No Ordinary Time,* 279–280.

4. Sousloff, *The Subject in Art,* 10.

5. Kemp, *Christ to Coke*, 3–5.

6. O'Ryan, *The Making of Jorge Luis Borges*, 7.

7. Culler, *Literary Theory*, 72.

8. Bodnar, *The "Good War" in American Memory*, 227.

9. Terkel, "The Good War"; Brokaw, *The Greatest Generation*; Burns, dir., *The War*.

10. Brokaw, *The Greatest Generation*, 3; Roosevelt, "Acceptance Speech for the Renomination for the Presidency, June 27, 1936."

11. Brokaw, *The Greatest Generation*, xxx.

12. Rothberg, *Multidirectional Memory*.

13. Rothberg, *Multidirectional Memory*, xiii.

14. Rothberg, *Multidirectional Memory*, 278.

15. Rothberg, *Multidirectional Memory*, 273.

16. Burgoyne, *Film Nation*, 3, 6.

17. Burgoyne, *Film Nation*, 7.

18. Mitchell et al., *Narrative Prosthesis*, 47.

19. Mitchell et al., *Narrative Prosthesis*, 47–48.

20. Mitchell et al., *Narrative Prosthesis*, 61.

21. Kantorowicz, *The King's Two Bodies*, 21–24.

22. Interview with Ross Patterson, September 3, 2014.

23. Burgoyne, *Film Nation*, 108.

24. Smith, "Dis-afection," 125.

25. Interview with Ross Patterson, September 3, 2014.

26. Brian, "Mythological Pedagogies, or Suicide Clubs," 235.

27. Bay, dir., *Pearl Harbor*.

28. Hobsbawm, *On Empire*, 55–59.

29. Rosenberg, *Spreading the American Dream*, 10.

30. Roosevelt, "Address to Congress Requesting a Declaration of War, December 8, 1941."

31. Bay, dir., *Pearl Harbor*, 33:00.

32. Gallagher, *FDR's Splendid Deception*, 64.

33. Roth, *The Plot Against America*, 1.

34. Roth, "The Story Behind 'The Plot Against America.'"

35. Kaufmann, "Heil to the Chief."

36. Theodoracopulos, "Roth's Counter-History and Mine."

37. Roth, *The Plot Against America*, 113.

38. Vidal, *The Golden Age*, 178.

39. Vidal, *The Golden Age*, 81.

40. Vidal, *The Golden Age*, 124.

41. Vidal, *The Golden Age*, 124.

42. The argument Beard made in *President Roosevelt and the Coming of War* is echoed in Tansill's still popular *Back Door to War*. The same arguments and sources are also to be found in Stinnett's *Day of Deceit* and Prange's *At Dawn We Slept*.

43. Rothberg, *Multidirectional Memory*, 3. Rothberg posits that cultural memories of one event can strengthen or reinforce cultural memories of another event: for example, an expression like "the Black Holocaust" to refer to slavery and the Middle Passage reinforces the idea of transatlantic slavery as a form of genocide without "taking away" from the memory of the Holocaust (indeed, arguably strengthening that, too).

44. Of course, this notion of FDR as a "common man" is, however attractive and well-used both in his own autofabrication and in later representations, quite simplistic, as Brands, *FDR: Traitor to His Class*, has shown in detail.

Conclusion · A Rooseveltian Century?

1. Schlesinger Jr., "Franklin Delano Roosevelt."
2. Bacevich, *The Short American Century.*
3. Ricard, ed., *A Companion to Theodore Roosevelt*, 521–526.
4. Burns, dir., *The Plot Against America.*
5. Frum, *The Right Man.* Although Frum's words make explicit that the Bush administration tried to identify Iraq and Iran with the Axis of the 1940s, the connection with Jörg Haider and "transplanted fascism" is actually more in the direction of Trump's rhetoric and position. I would argue that the regimes in Iraq and Iran at that time, however horrific they were, have never been "transplanted fascism" and Haider himself actually represents a homegrown Austrian neo-fascism.
6. Friedländer, *The Origins of Nazi Genocide*, 8–23; Mitchell et al., "The Eugenic Atlantic," 857.
7. Friedländer, *The Origins of Nazi Genocide*, 86–110.
8. Clinton, "Remarks by the President at the Dedication Ceremony of the Franklin Delano Roosevelt Memorial, May 2, 1997."
9. Clinton, "Remarks on the Unveiling of a Statue at the Franklin D. Roosevelt Memorial January 10, 2001."

"About the Roosevelt Institute." The Roosevelt Institute. Accessed November 11, 2019. https://www.rooseveltinstitute.org/about.

Albee, Peggy A. *Home of Franklin D. Roosevelt: Roosevelt-Vanderbilt Sites, Hyde Park, New York.* Lowell, MA: Department of the Interior, Building Conservation Branch, 1996.

Alter, Jonathan. *The Defining Moment: FDR's Hundred Days and the Triumph of Hope.* New York: Simon and Schuster, 2006.

Anderson, Benedict. *Imagined Communities: Reflections on the Origin and Spread of Nationalism.* New York: Verso, 1991.

Arendt, Hannah. *The Human Condition.* 2nd ed. Chicago: University of Chicago Press, 1998.

Assmann, Aleida. *Der lange Schatten der Vergangenheit.* Munich: C. H. Beck, 2006.

Assmann, Jan. "Collective Memory and Cultural Identity." Translated by John Czaplicka. *New German Critique* 65 (1995): 125–133.

Bacevich, Andrew. *The Short American Century: A Postmortem.* Cambridge, MA: Harvard University Press, 2012.

Badger, Anthony. *The New Deal: The Depression Years, 1933–1940.* Basingstoke: Macmillan, 1989.

Badger, Anthony. "The New Deal Without FDR: What Biographies of Roosevelt Cannot Tell Us." In *History and Biography: Essays in Honour of Derek Beales,* edited by T. Blanning and David Cannadine, 243–65. Cambridge: Cambridge University Press, 2002.

Bay, Michael, dir. *Pearl Harbor.* Burbank, CA: Touchstone Pictures, 2001. DVD. 183 min.

Beard, Charles Austin. *President Roosevelt and the Coming of War, 1941: A Study in Appearances and Realities.* New Haven: Yale University Press, 1948.

Beasley, Maurine. *Eleanor Roosevelt and the Media.* Chicago: University of Illinois, 1987.

Beasley, Maurine, Holly Shulman, and Henry Beasley, eds. *The Eleanor Roosevelt Encyclopedia.* Westport, CT: Greenwood Press, 2001.

Bellah, Robert, Richard Madsen, William M. Sullivan, Ann Swidler, and Steven M. Tipton. *Habits of the Heart: Individualism and Commitment in American Life.* Berkeley: University of California Press, 1985.

Binker, Mary Jo, and Brigid O'Farrell. "This Is What Ken Burns Neglected to Tell You about Eleanor Roosevelt." *History News Network,* July 12, 2014. http://historynewsnetwork.org/article/157795.

"Biography of Fala D. Roosevelt." Franklin D. Roosevelt Presidential Library and Museum. Accessed November 11, 2019. https://www.fdrlibrary.org/fala.

Black, Allida. *Casting Her Own Shadow: Eleanor Roosevelt and the Shaping of Post-war Liberalism.* New York: Columbia University Press, 1996.

Black, Conrad. *Franklin Delano Roosevelt: Champion of Freedom.* New York: Public Affairs, 2003.

Bodnar, John. *The "Good War" in American Memory*. Baltimore: Johns Hopkins University Press, 2010.

Boettiger, Anna Roosevelt. "My Life with FDR: How Polio Helped Father." *The Woman*, July 1949, 53–54.

Boller, Paul. *Presidential Campaigns: From George Washington to George W. Bush*. New York: Oxford University Press, 2004.

Boorstin, Daniel J. *The Image—or What Happened to the American Dream*. New York: Atheneum, 1962.

Borgwardt, Elizabeth. *A New Deal for the World: America's Vision for Human Rights*. Cambridge, MA: Harvard University Press, 2005.

Brands, H. W. *FDR: Traitor to His Class: The Privileged Life and Radical Presidency of Franklin Delano Roosevelt*. New York: Doubleday, 2008.

Brecht, Bertolt. "Der Rundfunk als Kommunikationsapparat." In *Gesammelte Werke in 20 Bänden*, vol. 18. Frankfurt am Main: Suhrkamp, 1932, 127–134.

Breitman, Richard, and Allan Lichtman Jr. *FDR and the Jews*. Cambridge, MA: Harvard University Press, 2013.

Brian, Kathleen M. "Mythological Pedagogies, or Suicide Clubs as Eugenic Alibi." In *Phallacies: Historical Intersections of Disability and Masculinity*, edited by Kathleen M. Brian and James W. Trent Jr., 235–262. Oxford: Oxford University Press, 2018.

Brokaw, Tom. *The Greatest Generation*. New York: Random House, 1998.

Brune, Jeffrey, and Daniel Wilson. *Disability and Passing: Blurring the Lines of Identity*. Philadelphia: Temple University Press, 2013.

Buhite, Russell, and David Levy. *FDR's Fireside Chats*. Norman: University of Oklahoma Press, 1992.

Burgoyne, Robert. *Film Nation: Hollywood Looks at U.S. History*, rev. ed. Minneapolis: University of Minnesota Press, 2010.

Burke, Peter. *The Fabrication of Louis XIV*. New Haven: Yale University Press, 1992.

Burns, Ed, and David Simon., dirs. *The Plot Against America*. TV Miniseries. HBO, 2020.

Burns, James MacGregor, and Susan Dunn. *The Three Roosevelts: Patrician Leaders Who Transformed America*. New York: Atlantic Monthly Press, 2001.

Burns, Kenneth L., dir. *The Roosevelts: An Intimate History*. PBS, 2014. DVD.

Burns, Kenneth L., and Lynn Novick, dirs. *The War*. TV Miniseries. PBS, 2007.

Carcasson, Martin. "Herbert Hoover and the Presidential Campaign of 1932: The Failure of Apologia." *Presidential Studies Quarterly* 28, no. 2 (1998): 349–365.

Clark, Anthony. *The Last Campaign: How Presidents Rewrite History, Run for Posterity and Enshrine Their Legacies*. Lexington, KY: Anthony Clark, 2015.

Clausen, Christopher. "The President and the Wheelchair." *Wilson Quarterly* 29, no. 3 (Summer 2005): 24–29.

Clinton, William J. "Remarks by the President at the Dedication Ceremony of the Franklin Delano Roosevelt Memorial, May 2, 1997." The American Presidency Project, edited by Gerhard Peters and John T. Woolley. https://www.presidency.ucsb.edu/documents/remarks-the -dedication-the-franklin-delano-roosevelt-memorial.

Clinton, William J. "Remarks on the Unveiling of a Statue at the Franklin D. Roosevelt Memorial January 10, 2001." The American Presidency Project, edited by Gerhard Peters and John T. Woolley. https://www.presidency.ucsb.edu/documents/remarks-the-unveiling-statue-the -franklin-d-roosevelt-memorial.

Cohen, Adam. *Nothing to Fear: FDR's Inner Circle and the Hundred Days that Created Modern America*. New York: Penguin, 2009.

Cook, Blanche Wiesen. *Eleanor Roosevelt, Vol. 2: The Defining Years 1933–1938*. New York: Viking Penguin, 1992.

Cook, Blanche Wiesen. Foreword to *The Eleanor Roosevelt Encyclopedia*, edited by Maurine Beasley, Holly Shulman, and Henry Beasley, xi–xiv. Westport: Greenwood Press, 2001.

Costigliola, Frank. "Personal Dynamics and Presidential Transitions: The Case of Roosevelt and Truman." In *Recapturing the Oval Office: New Historical Approaches to the American Presidency*, edited by Brian Balogh and Bruce J. Schulman, 34–50. Ithaca, NY: Cornell University Press, 2015.

Costigliola, Frank. "Roosevelt's Body and National Power." In *Body and Nation: The Global Realm of U. S. Body Politics in the Twentieth Century*, edited by Emily Rosenberg and Shanon Fitzpatrick, 125–146. Durham: Duke University Press, 2014.

Cover, Robert. *Narrative, Violence and the Law: The Essays of Robert Cover*, edited by Martha Minow, Michael Ryan, and Austin Sarat. Ann Arbor: University of Michigan Press, 1993.

Craig, Douglas B. *Fireside Politics: Radio and Political Culture in the United States, 1920–1940*. Baltimore: Johns Hopkins University Press, 2000.

Cullen, Jim. *The American Dream: A Short History of an Idea that Shaped a Nation*. Oxford: Oxford University Press, 2004.

Culler, Jonathan. *Literary Theory: A Very Short Introduction*. Oxford: Oxford University Press, 2011.

Daly, Christopher B. "How Woodrow Wilson's Propaganda Machine Changed American Journalism." *Smithsonian Magazine*, April 28, 2017. https://www.smithsonianmag.com/history/how-woodrow-wilsons-propaganda-machine-changed-american-journalism-180963082/.

Davis, Kenneth S. *FDR: The Beckoning of Destiny, 1882–1928: A History*. New York: Putnam, 1972.

Davis, Kenneth S. *FDR: The New Deal Years, 1933–1938: A History*. New York: Putnam, 1986.

De Certeau, Michel. *The Practice of Everyday Life*. Translated by Steven Rendall. Berkeley: University of California Press, 1984.

Eleanor Roosevelt Papers Project, The. Accessed November 11, 2020. https://erpapers.columbian.gwu.edu/.

Engel, Jeffrey A., ed. *The Four Freedoms: Franklin D. Roosevelt and the Evolution of an American Idea*. New York: Oxford University Press, 2016.

Fazzi, Dario. *Eleanor Roosevelt and the Anti-Nuclear Movement: The Voice of Conscience*. New York: Palgrave Macmillan, 2016.

"FDR Hope Memorial." Accessed November 12, 2019. http://www.fdrhopememorial.org/.

Ferguson, Andrew. *Land of Lincoln, Adventures in Abe's America*. New York: Atlantic Monthly Press, 2007.

Ferguson, Niall, Charles Maier, Erez Manela, and Daniel Sargent, eds. *The Shock of the Global: The 1970s in Perspective*. Cambridge, MA: Harvard University Press, 2011.

Floyd, Barbara. "Hugh Gregory Gallagher's Splendid Reception." *Disability Studies Quarterly* 30, no. 3–4 (2010). https://dsq-sds.org/article/view/1285/.

Flynt, Larry, and David Eisenbach. *One Nation Under Sex*. New York: Palgrave Macmillan, 2011.

Frankfurter, Felix. "The Memorial to F.D.R.: What the President Wanted." *Atlantic Monthly*, March 1961, 39–40.

"Franklin D. Roosevelt Four Freedoms Awards." Roosevelt Institute, September 29, 2015. https://rooseveltinstitute.org/fdr-four-freedoms-awards-1/.

Freidel, Frank. *Franklin D. Roosevelt: A Rendezvous with Destiny*. Boston: Little, Brown and Company, 1990.

Friedländer, Harry. *The Origins of Nazi Genocide: From Euthanasia to the Final Solution*. Chapel Hill: University of North Carolina Press, 1995.

Frisch, Michael. *A Shared Authority: Essays on the Craft and Meaning of Oral and Public History*. Albany: State University of New York Press, 1990.

Frum, David. *The Right Man: The Surprise Presidency of Georg W. Bush*. New York: Random House, 2003.

Gallagher, Hugh Gregory. *Black Bird Fly Away: Disabled in an Able-Bodied World*. Arlington, VA: Vandamere Press, 1998.

Gallagher, Hugh Gregory. *FDR's Splendid Deception: The Moving Story of Roosevelt's Massive Disability and the Intense Efforts to Conceal It from the Public*, rev. 1st ed. Arlington, VA: Vandamere Press, 1985.

Garland-Thomson, Rosemarie. *Staring: How We Look*. Oxford: Oxford University Press, 2009.

Goldman, Armond S., Elisabeth J. Schmalstieg, Daniel H. Freeman Jr., Daniel A. Goldman, and Frank C. Schmalstieg Jr. "What Was the Cause of Franklin D. Roosevelt's Paralytic Illness?" *Journal of Medical Biography* 11, no. 4 (November 1, 2003), 232–240.

Goodwin, Doris Kearns. *No Ordinary Time: Franklin and Eleanor Roosevelt—The Home Front in World War II*. New York: Simon and Schuster, 1994.

Greenblatt, Stephen. *Renaissance Self-Fashioning, from More to Shakespeare*. Chicago: The University of Chicago Press, 1980.

Gunther, John. *Roosevelt in Retrospect: A Profile in History*. New York: Harper and Brothers, 1950.

Hamby, Alonzo L. *Harry S. Truman and the Fair Deal*. Washington, DC: Heath, 1974.

Hand, Samuel B. *Counsel and Advise: A Political Biography of Samuel I. Rosenman*. New York: Garland, 1979.

Hand, Samuel B. "Rosenman, Thucydides, and the New Deal." *Journal of American History* 55, no. 2 (September 1968): 334–348.

Heer, Jeet. "Dear Orphan Annie: Why Cartoon Characters Get All the Best Mail." *Boston Globe Ideas*, September 15, 2002. https://web.archive.org/web/20101211113026/http://www.jeetheer .com/comics/dearannie.htm.

Hobbs, Allyson. *A Chosen Exile: A History of Racial Passing in American Life*. Cambridge, MA: Harvard University Press, 2014.

Hobsbawm, Eric. *On Empire: America, War and Global Supremacy*. New York: Pantheon, 2008.

Hobsbawm, Eric, and Terence Ranger, eds. *The Invention of Tradition*. Cambridge: Cambridge University Press, 1983.

Holli, Melvin G. *The Wizard of Washington: Emil Hurja, Franklin Roosevelt, and the Birth of Public Opinion Polling*. New York: Palgrave, 2002.

Holmes, Su, and Sean Redmond, eds. *Framing Celebrity: New Directions in Celebrity Culture*. New York: Routledge, 2006.

Houck, Davis W. *FDR and Fear Itself: The First Inaugural Address*. College Station: Texas A&M University Press, 2002.

Houck, Davis W., and Amos Kiewe. *FDR's Body Politics: The Rhetoric of Disability*. College Park: Texas A&M University Press, 2002.

Howe, Louis McHenry. "The President's Mail Bag." *American Magazine*, June 23, 1934.

Hufbauer, Benjamin. *Presidential Temples: How Memorials and Libraries Shape Public Memory*. Lawrence: University Press of Kansas, 2005.

Hufbauer, Benjamin. "The Roosevelt Presidential Library: A Shift in Commemoration." *Journal of American Studies* 42, no. 3 (2001): 173–193.

Huston, John, dir. *Annie*. Los Angeles: Columbia Pictures, 1982. DVD. 126 min.

Hyland, Pat. *Presidential Libraries and Museums: An Illustrated Guide*. Washington, DC: Congressional Quarterly Inc., 1995.

Jarvis, Christina. *The Male Body at War: American Masculinity during World War II*. DeKalb, IL: Northern Illinois University Press, 2010.

Kafer, Alison. *Feminist, Queer, Crip*. Bloomington: Indiana University Press, 2013.

Kammen, Michael. *The Mystic Chords of Memory: The Transformation of Tradition in American Culture*. New York: Vintage Books, 1991.

Kantorowicz, Ernst. *The King's Two Bodies: A Study in Mediaeval Political Theology*. Princeton: Princeton University Press, 1957.

Katznelson, Ira. *Fear Itself: The New Deal and the Origins of Our Time*. New York: W. W. Norton, 2013.

Katznelson, Ira, Kim Geiger, and Daniel Kryder. "Limiting Liberalism: The Southern Veto in Congress, 1933–1950." *Political Science Quarterly* 108, no. 2. (Summer 1993): 283–306.

Kaufmann, Bill. "Heil to the Chief." *The American Conservative*, September 27, 2004. https://www.theamericanconservative.com/articles/heil-to-the-chief/.

Kay, Harvey. *The Fight for the Four Freedoms: What Made FDR and the Greatest Generation Truly Great*. New York: Simon and Schuster, 2015.

Kemp, Martin. *Christ to Coke: How Image Becomes Icon*. Oxford: Oxford University Press, 2012.

Kennedy, David. "What Barack Obama Can Learn From FDR." *Time Magazine*, June 24, 2009.

Kimball, Warren. *The Juggler: Franklin Roosevelt as Wartime Statesman*. Princeton: Princeton University Press, 1994.

Koch, Cynthia M., and Lynn A. Bassanese. "Roosevelt and His Library." *Prologue* 33, no. 2 (2001). https://www.archives.gov/publications/prologue/2001/summer/roosevelt-and-his-library-1.html.

Kudlick, Catherine. "Social History of Medicine and Disability History." In *The Oxford Handbook of Disability History*, edited by Michael Rembis, Catherine Kudlick, and Kim E. Nielsen, 105–120. New York: Oxford University Press, 2018.

Landsberg, Alison. *Prosthetic Memory: The Transformation of American Remembrance in the Age of Mass Culture*. New York: Columbia University Press, 2004.

Laning, Edward. "The New Deal Mural Projects." In *The New Deal Art Projects: An Anthology of Memoirs*, edited by Francis O'Connor, 79–113. Washington, DC: Smithsonian Institution Press, 1972.

Leuchtenburg, William. *In the Shadow of FDR: From Harry Truman to George W. Bush*, 3rd ed. Ithaca, NY: Cornell University Press, 2001.

Leuchtenburg, William. *The Supreme Court Reborn: The Constitutional Revolution in the Age of Roosevelt*. Oxford: Oxford University Press, 1996.

Levine, Lawrence, and Cornelia Levine. *The People and the President: America's Conversation with FDR*. Boston. Beacon Press, 2002.

Lim, Elvin T. "The Lion and the Lamb: De-mythologizing Franklin Roosevelt's Fireside Chats." *Rhetoric & Public Affairs* 6, no. 3 (2003): 437–464.

Linenthal, Edward T., and Tom Engelhardt. *History Wars: The Enola Gay and other Battles for the American Past*. New York: Macmillan, 1996.

Linker, Beth. "On the Borderland of Medical and Disability History: A Survey of the Fields." *Bulletin of the History of Medicine* 87, no. 4 (Winter 2013): 499–535.

Lippard, Lucy. "Homage to the Square." *Art in America* 55, no. 4 (July August 1967): 50–54.

Lippman, Theodore Jr. *The Squire of Warm Springs: FDR in Georgia 1924–1945*. New York: Playboy Press, 1977.

Liu, Catharine. "Lacan's Afterlife: Jacques Lacan Meets Andy Warhol." In *Cambridge Companion to Lacan*, edited by Jean-Michel Rabaté. Cambridge: Cambridge University Press, 2003, 253–271.

Lomazow, Steven, and Eric Fettmann. *FDR's Deadly Secret*. New York: Public Affairs, 2009.

Longmore, Paul K. *Telethons: Spectacle, Disability, and the Business of Charity*, edited by Catherine Kudlick. Oxford: Oxford University Press, 2016.

Longmore, Paul K. "The Cultural Framing of Disability: Telethons as a Case Study." *PMLA* 120, no. 2 (2005): 502–508.

Looker, Earle. "Is Franklin D. Roosevelt Fit to Be President?" *Liberty Magazine*, July 25, 1931.

Lorentz, Pare. *FDR's Moviemaker: Memoirs and Scripts*. Reno: University of Nevada Press, 1992.

Mackintosh, Barry. "The National Park Service Moves into Historical Interpretation." *The Public Historian* 9, no. 2 (Spring 1987): 50–63.

Maney, Patrick. *The Roosevelt Presence: The Life and Legacy of FDR*. Berkeley: University of California Press, 1992.

Mangione, Jerre. *The Dream and the Deal: The Federal Writer's Project, 1935–1943*. New York: Avon, 1972.

Marling, Karal Ann. *Wall-to-Wall America: A Cultural History of Post Office Murals in the Great Depression*. Minneapolis: University of Minnesota Press, 1982.

May, J. T., and R. F. Hill. "How Shall We See Them? Perspectives for Research with Disabled Organizations." *Social Science and Medicine* 19, no. 6 (1984): 603–608.

McMahon, Kevin J. *Reconsidering Roosevelt on Race. How the Presidency Paved the Road to Brown*. Chicago: University of Chicago Press, 2004.

Meehan, Thomas, Charles Strouse, and Martin Charnin. *Annie Libretto / Vocal Book*. New York: E. H. Morris & Co, 1977.

Mehta, Dhrumil. "Every President's Executive Orders in One Chart." FiveThirtyEight, November 20, 2014. Accessed November 11, 2019. http://fivethirtyeight.com/datalab/every-presidents-executive-actions-in-one-chart/.

Meldon, Perri. "Interpreting Access: A History of Accessibility and Disability Representations in the National Park Service," Master's thesis. University of Massachusetts. Amherst, 2019, 2/787. https://scholarworks.umass.edu/masters_theses_2/787.

Meringolo, Denise. *Museums, Monuments, and National Parks: Toward a New Genealogy of Public History*. Amherst: University of Massachusetts Press, 2012.

Michell, Roger, dir. *Hyde Park on Hudson*. Daybreak Pictures, 2012, DVD, 95 min.

Mitchell, David T., and Sharon L. Snyder. *Narrative Prosthesis: Disability and the Dependencies of Discourse*. Ann Arbor: University of Michigan Press, 2000.

Mitchell, David T., and Sharon L. Snyder. "The Eugenic Atlantic: Race, Disability, and the Making of an International Eugenic Science, 1800–1945." *Disability & Society* 18, no. 7 (2003): 843–864.

Morris, Edmund. *The Rise of Theodore Roosevelt*. New York: Random House, 1979.

Mouffe, Chantal. *The Democratic Paradox*. London: Verso, 2000.

Murray, Stuart, and James McCabe. *Norman Rockwell's Four Freedoms*. New York: Gramercy Books, 1993.

Mutchler, Meghan. "Roosevelt's Disability an Issue at Memorial." *New York Times*, April 10, 1995, A8.

"NAACP History: Costigan Wagner Bill." NAACP. Accessed November 11, 2019. https://www.naacp.org/naacp-history-costigan-wagner-act/.

Nielsen, Kim E. *A Disability History of the United States*. Boston: Beacon Press, 2012.

Nielsen, Kim E. "The Perils and Promises of Disability Biography." In *The Oxford Handbook of Disability History,* edited by Michael Rembis, Catherine Kudlick, and Kim E. Nielsen, 21–40. New York: Oxford University Press, 2018.

"'One Definite Locality': History of the FDR Presidential Library & Museum." Franklin D. Roosevelt Presidential Library and Museum. Accessed November 11, 2019. https://www.fdrlibrary.org/library-history.

Orlansky, Harold. "Reactions to the Death of President Roosevelt." *Journal of Social Psychology* 26, no. 2 (1947): 235–266.

O'Ryan, Mariana Casale. *The Making of Jorge Luis Borges as an Argentine Cultural Icon*. London: Modern Humanities Research Association, 2014.

Oshinsky, David M. *Polio: An American Story*. Oxford: Oxford University Press, 2005.

Ott, Katherine. "The Sum of Its Parts: An Introduction to Modern Histories of Prosthetics." Introduction to *Artificial Parts, Practical Lives: Modern Histories of Prosthetics,* edited by Katherine Ott, David Serlin, and Stephen Mihm, 1–42. New York: New York University Press, 2002.

Ott, Katherine, David Serlin, and Stephen Mihm, eds. *Artificial Parts, Practical Lives: Modern Histories of Prosthetics*. New York: New York University Press, 2002.

Paterson, Thomas G., J. Garry Clifford, Shane D. Maddock, Deborah Kisatsky, and Kenneth J. Hagan. *American Foreign Relations, Vol. 2: A History since 1895*, 7th ed. Boston: Wadsworth, 2009.

Peirce, Charles Sanders. *Collected Papers of Charles Sanders Peirce*, edited by Charles Hartshorne, Paul Weiss, and Arthur W. Burks, 8 vols. Cambridge, MA: Harvard University Press, 1931–1958.

Penkower, Monty Noam. *The Federal Writers' Project: A Study in Government Patronage of the Arts*. Urbana, Chicago, London: University of Illinois Press, 1977.

Perkins, Frances. *The Roosevelt I Knew*. New York: Viking Press, 1946.

Petrie, Daniel, dir. *Eleanor and Franklin: The White House Years*. ABC, 1977. DVD, 155 min.

Pletcher, David T., and Ashlee Diane Russeau-Pletcher. "History of the Civil Rights Movement for the Physically Disabled." Academia.edu. https://www.academia.edu/1862883/History_of_the_Civil_Rights_for_the_Physically_Disabled [Originally published in *The American Association of Behavioral and Social Sciences Journal*, 2008].

Polak, S. A. "Roosevelt in Zijn Eigen Museum" ["Roosevelt in His Own Museum"]. In *Tweede Levens: Over Personen en Personages in de Geschiedschrijving en Literatuur*, edited by Annemarie van Heerikhuizen, Irene de Jong, and Manet van Montfrans, 124–135 Amsterdam: Amsterdam University Press, 2010.

Polenberg, Richard. "The Decline of the New Deal, 1937–1940." In *The New Deal: The National Level*, edited by John Braeman, Robert H. Bremner, and David Brody, 246–266. Columbus: Ohio State University Press, 1975.

Polenberg, Richard. *The Era of Franklin D. Roosevelt: A Brief History with Documents*. Boston: Bedford / St. Martin's, 2000.

Pollak, Michael. "Name That Island." *New York Times*, December 14, 2012.

Powell, Jim. *FDR's Folly: How Roosevelt and His New Deal Prolonged the Great Depression*. New York: Crown Forum, 2003.

Prange, Gordon W., Donald M. Goldstein, and Katherine V. Dillon. *At Dawn We Slept: The Untold Story of Pearl Harbor*. New York: Penguin Books, 1982.

Rainey, Reuben M. "The Garden as Narrative: Lawrence Halprin's Franklin Delano Roosevelt memorial." In *Places of Commemoration: Search for Identity and Landscape Design*, edited by Joachim Wolschke-Bulmahn, 377 416. Washington, DC: Dumbarton Oaks, 2001.

Redmond, Sean, and Su Holmes, eds. *Stardom and Celebrity: A Reader*. Los Angeles: Sage, 2007.

Reid, Paul. *The Last Lion: Defender of the Realm*. New York: Little Brown and Company, 2012.

Renshaw, Patrick. *Franklin D. Roosevelt: Profiles in Power*. Harlow: Pearson, 2004.

Report to the President and Congress, 30 May 1978. The Franklin D. Roosevelt Memorial Commission. https://babel.hathitrust.org/cgi/pt?id=uc1.e0000450775&view=1up&seq=7.

Reynolds, David. "FDR's Foreign Policy and the Construction of American History, 1945–1955." In *FDR's World: War, Peace, and Legacies*, edited by David Woolner, Warren Kimball, and David Reynolds, 5–33. New York: Palgrave Macmillan, 2008.

Reynolds, David. *In Command of History: Fighting and Writing the Second World War*. London: Allen Lane, 2004.

Ricard, Serge, ed. *A Companion to Theodore Roosevelt*. Malden, MA: Blackwell & Wiley, 2011.

Rich, Motoko. "For Books, Is Obama New Oprah?" *New York Times*, November 17, 2008.

Rigney, Ann. *The Afterlives of Walter Scott: Memory on the Move*. Oxford: Oxford University Press, 2012.

Robinson, Greg. *By Order of the President: FDR and the Internment of Japanese Americans*. Cambridge, MA: Harvard University Press, 2001.

Rollins, Alfred B., Jr. *Roosevelt and Howe*. New York: Knopf, 1962.

Roosevelt, Eleanor. "Why I Do Not Choose to Run." *Look Magazine*, July 9, 1946.

Roosevelt, Franklin D. "Acceptance Speech for the Renomination for the Presidency, Philadelphia, PA., June 27, 1936." *The American Presidency Project*, edited by Gerhard Peters and John T. Woolley. https://www.presidency.ucsb.edu/documents/acceptance-speech-for-the-renomination-for-the-presidency-philadelphia-pa.

Roosevelt, Franklin D. "Address Accepting the Presidential Nomination at the Democratic National Convention in Chicago, July 2, 1932." *The American Presidency Project*, edited by Gerhard Peters and John T. Woolley. https://www.presidency.ucsb.edu/documents/address-accepting-the-presidential-nomination-the-democratic-national-convention-chicago-1.

Roosevelt, Franklin D. "Address at Chicago. October 5, 1937." ["Quarantine Speech"] *The American Presidency Project*, edited by Gerhard Peters and John T. Woolley. https://www.presidency.ucsb.edu/documents/address-chicago.

Roosevelt, Franklin D. "Address at the Cornerstone Laying of the Franklin D. Roosevelt Library, Hyde Park, New York, November 19, 1939." *The American Presidency Project*, edited by Gerhard Peters and John T. Woolley. https://www.presidency.ucsb.edu/node/210315.

Roosevelt, Franklin D. "Address to Congress on the Yalta Conference, March 1, 1945." *The American Presidency Project*, edited by Gerhard Peters and John T. Woolley. https://www.presidency.ucsb.edu/documents/address-congress-the-yalta-conference.

Roosevelt, Franklin D. "Address to Congress Requesting a Declaration of War with Japan, December 8, 1941." *The American Presidency Project*, edited by Gerhard Peters and John T. Woolley. https://www.presidency.ucsb.edu/documents/address-congress-requesting-declaration-war-with-japan.

Roosevelt, Franklin D. "Annual Message to Congress on the State of the Union, January 6, 1941." *The American Presidency Project*, edited by Gerhard Peters and John T. Woolley. https://www.presidency.ucsb.edu/documents/annual-message-congress-the-state-the-union.

Roosevelt, Franklin D. "Excerpts from the Press Conference, December 28, 1943." *The American Presidency Project*, edited by Gerhard Peters and John T. Woolley. https://www.presidency.ucsb.edu/documents/excerpts-from-the-press-conference-8.

Roosevelt, Franklin D. *FDR: His Personal Letters, 1928–1945*, edited by Elliott Roosevelt. 2 vols. New York: Duell, Sloane and Pearce, 1950.

Roosevelt, Franklin D. "Fireside Chat, July 24, 1933." *The American Presidency Project*, edited by Gerhard Peters and John T. Woolley. https://www.presidency.ucsb.edu/documents/fireside-chat-recovery-program.

Roosevelt, Franklin D. "Fireside Chat, October 22, 1933." *The American Presidency Project*, edited by Gerhard Peters and John T. Woolley. https://www.presidency.ucsb.edu/documents/fireside-chat-22.

Roosevelt, Franklin D. "Fireside Chat, June 28, 1934." *The American Presidency Project*, edited by Gerhard Peters and John T. Woolley. https://www.presidency.ucsb.edu/documents/fireside-chat-21.

Roosevelt, Franklin D. "Fireside Chat, June 24, 1938." *The American Presidency Project*, edited by Gerhard Peters and John T. Woolley. https://www.presidency.ucsb.edu/documents/fireside-chat-14.

Roosevelt, Franklin D. "Fireside Chat, September 3, 1939." *The American Presidency Project*, edited by Gerhard Peters and John T. Woolley. https://www.presidency.ucsb.edu/documents/fireside-chat-13.

Roosevelt, Franklin D. "Fireside Chat, December 29, 1940." *The American Presidency Project*, edited by Gerhard Peters and John T. Woolley. https://www.presidency.ucsb.edu/documents/fireside-chat-9.

Roosevelt, Franklin D. "Fireside Chat, February 23, 1942." *The American Presidency Project*, edited by Gerhard Peters and John T. Woolley. https://www.presidency.ucsb.edu/documents/fireside-chat-6.

Roosevelt, Franklin D. "Fireside Chat, April 28, 1942." *The American Presidency Project*, edited by Gerhard Peters and John T. Woolley. https://www.presidency.ucsb.edu/documents/fireside -chat-5.

Roosevelt, Franklin D. "Press Conference, December 10, 1938." *The American Presidency Project*, edited by Gerhard Peters and John T. Woolley. https://www.presidency.ucsb.edu /documents/press-conference-20.

Roosevelt, Franklin D. "Press Conference, March 8, 1933." *The American Presidency Project*, edited by Gerhard Peters and John T. Woolley. https://www.presidency.ucsb.edu/documents /press-conference-25.

Roosevelt, Franklin D. "Radio Address of the President—Herald Tribune Forum, October 24, 1940." http://www.fdrlibrary.marist.edu/_resources/images/msf/msf01370.

Roosevelt, Franklin D. "Remarks at Mount Rushmore National Memorial, August 30, 1936." *The American Presidency Project*, edited by Gerhard Peters and John T. Woolley. https://www .presidency.ucsb.edu/documents/remarks-mount-rushmore-national-memorial.

Roosevelt, Franklin D. "Remarks at the Dedication of the Franklin D. Roosevelt Library at Hyde Park, New York, June 30, 1941." *The American Presidency Project*, edited by Gerhard Peters and John T. Woolley. https://www.presidency.ucsb.edu/documents/remarks-the-dedication -the-franklin-d-roosevelt-library-hyde-park-new-york.

Roosevelt, Franklin D. *Selected Speeches, Messages, Press Conferences, and Letters*, edited by Basil Rauch. New York: Rinehart, 1957.

Roosevelt, Franklin D., and Samuel I. Rosenman. *The Public Papers and Addresses of Franklin D. Roosevelt*. 13 vols. New York: Random House, 1938–1969.

Rosenberg, Emily. *A Date Which Will Live: Pearl Harbor in American Memory*. Durham and London: Duke University Press, 2003.

Rosenberg, Emily. *Spreading the American Dream: American Economic and Cultural Expansion 1890–1945*. London, New York: Macmillan, 2011.

Rosenman, Samuel I. *Working with Roosevelt*. New York: Da Capo Press, 1952.

Rossiter, Clinton. *The American Presidency*. New York: Harcourt, Brace and World, 1956.

Roth, Philip. *The Plot Against America*. Boston: Houghton Mifflin, 2004.

Roth, Philip. "The Story Behind 'The Plot Against America'." *New York Times Book Review* 109, part 38, September 19, 2004, 10.

Rothberg, Michael. *Multidirectional Memory: Remembering the Holocaust in the Age of Decolonization*. Palo Alto: Stanford University Press, 2009.

Sargent, Joseph, dir. *Warm Springs*. HBO, DVD, 2005. 131 min.

Schary, Dore. *Sunrise at Campobello: A Play in Three Acts*. 1st ed. New York: Random House, 1958.

Schlesinger, Arthur M., Jr. "Franklin Delano Roosevelt." *Time 100: Leaders and Revolutionaries* [special issue] *Time Magazine*, April 18, 1998.

Schlesinger, Arthur M., Jr. *The Age of Roosevelt, Vol. 2: The Coming of the New Deal*. Boston: Mifflin, 1958.

Schlesinger, Arthur M., Jr. *The Imperial Presidency*, New York: Mariner Books, 2004; New York: Houghton Mifflin, 1973.

Schoenherr, Steven. *Selling the New Deal: Stephen T. Early's Role as Press Secretary to Franklin D. Roosevelt*. Newark: University of Delaware Press, 1976.

Schwartz, Barry. *Abraham Lincoln in the Post-Heroic Era: History and Memory in Late Twentieth Century America*. Chicago: University of Chicago Press, 2008.

Schwartz, Barry. *George Washington: The Making of an American Symbol*. New York: Free Press, 1987.

Schwartz, Joan, and Terry Cook. "Archives, Records, and Power: The Making of Modern Memory." *Archival Science* 2 (2002): 1–19.

Scotch, Richard K. "Medical Model of Disability." In *Encyclopedia of American Disability History*, edited by Susan Burch. 3 vols. New York: Facts on File, 2009.

Shell, Marc. *Polio and Its Aftermath: The Paralysis of Culture*. Cambridge, MA: Harvard University Press, 2005.

Shiller, Robert. "What Would Roosevelt Do?" *New York Times*, July 31, 2010.

Siebers, Tobin. "Disability as Masquerade." *Literature and Medicine* 23, no. 1 (2004): 1–22.

Smith, Angela. "Dis-affection: Disability Effects and Disabled Moves at the Movies." In *The Matter of Disability: Materiality, Biopolitics, Crip Affect*, edited by David Mitchell, Susan Antebi and Sharon Snyder, 118–140. Ann Arbor: University of Michigan Press, 2019.

Smith, Ira T., and Joe Alex Morris. *"Dear Mr. President . . .": The Story of Fifty Years in the White House Mail Room*. New York: Julian Messner, 1949.

Smith, Jean Edward. *FDR*. New York: Random House, 2007.

Snyder, Sharon L., and David T. Mitchell. *Narrative Prosthesis: Disability and the Dependencies of Discourse*. Ann Arbor: University of Michigan Press, 2001.

Sousloff, Catherine. *The Subject in Art: Portraiture and the Birth of the Modern*. Durham: Duke University Press, 2006.

Stein, Sally. "The President's Two Bodies: Stagings and Restagings of FDR and the New Deal Body Politic." *American Art* 18, no.1 (Spring 2004): 32–57.

Stiles, Lela. *The Man Behind Roosevelt: The Story of Louis McHenry Howe*. Cleveland: World Publishing Company, 1954.

Stinnett, Robert B. *Day of Deceit: The Truth About FDR and Pearl Harbor*. New York: Touchstone, 2000.

Sussmann, Leila A. *Dear FDR: A Study of Political Letter-writing*. Totowa, NJ: Bedminster Press, 1963.

Tajfel, Henri. "Social Identity and Intergroup Behavior." *Social Science Information* 13, no. 2 (1974): 65–93.

Tansill, Charles Callan. *Back Door to War: The Roosevelt Foreign Policy, 1933–1941*. Chicago: Henry Regnery Company, 1952.

Taylor, David C., dir. *FDR: A Presidency Revealed*. History Channel, 2005. DVD.

Tebbel, John. *The Media in America*. New York: Mentor Books, 1974.

Terkel, S. *"The Good War": An Oral History of World War II*. New York: Pantheon Books, 1984.

"The Four Freedoms." Franklin D. Roosevelt Four Freedoms Park. Accessed November 12, 2019. http://www.fdrfourfreedomspark.org/fourfreedoms.

Theodoracopulos, Taki. "Roth's Counter-History and Mine." *The American Conservative*, October 25, 2004.

Tilden, Freeman. *Interpreting Our Heritage*, 4th ed. Chapel Hill: The University of North Carolina Press, 2007.

Titchkosky, Tanya. *The Question of Access: Disability, Space, Meaning*. Toronto: University of Toronto Press, 2011.

Tuchman, Phyllis. "The Franklin Delano Roosevelt Memorial." In *Lawrence Halprin: Changing Places—San Francisco Museum of Modern Art, 3 July–24 August 1986*, 90–103. San Francisco: Museum of Modern Art, 1986.

Tully, Grace. *F. D. R., My Boss*. New York: C. Scribner and Sons, 1949.

Turner, Graeme. "Approaching Celebrity Studies." *Celebrity Studies* 1, no. 1 (2010): 11–20.

Vagnone, Franklin D., and Deborah E. Ryan, *Anarchist's Guide to Historic House Museums*. Walnut Creek, CA: Left Coast Press, 2016.

Vansina, Jan. *Oral Tradition as History*. Madison: University of Wisconsin Press, 1985.

Veit, Fritz. *Presidential Libraries and Collections*. New York: Greenwood Press, 1987.

Vidal, Gore. *The Golden Age*. London: Abacus, 2000.

Warber, Adam L. *Executive Orders and the Modern Presidency: Legislating From the Oval Office.* Boulder: Lynne Rienner Publishers, 2006.

Ward, Geoffrey C. *Closest Companion: The Unknown Story of the Intimate Friendship Between Franklin Roosevelt and Margaret Suckley.* Boston: Houghton Mifflin, 1995.

Ward, Geoffrey C., and Ken Burns. *The Roosevelts: An Intimate History.* New York: Alfred A. Knopf, 2014.

Wesseling, Henk, ed. *Plaatsen van herinnering,* 4 vols. Amsterdam: Bert Bakker, 2005–2006.

White, Graham J. *FDR and the Press.* Chicago: The University of Chicago Press, 1979.

Wilson, Daniel J. "Passing in the Shadow of FDR: Polio Survivors, Passing, and the Negotiation of Disability." In *Disability and Passing: Blurring the Lines of Identity,* edited by Jeffrey A. Brune and Daniel J. Wilson, 13–35. Philadelphia: Temple University Press, 2013.

Winfield, Betty Houchin. *FDR and the News Media.* Urbana: University of Illinois Press, 1990.

Winter, Jay. *Performing the Past: Memory, History, and Identity in Modern Europe.* Amsterdam: Amsterdam University Press, 2010.

Woolner, David, Warren Kimball, and David Reynolds, eds. *FDR's World: War, Peace, and Legacies.* New York: Palgrave Macmillan, 2008.

Young, William H., and Nancy K. Young. *The Great Depression in America: A Cultural Encyclopedia.* New York: Greenwood, 2007.